SIMULATION IN BUSINESS AND MANAGEMENT, 1991

Titles in the *Simulation Series*

Simulation in Business and Management, 1991

Proceedings of the SCS Multiconference on
Simulation in Business and Management
23-25 January 1991
Anaheim, California

Edited by
Jay Weinroth
Kent State University

Joe E. Hilber
AT&T

Simulation Series
Volume 23
Number 2

Sponsored by
The Society for Computer Simulation (SCS)

ISBN 0-911801-79-0

PRINTED IN THE UNITED STATES

CONTENTS

CONTENTS

Page   Authors

PREFACE

Last year, after a gap of eight years, a conference on Simulation in Business and Management was part of our Multiconference. It proved to be so popular that this conference was scheduled again for 1991.

The planning for this conference is the product of an enthusiastic team of session chairpersons, authors and tutorial presenters. They have planned a conference covering a wide range of topics of interest to Simulationists and their clients in the fields of business and management. In addition two tutorials are scheduled integral to the conference on simulation tools of STELLA and WITNESS.

There is an awakening realization by business leaders that significant increases in quality and reduction in cost and cycle time are necessary for American business to compete and be successful in the rapidly evolving Global marketplace. Government officials, likewise, see the need for these breakthroughs and have initiated incentives such as the Baldridge Award to encourage them. These influences may be an important part of the background driving the interest in using simulation in the achievement of these goals.

Jay Weinroth, General Chairman, and myself wish to compliment the team who planned this conference for their good work. I also wish to thank Melissa Launer, my secretary, for the coordination efforts that kept our confusion to a minimum and kept us close to schedule in preparing for the conference.

Joseph E. Hilber
Program Chairman
AT&T

SIMULATING ECONOMIC SYSTEMS

THE SIMULATED ECONOMIC IMPACT OF HIGHWAY EXPANSION IN NORTH CAROLINA UPON TOURISM IN SOUTH CAROLINA

Dr. Peter B. Barr, Dr. Dennis A. Rauch and Dr. Gerald V. Boyles
USC Coastal Carolina College
P.O. Box 1954
Conway, SC 29526

ABSTRACT

The Grand Strand, a South Carolina coastal resort area, is a sixty mile strip of land that is separated from the mainland by the Intercoastal Waterway. Millions of visitors come to South Carolina each year with the primary destination point being the intensely developed areas of Myrtle Beach and North Myrtle Beach. Tourism constitutes the major industry in the region and accounts for an annual projected economic impact of $2.1 billion.

Currently, the Grand Strand captures approximately four percent of the total tourist market in the southeast. But this market is one of high competition which promises little stability to the region. The nature of this environment is such that governmental entities and private concerns often join forces to expand market share. Consequently, given the sheer size of the proposed highway expansion in North Carolina, leaders in South Carolina have marshaled forces to examine the potential economic impact that this might exert upon tourism or the Grand Strand. The purpose of this paper is to demonstrate how simulation was used to measure the potential economic impact upon the region.

INTRODUCTION

The purpose of this study is to estimate, in terms of market share, the effect of the North Carolina road building program (North Carolina Department

*** All authors contributed equally in the development of this paper.

of Transportation 1989) on tourism along the Grand Strand of South Carolina. Essentially, we seek to answer the question: What effect will the opening up of North Carolina's beaches and other tourist attractions, in terms of accessibility and transportation, have on tourism on the Grand Strand? In order to answer this question we need to know what factors play a role in consumers' decisions regarding recreation destination choice and how changes on these attributes will affect peoples' choices of where to vacation. To this end we conducted a study to determine the importance of various attributes of resort destinations and used the results to develop a simulation model. This model enabled us to predict the effect on market share of changes in, for example, travel time to or facilities available at various resort areas. For the purposes of this study, the market share to be predicted was the Grand Strand's portion of all of the tourists visiting the entire coastal region of North Carolina plus the Grand Strand.

METHODOLOGY

The simulation model, which forms the basis of this study, was calibrated from data collected from tourists selected randomly at sites along the Grand Strand. The data was used to assess the impact of various attributes of resort areas on consumers' perceptions of the values of resort areas in general. In other words, the information was used to estimate how big a role each attribute plays in the consumers' decisions. These estimations were made based on a theory of human judgment called Hierarchical Information Integration Theory. Louviere (1984) first proposed this theory and modeling methodology. He postulated that decision makers integrate logically related salient stimulus attributes into psychological constructs which are then combined to form overall evaluations. The model suggests that individuals simplify the judgment process by first focusing on selected subsets of stimulus attributes separately and 'rating' or 'scoring' the stimulus on decision constructs comprised of these subsets. Then an overall judgment of the stimulus is based on this much smaller, and easier to process, set of composite scores. Algebraically:

$$R = f_{int}(X_1, X_2, \ldots, X_i), \qquad (1)$$

$$X_1 = f_1(x_{11}, x_{12}, \ldots, x_{1n1}),$$
$$X_2 = f_2(x_{21}, x_{22}, \ldots, x_{2n2}),$$
$$\ldots$$
$$X_i = f_i(x_{i1}, x_{i2}, \ldots, x_{ini}), \qquad (2)$$

where the overall judgment of a stimulus, R, is a function (1), f_{int}, of the scores, X_i, in the multiattribute decision constructs, (2). This function is the overall integrating function. The scores on the decision constructs are functions, f_i, of the attributes which form the decision constructs x_{i1}, $x_{i2}, \ldots, x_{ini}$. (See Louviere 1984 for a more formal development of the theory and the algebraic consequences arising from possible specification of the functional forms for f_{int} and the f_i.)

To illustrate, suppose a consumer evaluates personal computers on the basis of two general characteristics or decision constructs, capacity and economy. Under the theory of hierarchical information integration, the consumer would assign scores to a computer for both constructs based on the computer's characteristics. For example, random access memory, speed and expandability might be evaluated and combined to form a capacity score; and, purchase price, maintenance costs and training costs

could be the inputs to the economy score. These two scores would then be combined, through the overall integrating function, to arrive at an overall judgment on the computer.

Louviere (1984) as well as Rauch and Barr (1989) have shown that results from the hierarchical methodology correspond extremely well with those derived from a parallel full profile analysis. It has also been shown (Louviere and Gaeth 1987) that in a very complex decision environment, managerial implications arising from both types of analyses are quite similar. These tests provide measures of concurrent validity for the concept of hierarchical decision processing.

The broad decision constructs selected for this study are travel to the resort area, facilities available at the area, infrastructure utilization (or crowding) and cost per day. The travel construct was broken down in order to estimate the impacts of the attributes of driving time to the area, the type of road (four lane vs. two lane) and whether or not there were any toll roads involved. The facilities construct dealt with the impact of the quality and/or variety of beaches, accommodations, sporting facilities (golf, tennis, etc.), shopping, night life and amusements (rides, games, etc.). The infrastructure utilization construct was made up of the effects of traffic congestion on the roads in the immediate vicinity of the resort area (more specifically the amount of time required to drive the last ten miles into the area), restaurant waiting time, recreation waiting time (for tee times, tennis courts, etc.) and a general "Crowding" factor. The cost per day construct was presented as a single measure.

Four sets of resort profiles were designed in order to calibrate the overall integrating function, (1), and the decision constructs, (2), for travel, facilities and infrastructure utilization. For the sets of profiles used to calibrate the decision constructs, the attributes assumed to comprise the constructs were varied according to orthogonal fractional factorial designs. For example, on the facilities construct, the six attributes (beaches, accommodations, etc.) were varied over high and low levels according to a one-fourth fraction of a 2^6 factorial design which allows the estimation of all main effects independent of all two factor interactions. These sixteen profiles were then rated as to the desirability of the resorts they describe. In order to calibrate the integrating function, (1), overall measures of the four decision constructs were varied over high and low levels and judged in the same manner.

ANALYSIS AND RESULTS

The analysis of all four data sets was performed after all data were standardized within subject to zero mean and unit standard deviation. A two step procedure was used to model the hierarchical judgment process. First, the (standardized) resort profile ratings were regressed on the orthonormal predictors, yielding a set of beta weights for each of the decision construct submodels (2) and the integrating function model (1). Because of the orthonormality of the predictors, each beta weight equals the simple correlation between the predictor and the ratings. And, for each model, the sum of the squared betas equals R^2 for that model. Dividing the squared betas by R^2 yields the portion of systematic variance accounted for by that variable. This measure represents relative attribute importance or impact on the judgment. The integrating function and the decision constructs were then combined according to the methodology outlined by Louviere (1987).

The results of the analysis of the information collected from the tourists is presented in Table 1. These results are presented in the form of percentages of impact attributable to each construct

Table 1

Percent Of Impact Of The Resort Area Attributes On Overall Evaluations*

Travel		Facilities	
Travel Time	21.65%	Beaches	9.81%
Road Type	0.15%	Accom.	32.05%
Toll Roads	3.86%	Sports Fac.	4.73%
		Shopping	6.50%
		Night Life	8.15%
		Amusements	0.82%
	------		------
Total	25.65%		62.07%

Infrastructure		Utilization	
Last Ten Mi.	4.47%		
Rest. Wait	1.79%		
Rec. Wait	2.09%		
"Crowding"	0.54%		

Total	8.90%		

Cost Per Day 3.37%

*Numbers do not sum to 100% due to rounding.

and attributes within constructs. For instance, the overall travel construct accounts for 25.65% of the evaluation of the value of resort areas. This figure is made up of 21.65% due to travel time, 0.15% due to road type and 3.86% due to toll roads. The interpretation of this information is that, for instance, when a consumer is evaluating a resort area 21.65% of his/her evaluation is based on travel time. Likewise, facilities overall account for 62.07% of the evaluation with accommodations accounting for 32.05% by itself. The same type of interpretation can be applied to each of the attributes.

This information about the consumer judgment process was used to calibrate the statistical simulation model. The model is a variation of the Luce Choice Axiom (Luce 1959) which, in this case, asserts that the market share of a resort area (or the probability of anyone choosing a particular resort area) is proportional to its perceived value. Or,

$$P(a) = V_a/\Sigma V_j,$$

the probability of selecting destination a, $P(a)$, equals the perceived value of destination a, V_a, divided by the sum of the perceived values of all the resorts in the consumer's choice set, ΣV_j. Therefore, changes in a resort area's perceived value, relative to another resort area, will result in a change in its predicted market share. With this model, we can make assumptions about changes in the environment (improved transportation, expanded facilities, etc.) and determine their impact on factors such as market share and expected tourist expenditures.

The market share simulation model was then calibrated so that travel, facilities, infrastructure utilization and cost per day predicted market share and had the appropriate percentage impact on the estimate. For comparison purposes, and to validate the model, it was used to 'predict' the present situation. This is the base model. The base model utilized in this analysis consists of four distinct modules; the informational module to drive the process, the replica model of "real-world" activities, the validation component, and the comparative analyses module.

The informational module contains those elements necessary to drive the simulation process. These elements include historical information, subroutines for random number generation, and process generators. Historical information was derived from a variety of sources which include: Departments of Parks, Recreation and Tourism, tax commissions, the United

States Travel Data Center and area Chambers of Commerce.

The remaining elements of this module are the subroutines developed for random number and process generation. Multiplicative congruential formulas were used to supply the random numbers utilized throughout the process and tested to assure conformity within acceptable limits (alpha = .05). The process generators were based upon the Box-Mueller (Watson 1987) methods for normality which were also tested to assure conformity within acceptable limits.

The second module of the simulation program includes those steps which were necessary to effect replication of the current tourism expenditures (South Carolina 1990). Tracking variables included percentage market share (U.S. Travel Data Center 1990), lodging, food, transportation, entertainment, miscellaneous, and total expenses.

The third module encompasses the statistical procedures necessary to validate the generators utilized in the simulation. The Chi-Square procedure was employed to test the validity of the random number and process generators using an alpha level of .05.

The final module included in the simulation consisted of the different forms of comparative analyses. Four separate strategies were compared to the value of the tracking variables as reflected in the base model. These scenarios were:

1. Ten percent improvement in travel.

2. Ten percent improvement in travel and ten percent increase in the number of facilities available in North Carolina.

3. Travel was increased by one

percent per year for five years with an annual expansion of North Carolina facilities by 3.32%.

4. Travel was increased by one percent per year for five years. Facilities in North Carolina expanded by 3.32% per year for five years. Influence of facilities decreases and its influence is distributed proportionally over the remaining three decision constructs.

In order to illustrate the use of this model, these four scenarios were simulated. In each scenario we introduced a change and then estimated its impact on the Grand Strand's share of the tourist market and on gross tourist expenditures on the Grand Strand. Because the purpose of this study was to assess the impact of the North Carolina road improvement program and in order to simplify the simulation of this effect, the Grand Strand's share of the tourist market was divided into two segments, those who would naturally drive through North Carolina on their way to the Strand and those who would not. The basic concept is that people who drive through the state would be affected most by changes in the North Carolina road network, at least in the short run. If one assumes a static market growth rate overall so that a constant number of visitors who do not drive through North Carolina come to the Grand Strand, then we need only simulate the effect of environmental changes for that portion of the market that does. Another assumption is that improving the transportation to North Carolina's beaches, at least from the north also improves the transportation, to the Grand Strand by the same amount. For example, widening U.S. 17 from border to border in North Carolina would improve the northern access to South Carolina.

The outcome of scenario one in comparison to the base model is presented in Table 2. Remember, the base model is a reflection of the present situation. Scenario number one represents the outcome predicted by the model of a ten percent improvement in travel. As can be seen, the change resulted in a 0.59% decrease in the Grand Strand's share of the market and the concomitant decrease in tourist expenditures. While this change is small in percentage

Table 2
Market and Expenditure Changes Predicted Under Scenario 1

	Base Model	Scenario #1
Market share	54.19%	53.87%
Tourists	4,489,324	4,462,894
Expenditures		
Lodging	$709,089,900	$704,913,995
Food	706,988,600	702,824,744
Transp.	141,467,700	140,634,612
Entertain.	238,114,100	236,711,793
Misc.	347,015,900	344,972,717
Total	$2,142,676,200	$2,130,057,861

terms, it translates into a loss in excess of $12 million in expected total tourism revenues. While a small loss such as this is not any indication that some sort of drastic action is necessary, it is unreasonable to assume that travel improvement will be the only environmental effect from the North Carolina road improvement program.

In scenario number two (see Table 3) an added change is introduced - the change to be considered is an improvement in the facilities offered by North Carolina which is likely to occur along with the road improvement. In this case the facilities are increased by ten percent at the same time travel is improved by ten percent. Because facilities account for 62.07% of the tourists' decision processes, while travel makes up only 25.65%, a much larger decrease in market share and expenditures would be expected. In fact, the market share is predicted to fall by 2.63% which translates into a decrease in tourism revenue of more than $56 million.

Table 3

Market and Expenditure Changes Predicted Under Scenario Two

	Base Model	Scenario #2
Market Share	54.19%	52.76%
Tourists	4,489,324	4,371,258
Expenditures		
Lodging	$709,089,900	$690,439,995
Food	706,988,600	688,394,044
Transp.	141,467,700	137,746,912
Entertain.	238,114,100	231,851,393
Misc.	347,015,900	337,889,317
Total	$2,142,676,200	$2,086,321,661

Scenarios one and two illustrate the types of "what if" situations that can be evaluated using the simulation model. But, in scenarios three and four, the effects of changes over time are predicted. Under scenario three, travel is improved by one percent each year for five years. At the same time, facilities in North Carolina are increased 3.32% annually over the same period while facilities are held constant on the Grand Strand. The one percent increase in travel was arbitrarily set as a conservative and realistic figure. The 3.32% facilities growth rate was selected for two reasons. First, over a five year period this growth rate would allow the entire coastal region of North Carolina to approximately catch up with the Grand Strand in terms of facilities. And, second, it is not significantly different from the growth rate experienced along the Grand Strand over the past several years. The results are in Table 4.

The simulation model predicts that at the end of the first year the Grand Strand would lose 0.71% of its market and over $15 million. These losses escalate over the five year period until in the last year the Grand Strand would lose 3.74% of its market and over $80 million. In fact the non-discounted total losses over the five year period total nearly $235 million.

While the results of the simulation for scenario three are dramatic, it represents a quite conservative prediction. Previous research as well as conventional wisdom indicate that when all of the options of a particular feature are not noticeably different, then that feature no longer plays a meaningful role in the decision process.

Table 4

Market and Expenditure Changes Predicted Under Scenario 3

	Base Model	Year 1
Market share	54.19%	53.80%
Tourists	4,489,324	4,457,458
Expenditures		
Lodging	$709,089,900	$704,055,695
Food	706,988,600	701,969,441
Transp.	141,467,700	140,463,412
Enter.	238,114,100	236,423,793
Misc.	347,015,900	344,552,717
Total	$2,142,676,200	$2,127,465,058

	Base Model	Year 2
Market Share	54.19%	53.41%
Tourists	4,489,324	4,424,759
Expenditures		
Lodging	$709,089,900	$698,890,795
Food	706,988,600	696,819,744
Transp.	141,467,700	139,432,982
Enter.	238,114,100	234,689,193
Misc.	347,015,900	342,024,917
Total	$2,142,676,200	$2,111,857,631

Base Model		Year 3
Market Share	54.19%	53.00%
Tourists	4,489,324	4,391,195
Expenditures		
Lodging	$709,089,900	$693,589,195
Food	706,988,600	691,534,344
Transp.	141,467,700	138,375,292
Enter.	238,114,100	232,909,093
Misc.	347,015,900	339,430,417
Total	$2,142,676,200	$2,095,838,341

Base Model		Year 4
Market Share	54.19%	52.62%
Tourists	4,489,324	4,359,758
Expenditures		
Lodging	$709,089,900	$688,624,495
Food	706,988,600	686,583,344
Transp.	141,467,700	137,384,742
Enter.	238,114,100	231,241,593
Misc.	347,015,900	337,000,617
Total	$2,142,676,200	$2,080,834,791

Base Model		Year 5
Market Share	54.19%	52.16%
Tourists	4,489,324	4,321,336
Expenditures		
Lodging	$709,089,900	$682,554,895
Food	706,988,600	680,532,444
Transp.	141,467,700	136,173,812
Enter.	238,114,100	229,203,593
Misc.	347,015,900	334,030,517
Total	$2,142,676,200	$2,062,495,261

For example, if one is asked to choose between two red automobiles color would play no role in the decision because the options are tied on that attribute. In scenario three the growth rate assumed for North Carolina would allow it to catch up to the Grand Strand in five years, all else being equal. If this were the case, the facilities offered would probably no longer play a role in the decision and the influence once attributed to facilities would be distributed among the remaining attributes.

This situation, mentioned above, is simulated in scenario four. Specifically, transportation is improved by 1% per year while North Carolina's facilities grow at 3.32%. This growth rate allows them to catch up with the Grand Strand in terms of facilities in approximately five years. As they catch up the importance of facilities decreases and its influence is distributed proportionally over the remaining three decision constructs. The influence of facilities is diminished at a steady rate over the five years to zero and the importance of travel, infrastructure utilization and cost per day increase to 67.65%, 23.46% and 8.89% respectively. The results of simulating this process are presented in Table 5.

Table 5
Market and Expenditure Changes Predicted
under Scenario 4

Base Model		Year 1
Market Share	54.19%	51.60%
Tourists	4,489,324	4,275,465
Expenditures		
Lodging	$709,089,900	$675,309,895
Food	706,988,600	673,308,644
Transp.	141,467,700	134,728,462
Enter.	238,114,100	226,770,793
Misc.	347,015,900	330,484,817
Total	$2,142,676,200	$2,040,602,611

Base Model		Year 2
Market Share	54.19%	48.72%
Tourists	4,489,324	4,036,615
Expenditures		
Lodging	$709,089,900	$637,583,395
Food	706,988,600	635,694,244
Transp.	141,467,700	127,201,802
Enter.	238,114,100	214,102,193
Misc.	347,015,900	312,022,117
Total	$2,142,676,200	$1,926,603,751

	Base Model	Year 3
Market Share	54.19%	45.50%
Tourists	4,489,324	3,769,608
Expenditures		
Lodging	$709,089,900	$595,409,995
Food	706,988,600	593,645,744
Transp.	141,467,700	118,787,872
Enter.	238,114,100	199,940,193
Misc.	347,015,900	291,383,217
Total	$2,142,676,200	$1,799,167,021

	Base Model	Year 4
Market Share	54.19%	41.90%
Tourists	4,489,324	3,471,032
Expenditures		
Lodging	$709,089,900	$548,249,695
Food	706,988,600	546,625,244
Transp.	141,467,700	109,379,102
Enter.	238,114,100	184,103,493
Misc.	347,015,900	268,303,817
Total	$2,142,676,200	$1,656,661,351

	Base Model	Year 5
Market Share	54.19%	37.87%
Tourists	4,489,324	3,137,317
Expenditures		
Lodging	$709,089,900	$495,539,095
Food	706,988,600	494,071,044
Transp.	141,467,700	98,863,082
Enter.	238,114,100	166,403,293
Misc.	347,015,900	242,508,317
Total	$2,142,676,200	$1,497,384,831

The results from scenario four are even more dramatic than those in number three. These results show that even after only one year the Grand Strand would lose 4.76% of its market and more than $102 million. In the fifth year, the losses would be 30.12% of market share and over $640 million. The total non-discounted losses over the five year period are almost $1.8 billion.

Scenarios three and four present the most conservative and liberal esti-

mates, respectively, of the effect of the North Carolina road improvement program on Grand Strand tourism, given the assumptions that are made. The truth may lie somewhere in between the two. Of course, the assumptions that were made for purposes of this report are only representative of the possible scenarios. Probably the greatest value of this research is that, the simulation model provides a flexible tool for evaluating a variety of situations.

ECONOMIC IMPACT

One must also recognize that the level of tourism expenditures, cited above, is a conservative estimate, and really only an approximation, of the real economic impact of tourism on the Grand Strand. Dollars spent by tourists when in the Grand Strand area become the income of individuals in the area. As these income recipients, in turn, spend some of their earnings, this spending becomes the income of other individuals. This spending-income linkage may continue through subsequent rounds, causing income to rise by a multiple of the initial injection of spending into the income stream. The multiplier is the number by which the initial expenditures by tourists would be multiplied in order to obtain the total amplified increase in income.

Estimating the size of the multiplier is difficult (at best). However the Bureau of Economic Analysis of the U.S. Department of Commerce provides estimates of the multiplier which can be used to estimate the impact of projects and program expenditures by industry on regional output (U.S. Dept. of Commerce 1977). The Bureau's estimates for the state of South Carolina for the major industry categories in the Grand Strand area range from about 1.90 to 2.0. Accordingly, each additional dollar of expenditures by tourists in the Grand Strand area will result in about a two dollar increase in output (i.e., gross receipts or sales).

Even after adjusting for the multiplier effect as noted above, there are clearly other, additional indirect benefits associated with (flow from) increased economic activity. Many of the amenities (attractions) which attract tourists to the Grand Strand area and which could not otherwise be supported by the permanent population base, are also enjoyed by residents of the area (e.g., restaurants, shopping, golfing, entertainment, amusement, etc.). Similarly, many social services which probably would not be feasible without the influx of tourists - improved water and sewage facilities as an example - benefit area residents. Although difficult to place a value on the amenities and services, they clearly enhance the "quality of life" of residents in the Grand Strand area.

CONCLUDING REMARKS

Admittedly, the true economic impact of planned road expansion in North Carolina cannot be measured directly but can only be approximated using available information. But these four scenarios have been presented as realistic assessments of a variety of outcomes. Other scenarios can also be tested within the confines of the simulation model.

However, one final point should be emphasized. The state of North Carolina has embarked upon an ambitious road expansion program. The reality is that these road improvements will impact upon tourism expenditures on the Grand Strand. The results of all four scenarios clearly illustrate adverse economic impacts. Consequently, the tourism industry in the Grand Strand cannot afford to become complacent. Improvement along the Grand Strand must be undertaken to remain competitive in this rapidly changing marketplace.

REFERENCES

Louviere, J. J. 1984. "Hierarchical Information Integration: A New Method for the Design and Analysis of Complex Multiattribute Judgement Problems", in Thomas E. Kinnear, ed., Advances in Consumer Research, XI, Provo, Utah: Association for Consumer Research, pp. 148-155.

Louviere, J. J. and G. J. Gaeth. 1987. "Decomposing the Determinants of Retail Facility Choice Using the Method of Hierarchical Information Integration: A Supermarket Illustration, Journal of Retailing, pp. 63, pp. 25-48.

Luce, R.D. 1959. Individual Choice Behavior, New York: John Wiley.

North Carolina Department of Transportation. 1989. 1990-1996 Transportation Improvement Program.

Rauch, D.A. and P.B. Barr. 1989. "A Test of the Equivalence of the Results of Two Consumer Modeling Methodologies: Full Profile Versus Hierarchical", in Marketing: Positioning for the 1990's Robert L. King, Ed., Charleston, SC: Southern Marketing Association.

South Carolina Department of Parks, Recreation and Tourism. 1990. South Carolina Out-of-State Visitor Survey By Region.

U.S. Dept. of Commerce. 1977. Industry-Specific Gross Output Multipliers for BEA Economic Areas.

Watson, H. J. 1981. Computer Simulation In Business. Wiley Publishing Co. NY.

Economic Simulation of Regional Economies Using Bayesian Vector Autoregression

Max E. Jerrell and James N. Morgan
Northern Arizona University
Flagstaff, AZ 86011
(602)523-7405

Abstract

Until recently structural econometric models (SEMs) have been the primary means of simulating economic activity. SEMs have been used to model national economies, international economies, state and local economies and economies made up of regional areas. There are certain difficulties inherent in SEMs which have led some econometricians to consider using time series models in their place. Multivariate time series models, however, tend to be characterized by a large number of parameters which must often be estimated with a relatively small number of observations - a data problem particularly common with sub-national economic databases. Bayesian methods offer a means of overcoming this loss of degrees of freedom, thus improving the statistical reliability of multivariate time series models. This paper will develop a time series model of the state of Arizona and use it to simulate the Arizona economy.

Structural Econometric Models

The process of constructing a SEM begins by developing a set of equations based on economic theory which are to represent economic activity in a region of interest. These equations will likely be simultaneous or block simultaneous and quite often are non-linear. Data is collected on the variables used in the equations and this data is used to statistically estimate the values of the parameters in the equations. The estimated equations are then solved for values of the endogenous equations in the SEM which are used to represent economic activity in the region. The resulting SEM may then be used for policy simulations. For example, the economic effects of a ten percent tax surcharge used to reduce the national deficit could be examined.

From a state modeling perspective the most useful simulation activity may be to forecast state economic activity and to understand how changes in national economic activity may affect the local economy.

There are difficulties, both practical and theoretical, in developing, using and maintaining SEMs. First of all they tend to have a large number of equations and variables. The Bureau of Economic Analysis models contains 117 equations and uses 117 variables, the Data Resources model contains 698 equations and uses an additional 184 exogenous variables and the Wharton III anticipations version model use 202 equations [2]. Note these figures were for the 1974 versions of the models and may have changed, they are presented only to give a feel of the size these models can reach. This means a substantial effort in developing the model equations, collecting data, estimating the parameters and maintaining the database. In short large scale econometric modeling is very costly.

A second concern in developing large scale SEM's involves the state of the economic theory and the equations representing that theory in the model. Consider the demand side of a SEM and equation(s) which model consumption behavior. Should the explanatory variables in the equation(s) contain current income or permanent income as the income measure? On the supply side should the production functions be Cobb-Douglas, constant elasticity of substitution, trans-log or just what? It is likely that most, if not all, of the behavioral equations in a SEM are subject to theoretical criticism.

Additional problems arise in estimating the parameters of SEM's. All of the difficulties in estimating single equation regression models such as misspecification, serial correlation and multicollinearity, are likely to be present. In addition systems methods of estimation require the imposition of apriori restrictions on the parameters, a process which Sims [8] has called "incredible".

Another consideration in using a SEM to study and forecast economic activity is the availability and quality of the data needed to estimate and evaluate the model. One may prefer, on the basis of theory, to use permanent income rather than current income in a consumption function. Permanent income cannot be directly measured. If an interest rate measure is included in a money demand function then a choice must be made between several different measures of interest rates.

Data availability becomes a critical concern for sub-national models. Demand side data is generally not available for most states. A dollar spent in Arizona may be from a resident (a possible measure of consumption) or may come from a tourist (an export). For this reason most state and regional models tend to be supply side oriented. Even this data tends to be incomplete - gross state product measures are available usually only on an annual basis which if used would lead to a model estimated with a very limited number of observations.

Multivariate Time Series Models

Multivariate time series models offer attractive alternatives to SEM's. This paper will examine the application of vector autoregressive (VAR) models to the study of the Arizona economy. A VAR model can be represented as

$$x_t = A_1 x_{t-1} + A_2 x_{t-2} + \ldots + A_k x_{t-k} + u_t$$

where x_t is a vector of economic variables, A_i is a matrix of parameters, and u_t a vector of innovations.

Consider a system with 5 variables and a lag k=6. Each equation in the system has 30 parameters to be estimated if no constant term is present. This would create a degrees of freedom problem for most state or regional models where large amounts of data are not available. Litterman has proposed estimating such a system of equations using Bayesian techniques [3], usually called Bayesian Vector Autoregression [BVAR]. Litterman's method imposes prior probability distributions on the model's parameters and using data as conditional information then producing a posterior probability distribution for the model parameters thus restoring all of the lost degrees of freedom in the estimation process. This process has been subject to the criticism that the prior distributions are obtained arbitrarily and without any particu

lar rationale. However, it should be noted that non Bayesian econometricians also incorporate prior information in SEM's, such as imposing constant returns to scale on Cobb-Douglas productions functions to avoid multicollinearity problems [9].

Time series models, TSMs, of all types have generally been considered to have a more limited range of application and effectiveness than SEMs because of their inability to forecast accurately over long term forecasting horizons, and because of their inability to support policy analysis applications. They have been seen as a forecasting tool useful almost exclusively for short term forecasting.

Studies comparing the forecasting performance of TSMs, such as ARIMA and VAR, with that of large scales SEMs have generally confirmed the view that TSMs can forecasts with reliability equivalent to or better than SEMs for periods up to six months, but that the reliability of TSMs deteriorates rapidly over longer forecast horizons [5] and [6]. Proponents of SEMs have argued that this is because of the SEM's superior ability to capture the effects of exogenous policy variables, while TSM proponents suggest that these results may be due to the extensive use of "judgmental adjustments" among users of SEMs.

Results to date for the BVAR model type are mixed. One study of Litterman's BVAR model of key variables in the U.S. national economy [7] found that his model provided more accurate estimates than prominent commercial judgmental forecasts over long term forecasting horizons, and that this BVAR model was actually more accurate in its year ahead forecasts than in its 1 and 2 quarter forecasts for some variables.. However, a recent study comparing forecasts based on models of the Italian economy [1] found the more traditional result that the BVAR model tended to provide more accurate results over time horizons of up to six months, while the large scale SEM dominated the forecasts of the BVAR model over longer time periods.

The second limitation noted above: that TSMs do not support policy analysis can also be addressed in multivariate TSMs. The natural forecasting process with TSMs produces unconditional forecasts in which the future value of each variable is based entirely on historical values of variables in the model. Uncon ditional forecasts do not provide a basis for assess the impact of policy changes, or evaluating hypotheses about economic behavior. However, a form of policy analysis can be performed on BVAR models by generating impulse response functions. This method in essence involves perturbing one variable by a specified amount and generating a forecast. This forecast is then compared with a base case forecast to assess the impact of the change in this variable on the system [4]. While this process can be criticized on theoretical grounds, an endogenous variable is exogenously perturbed and then becomes endogenous again as the model is resimulated, it does allow policy analysis. This technique also allows one to check the general conformity of model results against hypothesized economic relationships, although it obviously does not support formal hypothesis testing.

BVAR in Regional Modeling

Traditional SEM techniques are subject to some particular limitations in the regional context that make the BVAR approach a particularly attractive alternative for modeling regional economies. The costs of developing and maintaining large scales SEMs may be particularly burdensome for models of regional scope where the amount of resources that can be devoted to the modeling effort is more limited. This problem is exacerbated by the frequency and magnitude of adjustments that are made in regional economic data series. In a modeling environment in which historical data are frequently adjusted by substantial amounts, it is imperative that the model be re-estimated frequently, and the cost in time and effort to re-estimate is much lower with a BVAR model.

An additional limitation of SEMs in the regional modeling environment stems from the fact that they are usually "driven" by national economic variables, such as real GNP or disposable personal income, which are treated as exogenous in the regional model. These national variables are not truly policy variables, but are endogenous variables from national models. The accuracy of regional model forecasts often depends crucially upon the selection of a "driving" forecast of the national variables that proves to be accurate. In this environment it is difficult to accurately assess the forecast accuracy of the regional model or to provide confidence intervals on its forecasts. With a BVAR model any national variables included are endogenous to the system which makes evaluation of

error characteristics and generation of confidence intervals a relatively straight forward process.

The Arizona BVAR Model

In this study we present tentative results of a BVAR model of key variables in the Arizona economy. The focus will be on the parameters used and the process of generating the model and on analysis of impulse response functions generated by the model. Impulse response functions are an interesting simulation application, and they are a relatively overlooked feature of BVAR models in the literature.

The key to the process of BVAR modeling is the specification of the bayesian priors. This element of the BVAR modeling process involves the generation of prior estimates of the values of parameters and estimates of the degree of confidence we have about those values, as measured by the standard deviations of the estimated values. Litterman [3] has proposed some general guidelines for the priors used in BVAR models of most economic time series. He has suggested use of a modified random walk approach in which the estimated coefficient on the first own lag is one, the coefficients on all first cross lags are estimated to be zero (values around .2 or smaller are suggested), the prior parameter estimates for all lags greater than one period (own and cross) are zero, and the standard deviations of parameter estimates become smaller as the lag length increases. The later feature says that we become more sure that the coefficients on parameters are very close to zero as the lag length increases. BVAR models based on quarterly data have generally restricted the lag length to 4 to 8 quarters.

The model described here is based on quarterly data series for U.S. disposable personal income, and a set of key economic variables in the Arizona economy. The Arizona variables are, total personal income, employment in manufacturing, and average hours per week worked in manufacturing. Model runs are based on data for the time period from the second quarter of 1979 to the through the first quarter of 1989.

The RATS statistical package for microcomputers was used for the estimation of the model. The vector autoregressions component of this statistical package is specifically designed to accommodate Bayesian estimates of the type proposed by Litterman. A VAR specification requires the user to specify the variables to be used in the model, the maximum lag length to be considered, and whether or not a constant term should be included. However, RATS lets the user convert the VAR model to a BVAR model. The standard BVAR specification uses prior estimates of one for the first order own lag on each variable in the model and prior estimates of zero on all of the cross lags and higher order lags.

A set of parameters are used to estimate the structure of the standard deviations on the prior estimates. A tightness estimate, in the form of the estimated standard deviation of these prior estimates, is specified on the own first order lag terms. This parameter is expressed as a percentage of the mean and is applied to all of the estimated values of first order lag terms. A matrix of parameters can be used to specify the standard deviations of the first order cross lag terms. The matrix values are used to determine the estimated standard deviations of the cross lag coefficients as a percentage of the own lag standard deviations. Finally, a lag decay parameter can be used to cause the estimated standard deviation to decrease systematically as the lag length increases.

An example of a model specification for a set of key Arizona economic variables is presented in Table 1. Notice that a tightness parameter of .2 is used. This means that the standard deviation of each of the prior estimates of own first order lag parameters is estimated to be .2, while the prior estimate itself is 1 for each equation.

The first order cross lag estimates have been generated in the following way. We have used the random walk approach of specifying an a prior mean value of 1 for the parameter for the own first lag term, 0 on all other own lag terms, and 0 on all cross lag terms. The standard deviations of the first order cross lag terms have been have been specified by a set of parameters which express cross lag term standard deviations as a percentage of the standard deviation on the own first lag term.

A set of these estimates is also shown in Table 1. For some of the cross terms we are quite sure that the coefficient is very close to 0 while for others we are less sure, and this is reflected in these parameters. Notice that, the cross terms between Arizona income, AY, and manufacturing employment, EMG, variables are given relatively large prior esti-

mates, since they are expected to be highly interrelated. Also, notice that the priors on U.S. disposable income, USAY, and average hours in manufacturing, AHMG, are asymmetric; The possibility of U.S. income affecting the Arizona variables is much stronger than the possibility of the Arizona variables affecting U.S. income and Arizona personal income and manufacturing are seen as possibly having greater impact on hours in manufacturing than the latter could have on the former.

A harmonic decay function has been used to estimate the standard deviations for higher order lag terms. This decay function is of the form $1/L^i$. The estimated standard deviation for the second period lag is the estimated standard deviation of the first period lag times $1/2^i$, and so on. We have used a parameter of 2 to produce estimates of the standard deviations on higher order lag term estimates that decrease rapidly as the lag length increases.

A sample of the output produced for one variable in the model is shown in Table 2. The number of parameters is very large and it is difficult to interpret the meaning of individual coefficients. Only the own first lag, and the first lag on manufacturing employment are significant based on T-test values. The relative magnitudes of parameters can be used to get a feel for which variables are most important and for the lag structure of coefficients. The F-Tests at the bottom of the table give overall estimates of the significance of the sets of lag coefficients for each variable. In this case Arizona income is seen to be very significantly influenced by its own lagged values, and perhaps marginally influenced, .12 percent significance level, by lagged values of manufacturing employment. U.S. disposable income does not appear to have any significant influence on Arizona disposable income.

Impulse Response Functions

Impulse response functions measure the dynamic response of each endogenous variable in a system to a shock in the system. Impulse response functions can be generated for impulses of a variety of magnitudes, impulses to one, several, or all of the variables in a system, and impulses lasting a single period or multiple periods.

Impulse response functions are subject to criticism on conceptual grounds since they impose an exogenous shock on a variable endogenous to a system of equations. However, they do allow the generation of conditional forecasts based on multivariate time series models.

Perhaps the easiest form of impulse response function to understand and interpret is a one period impulse to a single variable. The impulse response functions presented here apply a one standard deviation shock to an individual variable in the system and generate a set of forecasts for the entire system for a number of periods following this impulse. This simulated forecast is compared to the variable values generated without the impulse in order to generate estimates of the dynamic multipliers for the system. All responses are measured as magnitudes relative to the standard deviation of the "shocked" variable.

The RATS statistical package has a built in instruction called impulse which can be used to generate this type of impulse response function and several others. The system's response to an impulse is depicted graphically. Graphs showing the response of each variable in the system to an impulse in one variable, and graphs showing the response of one variable to an impulses in each variable can be generated.

Table 3 shows a set of graphs of impulse response functions for this model. The graphs shown plot the response of each model variable to a one standard deviation impulse in a particular variable. The response is plotted over a ten quarter time horizon. The minimum and maximum values, as a ratio to the standard deviation of the impulse variable, are indicated and a set of + symbols indicates the line of zero response.

Notice that an increase in Arizona income causes increases in manufacturing hours, it is also associated with small increases in U.S. disposable income, and small decreases in manufacturing employment.

An impulse to Arizona manufacturing employment causes a relatively large increase in Arizona income, particularly after a lag of about a year, which is consistent with theory. Average hours in Arizona manufacturing also increase moderately, while a negative influence on U.S. disposable income is found.

An impulse to U.S. disposable income causes an initial increase in average hours in manufacturing, followed by increases in manufac-

turing employment and in disposable income in Arizona with a longer lag. These responses are small in magnitude, but are consistent with theory.

Finally, an impulse to Average hours worked in manufacturing causes mostly negative responses in Arizona income and manufacturing employment. Virtually no impact on U.S. disposable income is present.

Overall, it is fair to say that most of the largest influences between variables shown in the impulse response functions are consistent with theory. However, it is also clear that there are a number of smaller impacts which run counter to economic theory. This type of pattern seems to be fairly typical of BVAR models. Particularly noticeable in our model is the lack of influence of the national variable on Arizona variables. On the basis of the results of this model, the Arizona economy would appear to be almost countercyclical to the U.S. economy.

Summary

BVAR modeling methods have shown promising results in several recent studies, which suggest that BVAR models may be effective for longer term forecasting than traditional time series models, and that they can be used to generate conditional forecasts useful for policy analysis and testing of economic hypotheses. BVAR modeling is also substantially more economical than the use of structural modeling.

In this paper we have presented preliminary results for a BVAR model of the Arizona economy. Analysis of this model has been somewhat limited due to the short time horizon of the data series available. The model is presented as an example of the application of the BVAR technique. The best test of the effectiveness of this model will be its performance over time in ex-post forecasting applications. However, impulse response functions can be used to examine the character of model interrelationships, and assess its conformity with economic theory. Impulse response functions generated for the model show it to be generally consistent with economic theory, although almost no relationship between U.S. income and Arizona income and manufacturing employment is found. The model presented here is clearly a preliminary one, further experience with the specification of the priors for this and similar models, and a longer time horizon over which ex-post forecasts can be evaluated, will be required before the success of this approach in modeling the Arizona economy can be properly assessed. However, BVAR modeling does appear to be a promising, low cost alternative to the type of SEM commonly used in regional modeling.

References

[1] Boero, G., "Comparing Ex-ante Forecasts from a SEM and a VAR Model: an Application to the Italian Economy", Journal of Forecasting, 9(1990), 13-24.

[2] Christ, C. F., "Judging the Performance of Econometric Models of the U.S. Economy", in Econometric Model Performance, Lawrence R. Klein and Edwin Burmeister, eds., The University of Pennsylvania Press, 1976, p 322-342.

[3] Litterman R., "A Bayesian Procedure for Forecasting with Vector Autoregressions", Department of Economics MIT, Cambridge, Mass.

[4] Litterman, R., "Forecasting and Policy Analysis with Bayesian Vector Autoregression Models", Federal Reserve Bank of Minneapolis Quarterly Review, 8(4),(1984),30-41.

[5] Longbottom, J. A. and Holly S., "The Role of Time Series Analysis in the Evaluation of Econometric Models", Journal of Forecasting, 4(1985), 75-87.

[6] McNees, S. K., "The Role of Macroeconomic Models in Forecasting and Policy Analysis in the United States", Journal of Forecasting, 1(1982), 37-48.

[7] McNees, S. K., "Forecasting Accuracy of Alternative Techniques: a Comparisons of U.S. Macroeconomics Forecasts", Journal of Business and Economic Statistics, 4(1986), 5-15.

[8] Sims C. A., "Macroeconomics and Reality", Econometrica 48, 1-48.

[9] Zellner, A., Basic Issues in Econometrics, The University of Chicago Press, 1987, p 191.

Table 1

PRIOR SPECIFICATIONS IN AN ARIZONA BVAR MODEL

THE PRIOR IS....
TIGHTNESS PARAMETER   .20000
HARMONIC LAG DECAY WITH PARAMETER   1.00000
MEANS AND STANDARD DEVIATIONS AS PERCENTAGE OF OWN LAG
LISTED UNDER THE DEPENDENT VARIABLE

	AY	EMG	USAY	AHMG
AY	1.00000000	.80000000	.10000000	.80000000
EMG	.80000000	1.00000000	.10000000	.80000000
USAY	.50000000	.50000000	1.00000000	.50000000
AHMG	.80000000	.80000000	.10000000	1.00000000
MEAN	1.00000000	1.00000000	1.00000000	1.00000000

Table 2

SAMPLE BVAR OUTPUT FOR THE VARIABLE ARIZONA PERSONAL INCOME

FROM   1979: 2 UNTIL   1989: 1
TOTAL OBSERVATIONS   40   SKIPPED/MISSING   0
USABLE OBSERVATIONS   40   DEGREES OF FREEDOM   39
R**2   .99309016   RBAR**2   .99309016
SSR   .15947224E-03   SEE   .20221354E-02
DURBIN-WATSON 2.62968778
Q(18)=   15.2411   SIGNIFICANCE LEVEL .645351

NO.	LABEL	VAR	LAG	COEFFICIENT	STAND. ERROR	T-STATISTIC
***	*******	***	***	************	************	************
1	AY	1	1	.7879566	.8899911E-01	8.853534
2	AY	1	2	.2794200E-01	.6660010E-01	.4195490
3	AY	1	3	.1584969E-01	.4809125E-01	.3295754
4	AY	1	4	.7411572E-02	.3716050E-01	.1994476
5	AY	1	5	-.9114486E-04	.3017827E-01	-.3020214E-02
6	AY	1	6	-.2025735E-02	.2543472E-01	-.7964450E-01
7	AY	1	7	.6707180E-02	.2187608E-01	.3065989
8	AY	1	8	.3921758E-02	.1924520E-01	.2037785
9	EMG	8	1	.3799806E-01	.1297401E-01	2.928783
10	EMG	8	2	.4122700E-02	.1131494E-01	.3643591
11	EMG	8	3	-.2914903E-02	.7907262E-02	-.3686362
12	EMG	8	4	-.9782275E-03	.6039011E-02	-.1619847
13	EMG	8	5	-.2442755E-02	.4892918E-02	-.4992430
14	EMG	8	6	-.9112877E-03	.4135820E-02	-.2203403
15	EMG	8	7	-.7793131E-03	.3574023E-02	-.2180493
16	EMG	8	8	.1997627E-03	.3140677E-02	.6360497E-01
17	USAY	5	1	-.2344452E-03	.1299704E-01	-.1803836E-01
18	USAY	5	2	.2513273E-02	.9830879E-02	.2556509
19	USAY	5	3	.2174253E-02	.6868683E-02	.3165458
20	USAY	5	4	-.3287019E-03	.5242744E-02	-.6269653E-01
21	USAY	5	5	.1399353E-02	.4222214E-02	.3314264
22	USAY	5	6	.1085296E-02	.3537839E-02	.3067679
23	USAY	5	7	.9982994E-03	.3049585E-02	.3273558
24	USAY	5	8	.9629174E-03	.2674763E-02	.3600010
25	AHMG	12	1	-.7046486E-03	.5579717E-03	-1.262875
26	AHMG	12	2	-.2136165E-03	.3465908E-03	-.6163364
27	AHMG	12	3	-.1224642E-03	.2447429E-03	-.5003790
28	AHMG	12	4	.2292467E-04	.1881621E-03	.1218347
29	AHMG	12	5	-.5008424E-04	.1521122E-03	-.3292584
30	AHMG	12	6	-.4831965E-04	.1278085E-03	-.3780628
31	AHMG	12	7	.1104894E-04	.1100027E-03	.1004424
32	AHMG	12	8	.2876770E-04	.9670402E-04	.2974819
33	CONSTANT	0	0	.7008098E-01	.5541541E-01	1.264648

F-TESTS, DEPENDENT VARIABLE   AY

VARIABLE	F-STATISTIC	SIGNIF. LEVEL
AY	23.02007	.1618927E-11
EMG	1.72382	.1235161
USAY	.24115	.9802540
AHMG	.35120	.9394990

```
                                Table 3
                   PLOT OF IMPULSE RESPONSE FUNCTIONS

PLOT OF RESPONSES TO AY   (A)

MIN VALUE   -.15815      MAX VALUE   1.0000      SPACING    .23636E-01
          ++++++++++++++++++++++++++++++++++++++++++++++++++++++
   1976: 4+     B +      C              D                        A
   1977: 1+ B      +      C   D                     A            +
   1977: 2+B       +      CD               A                     +
   1977: 3+B       + D    C        A                             +
   1977: 4B        + D    C    A                                 +
   1978: 1B        D     C A                                     +
   1978: 2B        D+      &                                     + AC
   1978: 3+B    D + A  C                                         +
   1978: 4+B    D+ A   C                                         +
   1979: 1+ B   D+A   C                                          +
          ++++++++++++++++++++++++++++++++++++++++++++++++++++++

PLOT OF RESPONSES TO EMG   (B)

MIN VALUE   -.29192      MAX VALUE   1.0492      SPACING    .27370E-01
          ++++++++++++++++++++++++++++++++++++++++++++++++++++++
   1976: 4C          A         D                           B +
   1977: 1C          +       A D                           B
   1977: 2+C         +         D   A                        B
   1977: 3+  C       +            D      A                  B +
   1977: 4+    C     +            D        A        B       +
   1978: 1+     C    +            D          A    B         +
   1978: 2+      C + D                BA                    +
   1978: 3+      C + D          B     A                     +
   1978: 4+      C + D     B        A                       +
   1979: 1+        C +DB           A                        +
          ++++++++++++++++++++++++++++++++++++++++++++++++++++++

PLOT OF RESPONSES TO USAY   (C)

MIN VALUE   -.69159E-01  MAX VALUE   .99341      SPACING    .21685E-01
          +++++++++++++++++++++++++++++++++++++++++++++++++++++++
   1976: 4+   &    D                                  C + AB
   1977: 1+ BAD                                        C
   1977: 2+ &A                                         C+ BD
   1977: 3+DBA                                      C  +
   1977: 4D   BA                                  C      +
   1978: 1D  + BA                               C        +
   1978: 2+D +   BA                           C          +
   1978: 3+ D+      &                         C          + AB
   1978: 4+  D          &                     C          + AB
   1979: 1+  +D          BA                   C          +
          +++++++++++++++++++++++++++++++++++++++++++++++++++++++

PLOT OF RESPONSES TO AHMG   (D)

MIN VALUE   -.28570      MAX VALUE   .86849      SPACING    .23555E-01
          +++++++++++++++++++++++++++++++++++++++++++++++++++++++
   1976: 4+             &                              D ABC
   1977: 1+     A B  C                   D              +
   1977: 2+ A    B    +C         D                      +
   1977: 3+A     B    CD                                +
   1977: 4A     B    DC                                 +
   1978: 1A   B   D   C                                 +
   1978: 2A   B   D   C                                 +
   1978: 3+A   B D   C+                                 +
   1978: 4+ A   B D  C+                                 +
   1979: 1+  A    BD C+                                 +
          +++++++++++++++++++++++++++++++++++++++++++++++++++++++
```

SIMULATION IN LEARNING

A TEMPORAL ANALYSIS OF SIMULATION-TEAM ADAPTIVE BEHAVIOR

A. J. Faria; University of Windsor; Windsor, Ont., N9B 3P4; (519) 253-4232, Ext. 3101
John R. Dickinson; University of Windsor; Windsor, Ont., N9B 3P4; (519) 253-4232, Ext. 3104
T. Richard Whiteley; Mankato State University; Mankato, MN, 56002; (507) 389-5337

ABSTRACT

The present study, using a controlled experiment based on two experimentally manipulated environments, was designed to investigate the nature and the extent of the adaptive behavior of competitive teams in a marketing simulation game. If the players in such a game make decisions which are consistent with the environment with which they must contend, when during the game does such appropriate learning take place and how stable is such learning? The results of the study reveal that what limited appropriate adaptive behavior does take place occurs early in the game and reflects a high degree of stability. The same is also true for any inappropriate learning that takes place.

INTRODUCTION AND PAST RESEARCH

Since their inception in the middle 1950s, computer based simulation games have become a widely used learning tool. One source puts the number of business simulation games existing in 1980 at 228 (Horn and Cleaves 1980). A recent survey (Faria 1987) estimated that over 95 percent of AACSB schools incorporate simulation games into their curricula. As well, corporate business enterprise makes extensive use of computer simulations. Approximately 23 percent of the companies employing over 1,000 people currently use such games, while an additional 11 percent have used them in the past (Faria 1987).

As widely accepted as simulation games are, the effectiveness and validity of this approach to learning have been persistent issues of concern in the literature for some time. The effectiveness of simulation games has been addressed in dozens of empirical studies, as summarized in three major reviews (see Greenlaw and Wyman 1973; Miles, Biggs, and Schubert 1986; Wolfe 1985). The validity of such games also continues to be a focus of current research (see Mehrez, Reichel, and Olami 1987; Wolfe and Jackson [forthcoming]; Wolfe and Roberts 1986). In this vein, the present paper describes a controlled experiment investigating the adaptive behavior of simulation teams to an environment created in a simulation competition. Appropriate behavior of this nature is a necessary condition for simulation model validity.

Generally, a computer-based simulation game comprises an environment defined by the game's creators and, possibly, fine tuned by the game administrator. Players make decisions vis-a-vis this environment only (i.e., they compete against the simulation model) or, and perhaps more commonly, decisions may be made with regard to this environment in light of the decisions and performances of other players (i.e., players, in the guise of companies, compete against each other as well as adapt to the game environment). The premise of the present study is that if players do become meaningfully involved in a simulation gaming experience, then their decisions should at least in part reflect the environment defined by the simulation.

PURPOSE AND HYPOTHESES

It is recognized that the actual decisions made during a simulation game can be influenced by the dynamics of the game used, the company's changing state within the game context, the decisions and performances of competing companies, the objectives of the game, and the capabilities of the participants. Nevertheless, the simulated environment too must be considered and, _ceteris paribus_, players' decisions should reflect or adapt to the simulation environment. And if the participants in a simulation game make decisions which are consistent with the environment with which they must contend, _when_ during the game does such learning take place and _how stable_ is this newly acquired knowledge?

In order to investigate these concerns, a controlled experiment, using the marketing simulation game entitled "LAPTOP: A Marketing Simulation (Faria and Dickinson 1987), was carried out in a principles of marketing course. The identified game can be parameterized in such a way so as to define, from a marketing perspective, theoretically meaningful and distinctly different environments necessary for the specified experiment.

Experimental Environments

Strategy decisions in LAPTOP are made at the product-market level (4 levels), at the territorial level (2 levels), and at the company level. A total of 36 specific types of decisions must be made in the game in order to generate sales for the standard (Product 100) and deluxe (Product 200) versions of a laptop computer available for sale in each of the two territories (Territory 1 and Territory 2). Twelve different marketing research reports can also be ordered.

When initializing a new LAPTOP competition, the game administrator can specify the weights of the demand-affecting strategy elements, each of which can be weighted using an index ranging from 1 (low importance) to 10 (high importance). For the purposes of the present experiment, the parameter weighting feature of the game was used to define two distinct environments. One environment resulted in a situation that would reward the use of a "pull" strategy. The second environment resulted in a situation that would reward the use of a "push" strategy.

Under a pull strategy, the manufacturer attempts to stimulate consumer awareness and demand for a product by focusing its marketing efforts on the final consumer. In the case of a push strategy, the emphasis shifts to aggressive personal selling and trade promotion aimed at gaining the co-operation of distributors and retailers to carry a product (McDaniel and Darden 1987; Schewe 1987).

The strategy decision areas that were deemed to be "pull" variables in the study were (final household) price, broadcast and print advertising, and premiums. Weighted average price and exact competitive price research information were also considered to be pertinent to the decision-making process under such an environment. Trade advertising, co-operative advertising allowances, sales force size, trade show participation, and point-of-purchase sales promotion materials were deemed to be "push" variables. Co-operative advertising allowance and sales force size research information were also considered to be pertinent to companies in this latter environment.

In order to create an industry which would reward the use of a pull strategy, all of the identified pull variables were initialized with a weighting of 10 in one of the experimental conditions (i.e., the pull environment). The push variables in this environment were given a weighting of 1. The decision variables which did not fall within either a push or pull environment were given a middle weighting of 5.

In order to create an industry which would reward the use of a push strategy, all of the identified push variables were initialized with a weighting of 10 in the second experimental condition (i.e., the push environment). The pull variables in this environment were

given a weighting of 1. The decision variables which did not fall within either a push or pull environment were given a middle weighting of 5.

In total, the variable weight manipulations in the push and pull environments involved 20 of the 36 decision areas of the LAPTOP simulation. The parameter weights for each company were the same across all product-markets and between territories.

The marketing research information available to the companies under either of the environments did not require the assignment of weights. In this case, the company either requests or does not request the pertinent information.

Hypotheses

The nature of the dependent variables used in the study varies as a function of the decision area under consideration (e.g., actual price, dollar advertising expenditure, percentage of companies requesting a certain type of research) and the level of analysis (i.e., company level, product level, territorial level). Nonetheless, the general hypothesis is that, if marketing strategy formulation in a simulation environment is an internally valid experience, then the nature of the decisions should gravitate toward the more pertinent and more heavily weighted strategy elements. As a result, the nature of the decisions should vary as a function of the environment in which a company operates for each relevant period of play. Specifically, it is expected that

H1: The average price in the Pull environment will be lower than the average price in the Push environment.

H2: The average broadcast advertising expenditure in the Pull environment will be higher than the corresponding average in the Push environment.

H3: The average print advertising expenditure in the Pull environment will be higher than the corresponding average in the Push environment.

H4: The average trade advertising expenditure in the Pull environment will be lower than the corresponding average in the Push environment.

H5: The average co-operative advertising allowance percent in the Pull environment will be lower than the corresponding average in the Push environment.

H6: The average territorial sales force size in the Pull environment will be smaller than the corresponding average in the Push environment.

H7: The average per company selection rate of the sale promotion approaches of point-of-purchase (P.O.P) materials and/or trade shows in the Pull environment will be lower than the corresponding average in the Push environment.

H8: The average per company selection of the sales promotion approach of premiums in the Pull environment will be higher than the corresponding average in the Push environment.

H9: The percentage of companies requesting average price research and/or exact price research in the Pull environment will be higher than the corresponding percentage in the Push environment.

H10: The percentage of companies requesting cooperative advertising allowance research in the Pull environment will be lower than the corresponding percentage in the Push environment.

H11: The percentage of companies requesting sales force size research in the Pull environment will be lower than the corresponding percentage in the Push environment.

It should be noted that Hypothesis 7 reveals two consistent specific behaviors which are possible for companies in the push environment (i.e., using point-of-purchase sales promotion and/or using trade show sales promotion). Since only a single type of sales promotion can be selected for each of a company's four product-markets in a given decision period, the hypotheses is phrased so as to take this fact into account.

In the case of Hypothesis 9, even though a company can order average and exact price research in a given period, carrying out either behavior is consistent with a pull environment. A company may therefore feel that requesting both types of research information results in the acquisition of redundant and costly information. For this reason, Hypothesis 9 is phrased so as only to expect a request for at least one form of this type of research.

The investigation of the general hypothesis reflected by the preceding 11 specific hypotheses requires a between-environment comparison based on 11 dependent variables. In each case, the values to be used are the actual company-wide value, the average territorial value, or the average product-market value, as is appropriate. Thus, there is only one value for each dependent variable for each company per

period. In all cases, except for the very first period of play, the same analysis will be carried out for each period of play in the game, with a specific focus on identifying between-environment decision-making trends as the game progresses.

With respect to the very first period, all of the hypotheses need to be modified to reflect an expectation of no significant differences between environments. This modification is appropriate since all of the participants were randomly assigned to conditions, none of them were aware that an experiment of the nature identified was being conducted, and none of the participants in the two environments would have had any reason to make decisions of a differential nature. Once the results from the first period are obtained, then differential decisions would be expected.

METHODOLOGY

The simulation competition executed in the study involved approximately 260 undergraduate students enrolled in two sections of a one-semester principles of marketing course. The students were advised that the game was worth 20% of the course grade and that the performance objective of the game was to maximize the company's earnings per share relative to the competition in the same industry.

The students were assigned to teams (companies) of up to four players on the basis of self-selection or, when necessary, on a random basis. Sixty of the formed teams were randomly assigned to 12 industries consisting of 5 companies each. The remaining six teams were assigned to an industry that was not included in the study. This latter industry was used to handle administrative problems encountered during the course (e.g., late enrollees).

Each of the 12 industries in the study was randomly assigned to one of two environments. Six industries (i.e., 30 companies) were assigned to the "push" environment and a similar number of industries (i.e., 30 companies) were assigned to the "pull" environment. At no time during the game did the game administrator inform the players about the nature of the environment which they faced or that an experiment was being run.

The first weekly decision of the game was made during the third week of the course. This decision and the subsequent one served as trial decisions [i.e., Trial Period 1 (T1) and Trial Period 2 (T2)], thereby providing the players with the oppportunity to become familiar with the technical aspects of the game and to try various strategies without risk.

At the end of the trial period, a new game was started, but the environment and the competition faced by each company during the trial periods remained the same. The knowledge which the teams acquired during the trial sessions therefore had the potential of being relevant to the new game. The new game consisted of eight weekly decisions [i.e., Real Period 1 (R1) to Real Period 8 (R8)].

Since the focus of the study is to identify between-environment decision-making trends as the game progresses, the decisions for each period of play were analyzed independently.

RESULTS

Statistical Analysis Approach

For each of the periods of play, the participants in the game were required to make 36 specific types of decisions as well as to determine which of 12 areas of research information to request. Each of these decisions can be considered to involve theoretically unrelated variables, even though some variables may be statistically correlated. For example, a price decision in one product-market is conceptually unrelated to a price decision in another product-market and a request for one type of research is conceptually unrelated to a request for another type of research. Similarly, a price decision is conceptually unrelated to a broadcast advertising expenditure decision. This decision independence focus is also reflected by the fact that the importance weights for each variable can be (and were) set independently by the game administrators.

In an experiment of this nature, it is appropriate to analyze each dependent variable separately (see Biskin 1980, 1983). Furthermore, since all of the hypotheses in the study are directional in nature for Trial Period 2 and Real Periods 1 to 8, analyzing each dependent variable separately prevents the possibility of an unacceptable loss of power which could otherwise occur under a multivariate type of analysis (Tabachnick and Fidell 1983). For these reasons, the data collected for each dependent variable in all periods of the study, except Trial Period 1, were analyzed using independent, one-tailed t-tests. Since no between environment differences were expected for Trial Period 1, an independent, two-tailed t-test was used.

Tests of Hypotheses

The results and summary data analyses are presented in Tables 1 and 2 and Figures 1 to 11. There is a one-to-one correspondence between a figure number and each similarly numbered hypothesis.

TABLE 1
SUMMARY OF TESTS OF HYPOTHESES

Hypotheses	T1	T2	R1	R2	R3	R4	R5	R6	R7	R8
1. Price		SC	SC							
2. Broadcast advertising		SI	SI	SI	SI	SI	SI			
3. Print advertising			SI	SI	SI	SI	SI	SI	SI	SI
4. Trade advertising		SC	SC	SC	SC	SC	SC	SC	SC	
5. Co-op allowance										
6. Sales force size										
7. P.O.P./Trade shows	SI	SC	SC							
8. Premiums										
9. Price research										
10. Co-op research		SC								
11. Sales force research		SC								

Notes: "T1" represents Trial Period 1. "R1" represents Real Period 1. "SC" indicates result is significant and consistent with hypothesis. "SI" indicates result is significant but inconsistent with hypothesis. An empty cell indicates result is not significant.

The results for Trial Period 1 are generally consistent with expectations. For 10 of the 11 decision areas, no significant differences between environments are uncovered. The only inconsistent result during this period involves Hypothesis 7: The per company selection rate for the P.O.P. and/or trade show sales promotion approach in the pull environment is significantly higher than the corresponding value for the push environment. No between-environment difference was expected.

For the remaining nine decision periods (i.e., Trial Period 2 to Real Period 8), there is very limited support for the hypotheses of the study. Only for Hypothesis 4 can the results be considered to be consistent with expectations. For eight of the identified nine periods, the push environment companies spent significantly more on trade advertising than did the pull environment companies. No between-environment difference exists for Real Period 8 in this expenditure area.

In the decision areas of broadcast and print advertising (Hypotheses 2 and 3 respectively), the results reveal significant differences which are inconsistent with expectations. For six decision periods (Trial Period 2 to Real Period 5), the average broadcast advertising expenditure in the push environment is significantly higher than the corresponding pull environment value. No such difference exists for any of the final three decision periods. Similarly, for eight decision periods (Real Periods 1 to 8), the average print advertising expenditure in the push environment is significantly higher than the corresponding pull environment value.

Other consistent results are revealed in Trial Period 2 and Real Period 1 for Hypothesis 1 (price level)

26

TABLE 2
COMPARISON OF MEAN DECISION VARIABLE VALUES

		PERIOD								
		Trial 1		Trial 2		Real 1		Real 2		Real 3	
Variable	Environment	$\bar{X}$	SD	$\bar{X}$	SD	$\bar{X}$	SD	$\bar{X}$	SD	$\bar{X}$	SD
Price ($)	Push	1332.78	(1522.68)	1225.99	(760.26)	1004.22	(169.89)	1030.76	(195.65)	1021.46	(158.20)
	Pull	1026.03	(263.46)	977.37	(139.60)	938.27	(103.56)	964.24	(126.74)	946.46	(119.82)
	t-value	1.09	NS	1.76	p < .05	1.82	p < .05	1.56	NS	1.57	NS
Broadcast advertising ('000)	Push	79.78	(187.74)	62.66	(95.98)	42.96	(27.96)	44.67	(25.37)	45.33	(28.20)
	Pull	41.79	(127.63)	22.68	(19.87)	25.11	(21.44)	27.12	(16.03)	28.43	(18.72)
	t-value	0.90	NS	2.33	p < .05	2.76	p < .01	3.20	p < .01	2.74	p < .01
Print advertising ($'000)	Push	58.25	(173.20)	48.52	(115.28)	24.35	(14.84)	29.00	(13.41)	32.81	(19.45)
	Pull	27.26	(72.47)	14.06	(7.84)	14.86	(8.56)	18.17	(11.23)	17.78	(9.28)
	t-value	0.90	NS	1.63	NS	3.04	p < .01	3.39	p < .001	3.82	p < .001
Trade advertising ($'000)	Push	48.35	(158.50)	32.14	(62.03)	17.77	(17.56)	21.60	(19.23)	20.78	(18.14)
	Pull	16.57	(48.40)	7.20	(5.95)	7.28	(4.92)	8.01	(5.58)	7.21	(4.18)
	t-value	1.05	NS	2.19	p < .05	3.15	p < .01	3.72	p < .001	4.00	p < .001
Co-operative advertising allowance (%)	Push	2.28	(1.54)	2.58	(2.31)	2.65	(1.82)	2.65	(1.66)	2.93	(2.17)
	Pull	1.78	(1.36)	2.02	(1.60)	2.08	(1.62)	2.55	(1.65)	2.42	(1.55)
	t-value	1.33	NS	1.11	NS	1.27	NS	0.23	NS	1.06	NS
Sales force size	Push	10.75	(4.41)	11.18	(4.26)	9.73	(1.44)	10.15	(2.44)	10.52	(3.96)
	Pull	9.85	(3.97)	10.25	(4.21)	10.18	(2.69)	10.63	(2.76)	12.88	(11.94)
	t-value	0.83	NS	0.85	NS	- 0.81	NS	- 0.72	NS	- 1.03	NS
P.O.P/trade shows (% of use)	Push	46.67	(33.95)	42.50	(30.90)	42.50	(33.57)	38.33	(37.56)	31.67	(38.24)
	Pull	26.67	(29.31)	28.33	(29.89)	22.50	(24.87)	27.50	(28.12)	25.00	(28.62)
	t-value	2.44	p < .05	1.80	p < .05	2.62	p < .01	1.26	NS	0.76	NS
Premiums sales promotion (% of use)	Push	25.00	(26.26)	35.00	(31.21)	39.17	(31.27)	33.33	(33.04)	30.83	(36.37)
	Pull	15.83	(24.99)	28.33	(27.65)	36.67	(31.30)	42.50	(32.26)	44.17	(34.54)
	t-value	1.39	NS	0.88	NS	0.31	NS	- 1.09	NS	- 1.46	NS
Price research (% of use)	Push	93.33	(25.37)	93.33	(25.37)	100.00	(0.00)	90.00	(30.51)	90.00	(30.51)
	Pull	90.00	(30.51)	93.33	(25.37)	93.33	(25.37)	93.33	(25.37)	90.00	(30.51)
	t-value	0.46	NS	0.00	NS	1.44	NS	- 0.46	NS	0.00	NS
Co-operative advertising research (% of use)	Push	43.33	(50.40)	53.33	(50.74)	6.67	(25.37)	0.00	(0.00)	6.67	(25.37)
	Pull	20.00	(40.68)	10.00	(30.51)	3.33	(18.26)	0.00	(0.00)	0.00	(00.00)
	t-value	1.97	NS	4.01	p < .001	0.58	NS	0.00	NS	1.44	NS
Sales force size research (% of use)	Push	56.67	(50.40)	70.00	(46.61)	16.67	(37.90)	20.00	(40.68)	13.33	(34.57)
	Pull	36.67	(49.01)	30.00	(46.61)	6.67	(25.37)	6.67	(25.37)	6.67	(25.37)
	t-value	1.56	NS	3.32	p < .001	1.20	NS	1.52	NS	0.85	NS

27

TABLE 2 -- CONTINUED.

		Real 4		Real 5		Real 6		Real 7		Real 8	
Variable	Environment	$\bar{X}$	SD	$\bar{X}$	SD	$\bar{X}$	SD	$\bar{X}$	SD	$\bar{X}$	SD
Price ($)	Push	1041.92	(164.95)	1074.03	(198.03)	1085.28	(215.73)	1098.22	(214.82)	1107.62	(249.77)
	Pull	1005.93	(169.46)	1021.28	(187.30)	1064.35	(213.68)	1102.85	(237.07)	1021.56	(208.32)
	t-value	0.83	NS	1.06	NS	0.38	NS	- 0.08	NS	1.45	NS
Broadcast	Push	48.34	(31.91)	56.58	(32.77)	55.12	(36.29)	53.06	(35.96)	53.74	(44.16)
advertising	Pull	30.46	(19.07)	36.15	(24.55)	42.29	(32.90)	42.41	(31.01)	39.72	(31.49)
($'000)	t-value	2.63	$p < .05$	2.73	$p < .01$	1.43	NS	1.23	NS	1.44	NS
Print	Push	32.66	(22.27)	39.03	(21.17)	36.38	(20.53)	34.27	(21.07)	34.98	(26.42)
advertising	Pull	19.26	(12.23)	21.17	(12.26)	25.09	(19.38)	23.96	(15.96)	20.90	(11.07)
($'000)	t-value	2.89	$p < .01$	3.58	$p < .001$	2.19	$p < .05$	2.18	$p < .05$	2.69	$p < .01$
Trade	Push	20.23	(18.08)	20.78	(19.53)	18.72	(20.85)	13.38	(10.83)	13.83	(14.33)
advertising	Pull	7.08	(4.71)	7.71	(5.21)	7.38	(6.05)	7.83	(6.12)	8.12	(9.32)
($'000)	t-value	3.85	$p < .001$	3.54	$p < .001$	2.88	$p < .01$	2.45	$p < .01$	1.83	NS
Co-operative	Push	3.05	(2.11)	3.47	(2.19)	3.48	(2.16)	3.80	(2.36)	4.07	(2.07)
advertising	Pull	2.58	(1.84)	2.77	(2.00)	2.90	(2.36)	3.43	(2.46)	3.23	(3.11)
allowance	t-value	0.91	NS	1.29	NS	1.00	NS	.59	NS	1.11	NS
(%)											
Sales force	Push	10.67	(4.19)	10.88	(3.76)	10.43	(2.67)	10.53	(2.63)	10.02	(2.97)
size	Pull	12.58	(11.89)	11.43	(6.49)	10.50	(2.04)	10.38	(1.87)	10.07	(1.69)
(#)	t-value	- 0.83	NS	- 0.40	NS	- 0.11	NS	0.25	NS	- 0.08	NS
P.O.P/trade	Push	30.83	(37.53)	43.33	(38.24)	35.00	(34.49)	33.33	(34.32)	21.67	(33.95)
shows	Pull	30.00	(30.37)	35.83	(36.95)	26.67	(34.70)	25.00	(38.28)	21.67	(35.80)
(% of use)	t-value	0.09	NS	0.78	NS	0.93	NS	0.89	NS	0.00	NS
Premiums	Push	28.33	(37.56)	30.83	(36.95)	39.17	(31.95)	37.50	(37.57)	35.87	(36.95)
sales	Pull	29.17	(29.42)	37.50	(36.41)	43.33	(37.68)	47.50	(37.91)	35.83	(40.83)
promotion	t-value	- 0.10	NS	- 0.70	NS	- 0.46	NS	- 1.03	NS	0.00	NS
(% of use)											
Price	Push	86.67	(34.57)	76.67	(43.02)	80.00	(40.68)	80.00	(40.68)	6.67	(25.37)
research	Pull	83.33	(37.90)	86.67	(34.57)	83.33	(37.90)	73.33	(44.98)	6.67	(25.37)
(% of use)	t-value	0.02	NS	- 0.99	NS	- 0.33	NS	0.60	NS	0.00	NS
Co-operative	Push	6.67	(25.37)	6.67	(25.37)	13.33	(34.57)	13.33	(34.57)	3.33	(18.26)
advertising	Pull	10.67	(30.51)	3.33	(18.26)	3.33	(18.26)	3.33	(18.26)	3.33	(18.26)
research	t-value	- 0.46	NS	0.58	NS	1.40	NS	1.40	NS	0.00	NS
(% of use)											
Sales force	Push	13.33	(34.57)	13.33	(34.57)	10.00	(30.51)	10.00	(30.51)	0.00	(0.00)
size	Pull	13.33	(34.57)	6.67	(25.37)	3.33	(18.26)	3.33	(18.26)	0.00	(0.00)
research	t-value	0.00	NS	0.85	NS	1.03	NS	1.03	NS	0.00	NS
(% of use)											

Notes: n = 30 for each group. Two-tailed, independent t-test conducted for Trial Period 1. One tailed, independent t-test conducted for all remaining periods.

FIGURE 1
PRICE LEVEL
(Average Company Value - Between Environments)

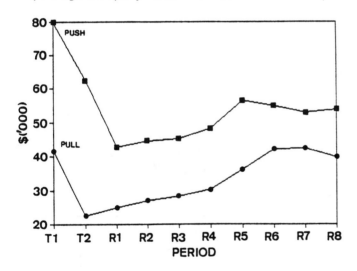

FIGURE 2
BROADCAST ADVERTISING EXPENDITURES
(Average Company Value - Between Environments)

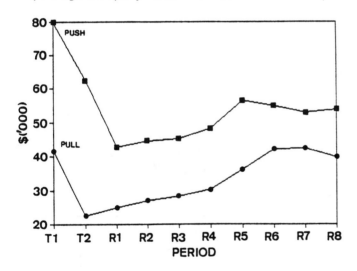

FIGURE 3
PRINT ADVERTISING EXPENDITURES
(Average Company Value - Between Environments)

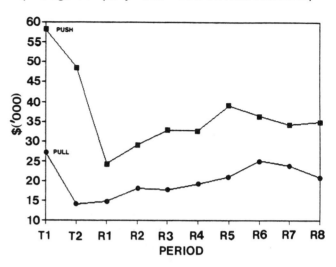

FIGURE 4
TRADE ADVERTISING EXPENDITURES
(Average Company Value - Between Environments)

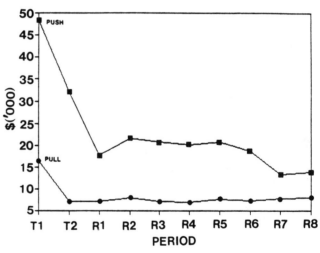

and Hypothesis 7 (per company selection rate for P.O.P. and/or trade show sales promotion) and in Trial Period 2 for Hypothesis 10 (request for co-operative advertising allowance research) and Hypothesis 11 (request for sales force size research). With respect to the price levels in Trial Period 2 and Real Period 1, the average prices for the pull environment companies are significantly lower than the corresponding push environment values. With respect to the per company selection rates for P.O.P. and/or trade show sales promotion in Trial Period 2 and Real period 1, the average selection rates for the push environment companies are significantly greater than

those for the pull environment companies. The latter relationship is also true for the level of requests for co-operative advertising allowance research and sales force size research in Trial Period 2: The levels of utilization are greater for the push environment companies.

At no time during the game did the companies in the two environments make significantly different decisions in the co-operative advertising allowance percent (Hypothesis 5), the sales force size (Hypothesis 6), the selection rate of the sales promotion approach of premiums (Hypothesis 8), and the use of price

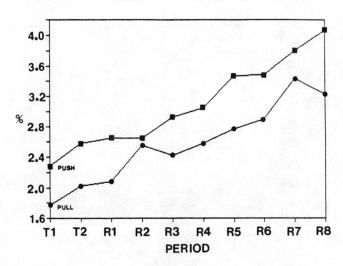

FIGURE 5
CO-OPERATIVE ADVERTISING ALLOWANCE
(Average Company Value - Between Environments)

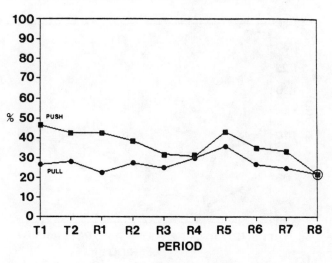

FIGURE 7
P.O.P./TRADE SHOW SALES PROMOTION
(Average Co. Selection Rate - Between Environments)

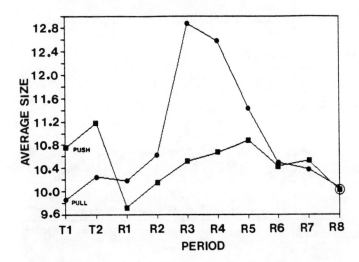

FIGURE 6
TERRITORIAL SALES FORCE SIZE
(Average Company Value - Between Environments)

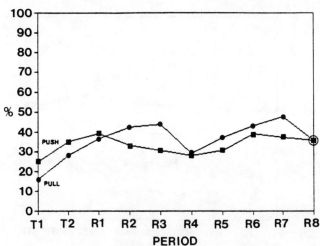

FIGURE 8
PREMIUMS SALES PROMOTION
(Average Co. Selection Rate - Between Environments)

research (Hypothesis 9).

DISCUSSION

Overall, the results of the study indicate that, throughout the game, the participants in the pull environment were not making very many operational and strategic decisions which were significantly different from those being made by the participants in the push environment. Furthermore, where significant differences did exist after Trial Period 1, the number of find-that were contrary to expectations equalled the number that were consistent with expectations (14

contrary and 14 consistent out of 99 comparisons).

Only with respect to the area of trade advertising expenditures is there strong evidence to indicate that the participants in the game were correctly adapting to the environment with which they had to contend. The learning of this correct form of decision making occurred early in the game (i.e., Trial Period 2) and remained stable until all but the final period of play. In this latter period, evidence of such learning disappeared; the push environment companies were no longer spending significantly more than the pull environment companies on trade advertising.

30

FIGURE 9
PRICE RESEARCH
(% of Co.'s Requesting - Between Environments)

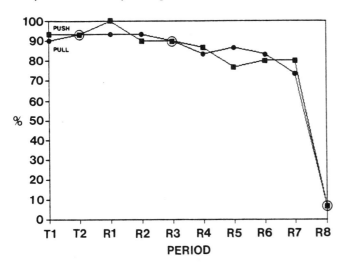

FIGURE 10
CO-OPERATIVE ADVERTISING RESEARCH
(% of Co.'s Requesting - Between Environments)

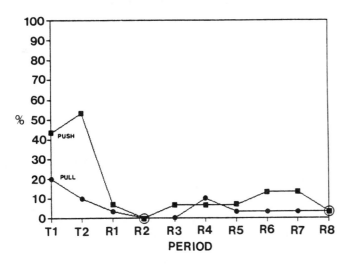

FIGURE 11
SALES FORCE SIZE RESEARCH
(% of Co.'s Requesting - Between Environments)

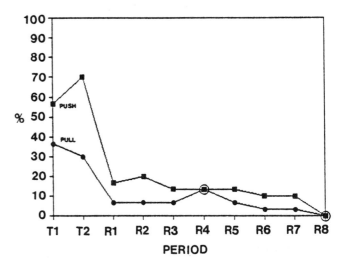

The occurrence of six other consistent decision-making episodes (i.e., for Hypotheses 1 and 7 in Trial Period 2 and Real Period 1 and Hypotheses 10 and 11 in Trial Period 2) can be considered to reflect nothing more than sporadic decision-making due to a lack of any sustained across-period continuity.

The stability of making inconsistent decisions appears to parallel that for consistent decision-making. The inconsistent decision-making for the variable of broadcast advertising has lasted as long as the consistent decision-making for the variable of trade advertising (i.e., for eight straight periods). For the

variable of print advertising, such inconsistent decision-making lasted for six straight periods of play. In this case, however, new learning appears to have occurred in Real Period 6, since the between-environment difference disappeared for the remainder of the game.

In total, the results of the study offer only very limited support for the general hypothesis that, if marketing strategy formulation in a simulation game is an internally valid experience, then the nature of the decisions should gravitate toward the more important strategy elements. The results also suggest that the initial learning and stability of appropriate <u>and</u> inappropriate decision-making are similar to one another. Both correct and incorrect forms of decision making occur early in the game and are sustained for a significant period of time, if not for the remainder of the game, as long as the identified nature of the decision continues for more than two consecutive periods of play.

<u>CONCLUSION</u>

The present study empirically investigated the internal validity of an experimentally manipulated simulation game environment with a specific focus on determining when during the play of the game the existence of such validity becomes evident and on determining the stability of the learning process on which such validity is based. The results offer only very limited support for the internal validity of the simulation environment to which the game participants had to react. Furthermore, when there is evidence of learning during the game, whether it reflects consistent or in-

31

consistent decision-making, if evidence of such learning continues beyond two periods of play, it will enjoy a sustained existence for the majority, if not for the remainder, of the game. Whether a longer game, the use of more advanced marketing students, and/or the use of alternate performance objectives would lead to different results than those obtained are issues that need to be addressed in future research.

REFERENCES

Biskin, B. H. 1980. "Multivariate Analysis in Experimental Counseling Research." The Counseling Psychologist 8 (4): 69-72.

_____. 1983. "Multivariate Analysis in Experimental Leisure Research." Journal of Leisure Research 15 (4): 344-358.

Faria, A. J. 1987. "A Survey of the Use of Business Games in Academia and Business." Simulation & Games 18 (2): 207-225.

Faria, A. J. and J. R. Dickinson. 1987. Laptop: A Marketing Simulation. Business Publications, Inc., Plano, TX.

Greenlaw, P. S. and F. P. Wyman. 1973. "The Teaching Effectiveness of Games in Collegiate Business Courses." Simulation & Games 4 (2): 259-294.

Horn, R. E. and A. Cleaves. 1980. The Guide to Simulations/Games for Education and Training. Sage, Beverly Hills, CA.

Keys, B. 1976. "A Review of Learning Research and Business Gaming." Developments in Business Simulation & Experiential Exercises 3: 173-185.

McDaniel, C. and W. R. Darden. 1987. Marketing. Allyn and Bacon, Boston, MA.

Miles, W.; W. Biggs; and J. Schubert. 1986. "Student Perceptions of Skill Acquisition Through Cases and a General Management Simulation: A Comparison." Simulation & Games 17 (1): 7-25.

Mehrez, A.; A. Reichel; and R. Olami. 1987. "The Business Game Versus Reality." Simulation & Games 18 (3): 488-500.

Schewe, C. D. 1987. Marketing. Random House, New York, NY.

Tabachnick, B. G. and L. S. Fidell. 1983. Using Multivariate Statistics. Harper & Row, New York, NY.

Wolfe, J. and R. Jackson. "An Investigation of the Need for Algorithmic Validity in Business Games." Simulation & Games, forthcoming.

Wolfe, J. and C. R. Roberts. 1986. "The External Validity of a Business Management Game." Simulation & Games 17 (3): 45-59.

THE IMPACT OF A MARKET LEADER ON SIMULATION COMPETITORS' STRATEGIES

W. J. Wellington, J. R. Dickinson and A. J. Faria
Faculty of Business Administration
University of Windsor
Windsor, Ontario, Canada N9B 3P4

ABSTRACT

This study continues a recent stream of research pursuing a new concept of simulation participation validity predicated on the extent to which participants respond to a simulation environment which is manipulated in meaningful ways. The present study investigates the impact of a market leading competitor on other competitors' strategies. The investigation is carried out in an experimental setting in which the responsiveness of the market to different strategy variables is also controlled. The findings provide substantial support that simulation players are sensitive to the presence of an industry-leading competitor and, correspondingly, to the environment created by the simulation administrator.

INTRODUCTION

Business managers must make important decisions in the face of different and constantly changing external and internal environments. Therefore, the ability to identify and adapt to different environments and then respond to environmental changes is an important attribute for effective business performance. Experiential learning is one way for business managers to develop these abilities and the use of business simulations is an excellent experiential learning tool because it allows for the construction of different environments and enables an objective test of the quality of business decision-making.

Among the major environmental factors affecting business performance are competitors. This research investigates the impact of a market leading competitor on other competitors' strategies. The investigation is carried out in an experimental setting in which the responsiveness of the market to different strategy variables is also controlled, thus bringing into the study a second major environmental factor.

PAST RESEARCH

This study continues a recent stream of research pursuing a new concept of simulation participation validity predicated on the extent to which participants respond to a simulation environment which is manipulated in meaningful ways. Here a researcher-run company was among the competing teams in several test industries. This "ringer" company was in a position to exploit both awareness of the true responsiveness of the simulation game markets and the concurrent knowledge of competitors' strategies. In this fashion, the ringer company was manipulated so as to maintain a market leadership position in terms of earnings per share, the measure used to identify industry leadership. Thus, it was generally theorized that if simulation participation is a valid learning experience, companies (1) should adapt to the differential responsiveness of markets to specific strategy variables, and (2) should learn from a market leading competitor whose strategy is specifically manipulated to reflect market responsiveness.

While no past research has used an artificial industry leader to examine participant responsiveness to the simulation environment, several studies have examined participant response to manipulated game parameters (Faria and Dickinson 1990; Faria, Whiteley and Dickinson 1990; Whiteley, Faria and Dickinson 1990). In these studies, the simulation game parameters were manipulated in a fashion that will be described below. Game participants' decisions were monitored to determine if they moved in the direction that would be suggested by the weighting of the game parameters.

The results reported in these studies suggested that the participants' decisions only moderately reflected the importance weightings of the game parameters. As such, it was concluded that some other variables may be influencing the actions of the game participants. One possibility is the action of competitors.

STUDY DESIGN

Four experimental conditions were defined comprising combinations of "push" and "pull" strategy responsive markets and industries with and without a market leading ringer company. While a market leading company would be expected to evolve during the play of any simulation game, this would normally take some time and market leadership may be less discernable due to minor and/or varying degrees of leadership as well as turnover in the leadership position. In this experiment, it was assured that a single company would assume and maintain a clear leadership position.

The simulation game used for this experiment was LAPTOP: A Marketing Simulation (Faria and Dickinson 1987). LAPTOP has been specifically designed for the principles of marketing course and lends itself to the creation of two meaningfully different marketing environments. Push and pull strategies are well known within the field of marketing and are prominently discussed in all principles of marketing textbooks.

Twelve simulation industries made up of four teams each were formed. Four treatment groups composed of three industries each were organized in a 2 X 2 experimental design as follows: 1) ringer industry - push responsive, 2) nonringer industry - push responsive, 3) ringer industry - pull responsive, and 4) nonringer industry - pull responsive. Ringer industries were composed of three actual student teams and an instructor operated ringer whose decisions would be based on knowledge of the environment created and of the decisons of all teams in the industry. The ringer team would, therefore, have advantages allowing it to lead the industry by making decisions which were correctly "tuned" to the industry environment.

To ensure that all of the student teams would be able to learn about the environment in which they were operating, all teams were provided a complete set of market research reports at the end of each period of competition. This would insure that all of the student teams would have the same information available and the same opportunity to learn about their environment.

Marketing decisions in LAPTOP are made in four product-market segments (two products by two geographic markets). The decision areas for each product-market include price, quantity of product to be shipped, advertising level, advertising media, advertising message, sales promotion spending, and type of sales promotion program. Geographic market decisions include co-operative advertising allowances and sales force size. Sales force salaries and commissions apply to both geographic territores while research and development decisions are specific to each of the products.

The LAPTOP simulation environment can be adjusted in terms of the relative impact of decisions in each of the above mentioned areas using a weighting of 1 to 10. A weighting of 1 minimizes the relative impact of a specific variable while a weighting of 10 maximizes the

impact of the variable. The push and pull environments were parameterized or weighted as follows:

	Pull	Push
Price	5	5
Advertising		
Broadcast	10	1
Print	10	1
Trade	1	10
Sales Promotion	1	10
Co-operative Advertising		
Percent	1	10
R & D Expenditures	10	1
Salesforce		
Size	1	10
Salary	1	10
Commission Percent	1	10

As is commonly described in all basic marketing textbooks, the push variables were identified as those whose most direct impact are on trade channel members. These were initialized as 10's to create the push environment. The pull variables (initialized as 10's for the pull environment) are those whose most direct impact is felt by the final consumer. In each environment, the opposite variables were given a weighting of 1. Demand levels for all industries were initialized at the same level.

As opposed to the competitive environment, the impact of the structural environment is not as clearly identifiable to the student teams. Reasonably, the industry leader is the best decision maker with regard to the environment in which the teams are competing. This would suggest that the industry leader is making decisions most in tune with the industry environment and vis-a-vis competitors. Therefore, the leader represents a barometer against which competitor teams can measure themselves and come to understand the industry environment.

The ringers or "artificial" leaders would have an advantage due to perfect knowledge of the industry environment. While nonringer industries would have leaders too, these leaders must learn from experience as they explore the industry environment. The ringers would not have to endure a discovery period and would lead from the start and continuously throughout the competition. In nonringer industries the lead could change a number of times as teams experiment with different strategies while ringer teams would always have the best strategy. Of course, the competitors of the ringers would be exposed to the optimal strategies through the market research studies provided to them and, reasonably, could imitate the ringer/leaders.

HYPOTHESES

In a simulation competition, the student teams are competing for industry leadership and are rewarded (graded) based on their performance. The student teams, therefore, are constantly searching for a marketing strategey that will work. As part of the environment in which each team is operating are a number of competitors. A well performing competitor, the industry leader, has presumably developed a marketplace strategy that is working. It is reasonable to believe that other companies, in their attempt to

develop a successful strategy, will monitor and copy the industry leader. As complete market research information was supplied to each company in every period of the competition, this was easy to do in the present study.

H1: Companies in pull environment industries will allocate greater resources to pull variables in ringer industries than will companies in nonringer industries.

H2: Companies in pull environment industries will allocate fewer resources to push variables in ringer industries than will companies in nonringer industries.

H3: Companies in push environment industries will allocate greater resources to push variables in ringer industries than will companies in nonringer industries.

H4: Companies in push environment industries will allocate fewer resources to pull variables in ringer industries than will companies in nonringer industries.

Allocation of resources to push and pull variables will be examined by product and region. The pull variables include broadcast and print advertising as well as research and development expenditures. The push variables include trade advertising, sales promotion, co-operative advertising and sales force size, salary and commission percentages. It has been hypothesized that teams in ringer industries will better assimilate the nature of the simulation environment since they have a leader that is "tuned in" to the environment of the simulation from the start.

METHODOLOGY

Data were gathered for a total of 42 companies made up of 153 students in an introductory marketing course required of all business students. Students were in two sections of the single introductory course taught by a single instructor.

Generally, three or four students formed each company on a self-selection basis. Four student companies were assigned to each nonringer industry. For ringer industries, the single experimenter-manipulated ringer company plus three student companies comprised each industry. Sample sizes, i.e., numbers of companies, for each experimental treatment group are as follows: pull, ringer 9; pull, nonringer 12; push, ringer 9; push, nonringer 12.

All criterion variables, being dollar amount allocations or, in the instance of sales force commission, a specified percent of dollar sales, are intervally scaled. Hypotheses underlying this study call for comparisons of criteria between ringer and nonringer industry companies in the pull simulation environment and, separately, comparisons between ringer and nonringer industry companies in the push environment.

Accordingly, the common one-tail t-test of two means was employed for each of the specific hypotheses.

LAPTOP is a dynamic simulation in that, depending on the strategies of their component companies, different industries may grow at different rates. Differences in absolute expenditures across industries, then, may be partly attributable to their different sizes and not necessarily to differences in underlying marketing strategies. To adjust for industry size differences, then, company expenditures for broadcast, print, and trade advertising were transformed to a percentage of industry sales.

Sample sizes, i.e., numbers of companies, in each experimental treatment group are typical if not larger than typical for simulation studies of this sort. However, sample sizes for purposes of achieving substantial power in statistical tests are small. Significance levels of t-tests are nevertheless reported in Table 1 as Glass and Hopkins (1984) have shown that confidence intervals for t-tests are quite accurate even for sample sizes as low as five.

Otherwise, results of this study are interpreted on the more descriptive basis of whether or not differences in company strategy decisions are in directions consistent or inconsistent with the hypotheses.

Means and percentages for each experimental treatment combination are presented in Table 1, broken down variously by product model (Standard 100 and Deluxe 200) and territory (Territory 1 and Territory 2) as

TABLE 1
MEAN STRATEGY DECISION VALUES

Criterion	Pull Environment Ringer	Nonringer		Push Environment Ringer	Nonringer	
Broadcast Adv						
S100, T1	1.01	0.85	*	0.42	0.61	**
S100, T2	0.70	0.60	*	0.28	0.47	**
D200, T1	0.84	0.66	*	0.32	0.43	*
D200, T2	0.46	0.50		0.18	0.31	**
Print Adv						
S100, T1	0.95	0.30	**	0.23	0.27	*
S100, T2	0.62	0.28	**	0.16	0.21	*
D200, T1	0.75	0.27	**	0.16	0.23	*
D200, T2	0.39	0.23	**	0.11	0.16	*
Trade Adv						
S100, T1	0.17	0.12	*	0.31	0.13	**
S100, T2	0.13	0.09		0.20	0.10	**
D200, T1	0.15	0.13		0.24	0.10	**
D200, T2	0.09	0.08		0.14	0.08	**
Co-operative Adv						
Territory 1	3.6	4.8	*	6.9	2.4	**
Territory 2	3.7	4.8	*	6.9	2.8	**
Salesforce Size						
Territory 1	12.3	17.0	**	12.1	10.6	**
Territory 2	16.3	22.8	**	18.0	15.8	**
Salesforce Salary	3638	4053	*	5706	3866	**
Sales Commission	3.76	6.10	**	6.90	4.50	**
R & D						
Standard 100	15.6	18.8		19.4	25.8	*
Deluxe 200	21.1	31.3		26.1	43.8	*

* = in hypothesized direction, p > .10
** = p < .10

appropriate.

DISCUSSION AND CONCLUSION

A total of 40 relationships were analyzed, 20 comparisons between ringer and nonringer industries in each of pull and push simulation environments. In the pull environment, 14 of the 20 comparisons were in the hypothesized direction. Of these 14, seven were statistically significant (p<.10). In the push environment, all 20 comparisons were in the hypothesized direction.

Thirteen of the 20 push environment comparisons were significant at the .10 level.

There is substantial descriptive support and material inferential support, then, that players are sensitive to the presence of an industry-leading competitor. They do, indeed, adjust their strategies to be, in this research design, simultaneously more like the leading competitor and more effective vis-a-vis the market environment. At a broader level, this general finding attests to the validity of the simulation experience. Players do appear to make their decisions on systematic and meaningful bases.

Notably, exceptions to this support are confined to just two of the eight strategy decision areas and then only in one of the two simulation environments. Trade advertising and research and development expenditure decisions in the pull environment are virtually all (5 out of 6) contrary to those hypothesized. In the push environment, however,

trade advertising expenditures were not only in the hypothesized direction, differences for all four product-territory combinations were statistically significant. Differences in research and development expenditures in the pull environment were not statistically significant, but both instances were in the hypothesized direction. Thus, it seems that it is not the decision areas themselves that account for the selected results that are contrary to that hypothesized.

In this study the responsiveness of companies' strategy decisions to the simulation environment is compounded with their responsiveness to the ringer company, a company manipulated by the experimenters to be both an industry leader and a leader in strategy directions appropriate for the environment. This was the planned research design. It is, however, a less rigorous test of the responsiveness of companies to the simulation environment per se, i.e., without the presence of a ringer company. Previous research of this more rigorous design has found mixed results (Faria and Dickinson 1990; Faria, Whiteley and Dickinson 1990; Whiteley, Faria and Dickinson 1990). The largely supportive results of this study, then, encourage the belief that participation in simulations is a meaningful exercise. Adaptation to the simulation environment, however, might be more subtle and difficult to isolate than the small sample sizes of earlier studies have allowed.

REFERENCES

Faria, A.J. and J.R. Dickinson. 1990. "Extant Measures of Simulation Validity and an Addition." In Proceedings of the 1990 SCS Multiconference in Business and Management (San Diego, CA, Jan. 17-19). Society for Computer Simulation, San Diego, CA, 66-71.

Faria, A.J. and J.R. Dickinson. 1987. LAPTOP: A Marketing Simulation. Richard D. Irwin, Inc., Homewood, ILL.

Faria, A.J.; T.R. Whiteley; and J.R. Dickinson. 1990. "A Measure of the Internal Validity of a Marketing Simulation Game." In Proceedings of the Southwest Decision Sciences Institute (Dallas, TX, March 23-25). Decision Sciences Institute, Atlanta, GA, 133-141.

Whiteley, T.R.; A.J. Faria; and J.R. Dickinson. 1990. "The Impact of Market Structure, Versus Competitor Strategy, on Simulation Outcomes." In Proceedings of the Thirteenth Annual Conference of the Academy of Marketing Science. (New Orleans, LA, April 25-29). Academy of Marketing Science, Miami Beach, FL, 279-288.

INTRODUCTION TO STELLA

An Introduction
to
STELLA II™
A Simulation

David B. Hoffman
School of Management
University of Alaska Fairbanks
Fairbanks, Alaska 99775-1070

ABSTRACT

This paper is an introduction to the simulation language **STELLA II™** by High Performance Systems. Version 2 includes several enhancements and is also available under the name: ithink™. This paper breifly describes the operating environment for modeling systems. The objects used to describe the relationship between components are similar to Jay Forrester's "rates" and "levels".

The language provides a diagrammatic approach to building models, with specific "tools" available for building,editing and enhancing. The built in functions available for use in the model's equations are also listed. A completed model is represented both as a diagram and as a series of equations. Output from the simulation is provided both in tables and as predefined graphs. There is also the capability to input data into the model for analysis and transporting simulated output for further analysis.

COMPONENTS

STELLA™ and ithink™ are Macintosh-based, object-oriented simulation language developed by High Performance Systems, Inc. (Richmond et. al., 1987). Models are built by first describing the system as components. These components are expressed as objects that represent **stocks, flows, converters,** and **connectors.** A simple example is shown in Figure 1

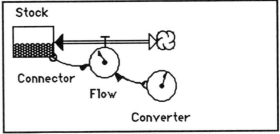

Figure 1. Components of STELLA™

In STELLA™, rectangle objects, called **stocks,** represent levels. The "rates" are represented as circular valves and are called **flows.** Dependencies are represented as connecting arrows. Each stock must be given an initial value and each flow must include an appropriate formula. Several editing icons are used in building, editing and enhancing the model.

Stocks are the rectangular blocks in the model diagram and represent the levels or amounts. At any point in time each stock represents a level or quantity. The value in a stock at any point in time is affected by inflows and outflows. Characteristics if stocks can be defined to function as a reservoir, a queue, a conveyor with a specified lag time or as an "oven". As an oven, the stock is affected by parameters of fill time, bunching debth, capacity and cook time. These choices provide a great deal of flexibility in how the language is used.

Flows are similar to a pipe and represent the conduit through which goal-seeking activities flow. The direction of positive flow is indicated by the arrow-head. There is the choice between uniflow or biflow. Flow relationships can be expressed either mathematically or as a graph. The graph option permits data input to the model. An important aspect of flows is that they have the same unit of measure as their associated stocks but they also include a time dimension. For example, if a stock represents barrels, than the flow could represent barrels per day. The circle attached to the pipe is the flow regulator.

Converters are represented as circles. They are called converters because they *convert* inputs to outputs. Converters do not represent any of the goal seeking aspects of the model but are valuable in giving the model its desired characteristics. Converters, like stocks exist at a point in time but unlike stocks, converters do not accumulate rates of flow. In the simulation described here, a converter, for example, was used to simulate daily average temperatures. Since the demand for heating oil was based on temperature, the simulation used a converter to simulate each days temperature. The simulated temperature generated was **connected** to a flow-related converter which computed that day's demand for heating oil.

In addition to the components, STELLA™ provides four tools to position, define, copy and delete elements in the diagram. The first tool, called a **hand** is for positioning model components. The second is called a **ghost** and is used for duplicating converters for use in several places in the model diagram. Ghosting is used to eliminate the need for running complex model "plumbing" all over the place. The third tool is represented as a camera. This tool enables the model to include **pictures**, labels and representations. The last tool is called **dynamite**. This tool is used for deleting components of a model. These four tools are available in the Diagram window as shown in Figure 2.

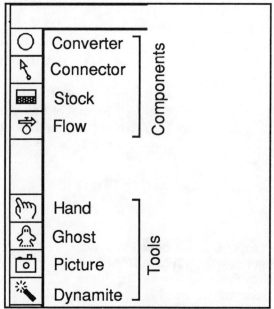

Figure 2. Components and Tools

Model building starts with a careful and thorough definition of the problem, the identification of the variables involved and the relationships that will apply in the situation. Programming the problem in STELLA™ requires using the hand to place the appropriate stocks, flows and linkages in the Diagram window. For each component, a formula is required, and in the case of the stocks, an initial value must be stated. As the relationships of the model are built with the components, the formulas with which the simulation will operate are developed by STELLA™. If the model lacks requisite information or defined relationships, the program will not run. The program will not accept an incomplete formula. For example, if an IF statement is being entered, and the value to follow the word ELSE is left out, the program will bring this to the programmer's attention.

The model is represented in the **Diagram** window. In addition, all formulas, relationships and initial states are given in the window called **Equations**. In addition to obtaining output in the form of data in the window called: **Table Pad**, a **Graph Pad** can be selected which offers multiple windows. Graph can both show data over time and XY relationships. For the purpose of multiple iterations of a model, **Sensitivity** selections can be made. These are all accessed with the the Windows menu is in Figure 3.

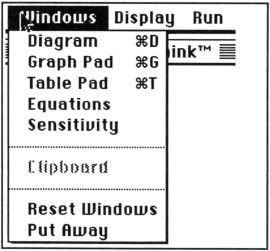

Figure 3. Program Windows

The STELLA™ and ithink™ programs not only creates a pictorial representation of the model in the form of the components mentioned above but also animates them. Assumptions and activities can be reviewed as the simulation is run. Both stocks and flows can be animated. Animation enhances error detection and allows one to observe over time the dynamic assumptions placed in the model.

Simulation output includes a simulation diagram, graphs of specified stocks, flows and converters; data tables and a listing of the formulas.

REFERENCES

Ahlgren, David J., and Stein, Alex C., *"Dynamic Models of the AIDS Epidemic"*, **SIMULATION**, Vol 54, No.1, Jan, 1990, pp7-20.

Forrester, Jay W. **Industrial Dynamics** (New York: John Wiley), 1961.

Richmond,B; Vescuso, P.; and Peterson, S. 1987. *STELLA™ for Business*. High Performance Systems, Inc., Lyme, N H.

David B. Hoffman teaches production management and computer simulation at the University of Alaska Fairbanks, School of Management. His research interests include simulation modeling and computer graphics as decision support tools for management. Dr. Hoffman has studied the computer graphics industry to evaluate its current makeup and future plans. His teaching and research emphasize the necessity for innovation in both product design and manufacturing strategies.

SIMULATION IN DECISION SUPPORT SYSTEMS

The Optimal Sonobuoy Pattern Decision

Ralph C. Hilzer, Jr.
Department of Computer Science
California State University, Chico
hilzer@csuchico.edu

ABSTRACT

A technique used by the U.S. Navy to detect and track submarines at sea is to place listening devices called "sonobuoys" in the water. If both water temperature by depth and noise levels emanating from the submarine are known, the principles of underwater physics can be used to predict sonobuoy detection ranges. Since sonobuoys are expensive, it is essential to limit the number used while engaged in detection and tracking. The sonobuoy pattern which has the best balance between providing a high probability-of-detection with a low sonobuoy usage is said to be "optimal." This paper will use unclassified techniques derived from probability theory and underwater physics to propose methods for designing computerized simulation models that determine optimal patterns based on current conditions.

INTRODUCTION

Some of the most critical decisions in the military are those involving the allocation of resources. Since budget dollars are scarce, every effort must be made to economize and optimize, while still maintaining an effective force.

A primary mission of the U. S. Navy is to maintain freedom of the seas. A huge commitment in terms of manpower and other resources is needed in order to guarantee that freedom.

One of the greatest threats to freedom of the seas is the submarine. Submarines were first used effectively by Germany during World War II where they raised havoc with allied supply lines. It is noteworthy that Germany's small force nearly turned the tide of the war.

After World War II, the main benefactor of Germany's submarine technology was the Soviet Union, due to its position as a conquering power. In the years since World War II, the Soviet Union has dramatically improved on that technology to the extent where their submarines represent the primary threat to freedom of the seas.

To counter the Soviet submarine threat, the U. S. Navy has developed Antisubmarine Warfare (ASW) forces that are comprised of both airborne and seagoing units. Airborne ASW units include helocopters, carrier-launched jets, and land-based reconnaissance aircraft. Seagoing units include many types of surface navy ships (such as the destroyer), and the most effective ASW platform of all, the U. S. submarine. So far, the U. S.'s combined air and sea ASW forces have contained the Soviet submarine threat by using a variety of techniques.

One technique airborne ASW units use to detect and track submarines is to drop listenening devices called "sonobuoys" in the water. Sonobuoys are actually radio transmitters deployed from an aircraft that float on the water with a microphone (called a hydrophone) hanging submerged in the water at the end of a wire cable. The transmitter relays underwater sound signals back to the aircraft where they are analyzed looking for sounds unique to Soviet submarines.

The problem with using sonobuoys for detecting and tracking submarines is that it is costly. It requires placing an expensive airborne unit and highly trained flight crew in the vicinity of the submarine. Typically, this is thousands of miles at sea. Also, sonobuoys are costly.

Therefore, airborne commanders must employ sonobuoy patterns that maximize the probability of detecting a submarine while minimizing the number of sonobuoys used. Such a pattern is referred to as an "optimized" or "optimal" sonobuoy pattern.

Little is known about the size and shape of an optimal pattern. Also, optimal pattern characteristics probably vary depending on existing conditions. However, if conditions affecting a pattern are known in advance, simulation can be used to compare all possible pattern alternatives. In that case, the aircraft commander's decision would be reduced to merely selecting the pattern reported as optimal.

The purpose of this paper is to discuss ideas that might be used to design an optimal sonobuoy pattern simulation program. Although several simulations have already been designed, none have been good enough to be useful so far.

BACKGROUND

Specifically, Tactical Airborne Sonar Decision Aid (TASDA) (Cole 1971) designed at the Naval Air Development Center, Warminster, Pennsylvania is old, cumbersome, and proven to be inaccurate. The first simulation effort completed by this author, "An Approach to Barrier Sonobuoy Pattern Optimization" (Hilzer 1974) does little more than accept a sonobuoy pattern as an input and calculate its probability of detecting the submarine. To determine the optimal pattern, the user must exhaustively enter all possible patterns and select the one with the highest probability-of-detection. Unfortunately, little time is available to do this since the submarine is slipping away down below.

It is preferable that a computer simulation make these comparisons for the aircraft commander and recommend an optimal pattern in a short enough time span to be used. The remainder of this paper will discuss such a simulation.

METHODOLOGY

Four factors influence the detectability of a submarine at a sonobuoy. They are:

1. Depth of the submarine.

2. Noise levels emanating from the submarine. Noise levels are most directly influenced by speed. The higher the speed, generally speaking, the higher the noise level (due to increased engine noise and collapsing bubbles near the propellers called cavitation).

3. Oceanographic (sea) conditions. Ambient noise caused by surface wave action, biological activity (fish noise), or transiting merchant ships can mask out weak submarine noises. Also, pressure and temperature changes-by-depth (called pressure and temperature gradients) tend to bend sound rays (detectable noise) either towards or away from the sonobuoy.

4. Sonobuoy characteristics. Is the sonobuoy being monitored? If it isn't, probability-of-detection at that sonobuoy is zero! Also, what is the depth of the hydrophone? Sometimes, hydrophone depth can be set to take advantage of temperature gradients.

Using the principles of probability and underwater physics, it is possible to compute a range from the sonobuoy at which the probability of detecting a submarine is fifty-percent. A submarine at that range from the sonobuoy, referred to as the Median Detection Range (MDR), would theoretically be detected fifty percent of the time and remain undetected fifty-percent of the time. Of course as the submarine gets closer to the sonobuoy the probability of detecting it goes up, and approaches one-hundred percent when the range between them is zero.

To compute MDR, the submarine's depth and speed, ambient sea noise, and temperature gradients must be predicted. Also, sonobuoy characteristics must be selected. Unfortunately, all of these but sonobuoy characteristics involve only predictions. Worse yet, the enemy controls submarine depth and speed, and can normally increase ambient sea noise by heading for merchant sea traffic. The point here is to be weary of those who place too much faith in the accuracy of MDR predictions. Since MDR is in question, and MDR is a basis for this author's method for determining the optimal pattern, the optimal pattern itself can be little more than a "best guess." However, with some care it can be a very educated guess.

Anyway, there are nice classified methods available to compute MDR. They must remain classified because they involve the use of submarine noise level predictions. However, it is certainly possible for the aircraft commander to compute MDR himself, and enter results into the simulation program interactively.

Other interactive inputs include the submarine's latest known area-of-probability (position and the reliability of that position), its course and speed, and depth (if known), and the number of sonobuoys the aircraft is able to monitor at one time.

The submarine position might be determined by knowledge that it must pass through a "choke point" (a restricted area such as between two islands) or by tactical information such as previous detection by other units. Similarly, the course, speed, and depth could have been reported by other tactical units, or that information might be inferred by prudent assumptions. For example, are there any surface units in the area which the submarine is likely to intercept? If not, what are other likely destinations of the submarine? Even something as large as the coast of the U. S. can be helpful. Remember, however, that course, speed, and depth are variables that the enemy controls. Even if they are known accurately at the start of the search, they can quickly be changed (and usually are).

The simulation initiates random submarine runs starting at locations inside the area-of-probability with random courses and speeds (refined by available tactical intelligence). Coincidentally, a sonobuoy pattern with some arbitrary geometry and spacing is placed either over the area-of-probability or in the path of the submarine. This pattern will compete with others for distinction as the optimal pattern.

Several simulated submarine runs will be made "through" the pattern. If a run passes through a single monitored sonobuoy at the MDR, a probability-of-detection of fifty-percent is registered for that pattern during that run. Submarine runs that pass either closer to or further away from a single monitored sonobuoy than MDR will register a probability-of-detection that is greater or less that fifty-percent respectively. Some runs will pass through two or more monitored sonobuoys. Using probabilistic techniques, probability-of-detection for these runs will be adjusted to some value over that of the highest detecting single sonobuoy. Still other runs will miss the pattern by a great enough distance or will pass entirely through unmonitored sonobuoys. Those runs will register a probability-of-detection of zero.

The probability-of-detection for a particular sonobuoy pattern geometry and spacing is an average of each probability-of-detection reported during individual runs through it. If every possible geometry and spacing is tested, the optimal pattern is the geometry and spacing with the highest average probability-of-detection.

Unfortunately, there are several problems that must be solved before this method is practical. The remainder of this paper discusses those problems.

First, uniform distributions will probably be used both to randomize the submarine's starting position inside the area-of-probability and the submarine's course within its probable direction of transit. The author feels the uniform distribution should be used, although other distributions should be investigated to see if they are more appropriate.

Should submarine speed also be randomized with some distribution function? If it is, then the simulation might reflect conditions that are better than the "worst-case" scenerio. Then, if the submarine assumed the worst-case speed, it might slip through the pattern undetected. It might be better to simply use the worst-case speed for all runs. However, what is the worst-case speed? A slow speed would generate the least noise, but a faster speed allows the submarine to exit the pattern area more quickly (a faster speed could allow the submarine to pass through a sonobuoy's detection area while it is not being monitored). This apparent quandary can be resolved by recognizing that the lowest possible speed was already used to determine the noise level when computing MDR. Nothing prevents the use of a higher speed for the simulation runs. That way MDR reflects the slowest possible speed and the simulation runs reflect a faster realistic speed.

Next, how can the number of pattern simulation runs be limited? If no effort is made to limit them, the program will execute too slowly to be useful. Intuitively, it seems that if the addition of one sonobuoy to a pattern does not improve probability-of-detection for a pattern, then patterns with the same spacing containing even more sonobuoys need not be tested. That is almost true. However, the original sonobuoy might have been added to the pattern at a poor position. By placing it somewhere else, the pattern detection capabilities might be improved. Only when all possible positions have been tested and found to yield no improvement can pattern configurations with more sonobuoys be ignored.

Ideally, geometries should be tested starting with a few sonobuoys at a given minimum spacing. Then, the number of sonobuoys should be increased until there is no improvement in detection capabilities for that geometry. Next, start with a few sonobuoys again, but this time with a wider spacing, and repeat the remainder of the above steps. In the end, the best geometry for each spacing will be computed. The optimal pattern is the one selected from that list that has the highest probability of detecting the submarine.

One last program enhancement should be considered. Notice that someone must guess where to place the pattern and provide that position as a program input. If the guess is wrong, the true optimal pattern might never be considered in the simulation. For that reason, it would be appropriate to both add and delete sonobuoys when running simulations. That way the pattern can grow away from its original position to its best position. "Optimal" would then be refined to mean the best geometry with the best spacing located at the best position. Doing this without undermining responsiveness is the problem. In fact, no solution is offered.

Someday, someone will solve this and all of the other problems associated with implementing this simulation program. It is hoped that your curiosity is aroused sufficiently to investigate the problem yourself.

REFERENCES

Cole, S. N. June 8, 1971. "TASDA III, Program for Optimal Geometric Selection." Naval Air Development Center, Functional Specification, N62269-72-C-0402.

Hilzer, R. C. June 1974. "An Approach to Barrier Sonobuoy Pattern Optimization." Naval Postgraduate School, Monterey California.

A COMPUTER-ASSISTED SIMULATION SYSTEM FOR FUTURES MODELING

Robert G. Main, Ph.D
George N. Arnovick
California State University, Chico
Chico, CA 95929-0504

Introduction

This paper reports the results of an extensive one-year study conducted by a team of researchers from California State University, Chico under contract with the California Peace Officer's Standards and Training (POST) Commission to develop the concept and specifications for using computer-assisted management simulation exercises for futures projection as a tool in strategic planning training for management students in their Command College curriculum. The recommended management training simulation system consists of two system models--a Command College Strategic/Futures Scenario Development system, and Law Enforcement Incident Command System (LEICS) interactive system. Both systems are identified by the term "Computer-Assisted Management Simulation System (CAMS).

Methodology

The study was organized into a series of manageable tasks that systematically examined the problem and development proposal. The primary tasks were:

o   Instructional Needs Assessment
o   Review of the Literature
o   Instructional Design
o   Concept Development and Functional Specifications

Throughout the project, a close coordination was maintained with the POST Center for Executive Development staff. The principal researchers also consulted with instructors in the Command College and the LEICS courses and attended classes of particular interest to application of computer-assisted management simulation exercises the driving force throughout the project was the instructional needs of the curriculum, instructors and students.

Specifically, the computer simulation provides application of the following elements contained in the Futures Workshop:

o Identifying Emerging Issues
-   Event Analysis (Chance)
        Identification: Indicators, Monitoring Probability/Time, Impact Evaluation, Relationship Analysis
-   Trend Analysis (Certainty)
        Identification: Indicators, Monitoring, Impact Evaluation, Prioritizing, Forecasting Ability
-   Policy Change (Choice)
        Pressures: Social, Political, Judicial, Administrative, Law Enforcement Discretionary
o Analysis of Emerging Issues
   - Structuring
   - Relationships, cross-impact analysis between events, trends, policy
   - Intervention Strategies
o Synthesis of Issues: Imaging the Future
   - Scenario Building
   - Strategic Planning
o Problem Solving
   - Transition Management
   - Intervention Strategies (Proactive Events)
   - Unexpected Events (Reactive)

A diligent effort was made to conduct a comprehensive review of the literature. The study group was especially interested in computer-based simulations in use by the military services as they had the most experience with simulation exercises. Information was collected on more than 200 games and simulations used by the military and other organizations.

Strategic Future Management Simulator

A modular concept for the Command College computer-assisted management simulation was derived from the instructional design. The variety of skills and knowledge contained in the Futures workshops preclude a single simulation concept. The exercise would be able to address only a small number of the learning objectives or it would have to be so complex it would need a very large computer on which to run and a full-time staff to load the variables and operate the system.

Modularizing the instructional design allows the learning objectives to be addressed by a less elaborate simulation. It also makes the development and operation of the simulations more flexible. Future curriculum changes can be accommodated without disabling the entire package and the modules can be sequenced in different ways to meet instructors' differing teaching strategies. Figure 1 illustrates the System Model and Concept.

The Command College Strategic/Futures management simulator provides a realistic exercise of the knowledge and skills taught in the "Defining the Futures" workshops. Eight distinct modules can be used independently as stand-alone learning exercises but are designed primarily for use as an integrated package where the simulation builds progressively as the player advances through the stages of futures scenario building. The first seven modules concentrate on the techniques needed for scanning, identifying and forecasting key trends and events for futures analysis. The simulation develops cross-impact analysis skills and requires the player to build a futures

scenario using the historical date/time approach. The final module of the simulation is a "futures revealed" exercise where the player is required to interact with his futures scenario as the computer unveils the events and trends of a future built upon the event probabilities and trend analyses developed during the previous modules. The simulation play is a stachostic model with probabilities established interactively by the players within program parameters.

The functional specifications allow event and trend combinations to vary randomly. This permits repeated simulations that provide novel experiences for the player that cannot be projected. The functional specifications also permit the mode and method of the simulation to be varied by the instructor from individual play to team play to group play.

Law Enforcement Incident Command System

The LEICS simulation is a completely different approach. The computer managed trainer is designed to provide a realistic interactive exercise of the knowledge

Figure 1 System Model and Concept

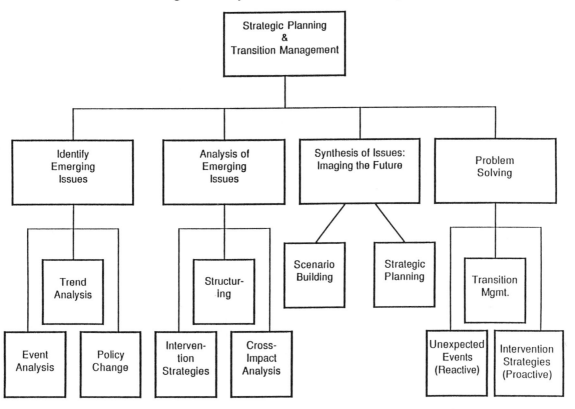

and skills taught in the Law Enforcement Incident Command System developed by the San Bernardino, California Sheriff's Department. The functional specifications prescribe a simulator that permits real time command and staff interaction. A series of scenarios allow students to play roles as the Incident Commander, Operations Officer, Planning/Intelligence Officer, Logistics Officer, and Finance Officer. A sixth station offers play as the Public Information Officer and liaison with a variety of agencies and higher headquarters, political figures, etc. The instructor can serve as the controller for the exercise or that function can be rotated among the trainees. The system documents the activities of the commander and each staff officer for a replay and critique of the exercise. Figure 2 illustrates the design concept. Scenarios that may be designed into the simulation might include fire (forest or structure), hazardous material spill, hostage or barricadement, and riot.

Each player has his own terminal and all terminals are interactive. As a result, a decision that the commander makes affects one or all of the other team members. While the screens are be interactive, it is the responsibility of each member to notify the others through a formal communication channel. In an actual incident the channel would probably be radio, telephone or face-to-face contact. For the purpose of the incident command simulation a system of "official memos" are used. This communication system prevents the players from making decisions based on what the other players might do and bases them more on actual moves.

System Configuration

The modular design of the instructional content is reflected in the specified computer hardware and software development. The same components and operating system

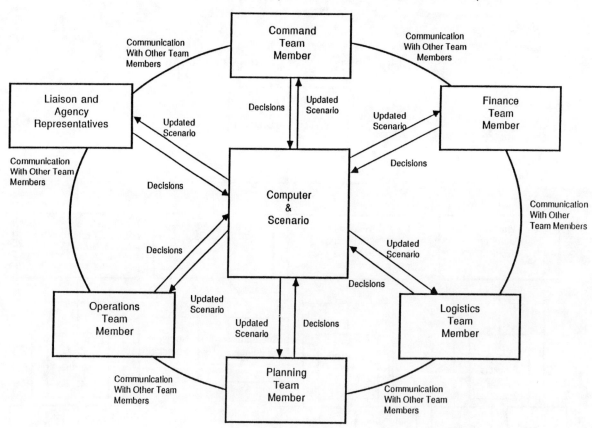

Figure 2 LEICS Module II (Interactive Incident Command)

are used throughout the modules. This reduces development costs because program algorithms are repeated and common data bases are used. Instructor and user training is also minimal and embedded rules and instructions require less development time and cost.

The functional design specifies an integrated classroom with an instructor's work station and 24 student stations for the CAMS installation. A local area network (LAN) would provide communication and control for the system. Visuals would be available from an interactive video player and computer graphics package. A large screen projection unit would permit visuals and screen displays to be viewed collectively by the students as well on their individual monitors. The instructor's station would be a mini-computer to host the control program. Student work stations would be microcomputers (PC's) that would operate either as smart terminals or independent from the network with a hard disk drive. This allows portability of a modified operation of the CAMS simulation to different geographic locations.

The LEICS installation involves a similar installation scheme with a mini-computer for the instructor/controller and a communication network to six microcomputer player stations comprising a command terminal and five staff terminals. The LEICS simulation is a team exercise where each participant's actions affect the screen of every other position console in a real-time interaction effect. The communication link between the instructor/control console and participant consoles could be provided either by a LAN or by a telecommunication link via telephone data connects that would allow the simulation to be exercised among players separated geographically.

Advantages of CAMS

The use of simulations are ideal methods for the higher level learning defined in Bloom's cognitive domain of educational objectives (Bloom, 1956). Simulations allow the review of concepts, rules, and principles and the application of knowledge and skills in a realistic manner. Skills of analysis, synthesis and evaluation can be exercised in novel and stimulating ways in either competitive or non-competitive computer-simulated exercises.

Benefits of CAMS

o Reduced Training Time. While time savings vary considerably, a median value is about 30% over conventional training approaches (Orlansky and String, 1979). This is well documented in the literature.

o Increased Learning Satisfaction. The CAMS is more motivating than other forms of instruction because of its interactive nature. Because of feedback provided

and the capability to assess progress, students are able to develop a sense of achievement during training (Kearsley, 1983).

o Problem-solving and Decision-making Skills. Simulation is best suited to training involving problem-solving or decision-making skills (Kearsley, 1983). Simulations are typically used for training purposes when increasing student motivation is desired.

o Achievement. The military has conducted numerous studies comparing computer-based training with conventional instruction. A review of 48 of these studies showed significantly greater student achievement (Orlanski and String, 1981). Furthermore, of the 39 studies that collected student attitude data, 29 reported more favorable attitudes toward computer simulation than conventional instruction.

Features of the POST Computer-Assisted Management Simulation (CAMS)

The CAMS simulation provides a richer educational experience for the Command College and LEICS students as summarized.

o Realism. Simulation allows the application of abstract principles and concepts to concrete situations.

o Modularized. Eight modules allow the students to build knowledge and skills incrementally--much like a part-task trainer.

o Flexibility. The simulation exercises are a combination of deterministic scenarios (the play and outcomes are established in advance) and stochastic processes (mathematical probabilities).

o Variable Mode. The simulation exercise can be varied by the instructor to operate as an individual player mode where each student plays against program-produced norms or it can be played in a team mode where four to six players form a team and make collective decisions.

o Repetition and Reinforcement. The number of variables in the data base allows the simulation to be repeated many times with a different combination of variables used each time.

o Control. The simulation specifications also permit instructor intervention during the play.

o Standards. The computer simulation by necessity imposes a certain amount of standardization to the instruction. It ensures each student in every class receives a common educational experience with a uniform measurement instrument regardless of the course instructor.

o Interaction. Simulations allow the student to actively participate in a scenario situation where they can experience the consequences of their decisions in a realistic, non-judgmental manner. The computer simulation requires the student interact with the learning material.

The progressive nature of the simulation modules enhances learning as well. Since each module builds upon the previous exercise, the learning objectives are reinforced.

Development Cost

Modularizing the simulation exercise allows the development cost to be spread over several years. Since the simulation modules are designed to be progressive, the costs are incremental; i.e., the data bases, software routines and hardware are shared among the modules. Development cost of the final "Futures Revealed" module should be about the same as for the previous modules even though it is much more complex and sophisticated in its operation. This is accomplished because many of the data bases and much of the software used in the previous modules are incorporated in the design. Also, the same hardware configurations are used throughout the modules.

The modular concept allows for future expansion as well. As new instructional needs become apparent, simulation modules can be added relatively inexpensively.

REFERENCES

Bloom, Benjamin S. Editor, 1956.
Taxonomy of Educational Objectives Handbook I: Cognitive Domain. David McKay Company, Inc. New York.

Kearsley, Gregg, 1983.
Computer-Based Training.
Addison-Wesley Publishing Co., Menlo Park, CA.

Orlansky, J. and String, J., April, 1979.
Cost-Effectiveness of Computer-Based Instruction in Military Training. IDAP-1375.
Arlington, VA: Institute for Defense Analyses.

Orlansky, J. and String, J. (2nd quarter, 1981).
"Computer-Based Instruction for Military Training",
Defense Management Journal, pp. 45-54.

BIOGRAPHY

Dr. Robert G. Main is a professor of instructional technology at California State University (CSU), Chico. He is an active consultant with industry in the area of computer-based training (CBT) and the design of interactive video systems, simulators, and part task trainers as well as individualized computer-assisted instruction and computer-assisted learning modules. Dr. Main's educational background includes a B.S. in journalism from the University of Missouri, and M.A. in communication from Stanford University, and a Ph.D. in educational technology from the University of Maryland. He has completed all course work toward his master's degree in computer science at CSU, Chico and is a graduate of the U.S. Army Command and General Staff College. A retired Army officer, Dr. Main spent 22 years on active duty in a variety of command and staff positions. He was named outstanding professor at CSU, Chico in 1987-88.

SIMULATION AND NETWORKING

Using Simulation Techniques to Model Local Area Network (LAN) Configurations

Jane M. Carey
Arizona State University - West

Leonard C. Lindstrom
LC Consultants, Inc.

Philip J. Mizzi
Arizona State University - West

INTRODUCTION

Telecommunication networks are proliferating throughout business organizations. Local area networks (LANs) and wide area networks (WANs) support business communications in all size businesses. WANs are equipped with very sophisticated algorithms which determine which branches have enough capacity for message transmission. LAN capacity management has received less focus and attention.

A simulation package by Chang and Sullivan (1986) called Quantitative Systems for Business (QSB) is used to demonstrate the effects of adding additional nodes on a local area network. The model is called NETwork modeling (NET) Decision Support System. It allows the drawing of a network with the numbering of the nodes and the application of the following algorithms:

1. Shortest Route (Path) Algorithm
2. Maximal Flow Algorithm
3. Minimal Spanning Tree Algorithm

BACKGROUND

Local Area Networks (LANS)

A local area network is a high-speed information transfer system that links intelligent devices over a common transmission medium within a confined geographical area. (Mizra & Belitsos, 1987: 117)

LANs are usually confined to a single building or even to a single floor of a building. Because of this geographical proximity and bridging of short distances, LANs can run hundreds of times faster than wide area networks (WANs) which use common phone lines for transmission media.

Several motivations exist for putting LANs in place. The first is cost saving through peripheral sharing. Items such as laser printers, high capacity secondary storage, plotters, and scanners are still relatively expensive and usage levels seldom dictate having one device for each workstation. A second reason is that file sharing can occur. Workgroups can access the same documents and project information from their own workstations rather than sending hard copies of documents from person to person. The third reason is to facilitate person-to-person communication. This is most frequently accomplished by using electronic mail packages that reside on the network. Most net-based e-mail packages also include other useful features such as meeting schedulers and calendars. In general, LANs can improve the individual and collective efficiency and effectiveness of workers.

There are negative aspects to LANs. Security and privacy can be issues. If inadequate controls are placed on the networks, users may gain access to data that has been previously inaccessible. Also, the management of LANs is a complex software issue. Contention for access to devices may be difficult to resolve, LANs may also grow too large for the current technology and throughput, reliability, and response-time may be degraded. Simulation techniques are ideal for testing out various configurations and LAN topologies. It is very difficult to recable a LAN once the cabling is in place. It is also too expensive to change the topology if a poor choice is made.

The Current System-SneakerNET

The target simulation environment is a university department. Currently the department houses 22 faculty members, 5 fulltime support-staff members, one administrator, and several part-time support-staff members. The department is anticipating moving into a new building and is at the planning stage for a network. The network will have a potential service base of 50 faculty members, 10 support staff member, two administrators, and several part-time support members in the coming years.

The current system is not supported by a LAN. Each of the faculty and staff members have stand alone workstations of various types. Some of the staff members and the administrator have broadband connection to a mainframe computer to access the student information system and the financial system. Most of the faculty have modem dial-up capabilities to connect them to the mainframe which they primarily use for statistical analyses.

The workstations are mainly DOS machines of various types including 8086, 8286, and 8386 architecture. At least three faculty members have MACintosh machines. Most of the faculty have dot matrix or ink jet printers at their workstations. There are six laser printers, one scanner, and one plotter scattered throughout the common work areas. The faculty create documents or execute runs at their standalone work stations and then save the files to disk. They then take their disks to one of the common workstations attached to a laser printer, insert the disk and print the document. This process is affectionately(?) referred to as "sneakerNET" since the transmission medium is foot travel. Besides the nuisance of having to leave the workstation and move to a remote site to print, often the single-user laser printers are in use by someone else. This creates frustration and is a tremendous waste of time.

The Proposed Environment

The new building has been wired with dual phone jacks. One connection is for normal phone transmission, the other can provide the transmission medium for the proposed network. Several decisions must be made in regard to the proposed network. Various criteria must be defined and issues resolved before the final decision can occur. Many times, the issues have trade offs. The following list contains many of the decision criteria that had to be considered in this decision:

1. Cost Constraints
2. Future Expandability
3. Performance or throughput
4. Interoperability (running UNIX, DOS, OS/2, and MACintoshes on the same network)
5. Security
6. Reliability and network management
7. Bridges or gateways to the outside world
8. Software compatibility
9. Intended use (type of software)
10. Ease of use
11. OSI (Open Systems Interconnection) standards

The floor plan for the new building with the nodes indicated by * is illustrated in figure 1.

NORTH

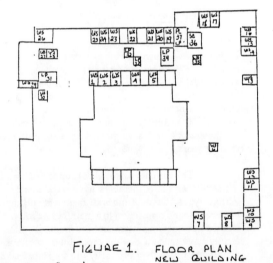

FIGURE 1.   FLOOR PLAN
NEW BUILDING

SCALE 1" = 33'

Network Topologies

Network topology refers to the overall shape or geometric arrangement of the LAN configuration. Topology influences a LAN's efficiency and effectiveness. There are four basic topologies: bus, tree, star, and ring. The type of topology dictates determination of maximal flow, shortest route, and minimal spanning tree.

The simplest topology is the bus topology (see figure 2). The attached workstations and peripherals share a common medium. There is no central controller. The biggest advantage of the bus topology is that if one or more of the attached devices malfunctions, the other nodes can still operate. Another

advantage is that new nodes and peripherals may be easily added to the network.

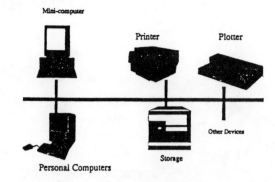

Figure 2. Bus Topology

The tree topology builds on the bus topology. It basically joins two or more buses together. The tree topology is used to link several floors in a building together or in the case of a campus, can link several buildings together if they are close in proximity.

The ring topology has a set of repeaters joined by point-to-point links (see figure 2). It gets it's name from the circular shape that it takes on. Stations are linked to the LAN at a repeater. Data circulates around the ring in one direction. The drawback of the ring topology is that when one workstation is down, the whole LAN may be affected.

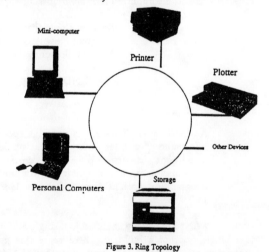

Figure 3. Ring Topology

The star topology has a central switching station (see figure 3). The nodes are attached to the central switching station by a point-to-point link. The whole system is dependent on the central switching station. If the switching station goes down, the whole LAN is down.

All LANs may be connected to other LANs or WANs through bridges and gateways. A bridge stores and forwards data to the proper destination between two or more LANs with identical topologies and software. Gateways can connect any two LANs or a LAN to non-LAN resources, regardless of topology or software. Interconnectivity is another issue that affects the LAN decision.

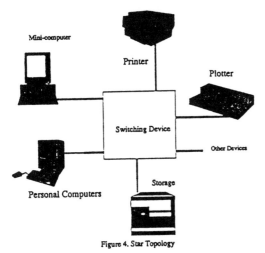

Figure 4. Star Topology

Several other terms need to be addressed within the LAN context. Two are baseband and broadband. Baseband in the LAN world refers to digital signaling. Broadband refers to analog transmission. Baseband does not have enough bandwidth to support video or audio whereas broadband does. Broadband is better suited for long distances because of the common carrier presence. The speed of broadband is slower than baseband.

Another issue is that of transmission medium. The typical LAN media include coaxial cable, twisted-pairs, and fiber optics. Coaxial cable has traditionally been the most frequent choice of medium for LANs. It has a high bandwidth and is resistent to outside interference or noise. It is expensive and very stiff which makes it difficult to install. Data rates for coaxial cable average around 10 megabits per second (mbps).

Twisted-pairs is the medium that the telephone companies use for transmission. It is easy to install and inexpensive; however, it is susceptible to noise. The newest approach is to sheath the twisted-pairs to protect from noise. This medium is called 10baseT wire. The data rate for 10baseT is between 700 kilobits to 1 megabit per second.

Fiber optics are based on light traveling through spun glass tubes. The bandwidth and noise protection are excellent. The cost is quite high. If LAN security is a primary concern, the best choice is fiber optics.

The last issue in LAN technology is that of controlling multiple access to LANs. The techniques are token passing ring, token passing bus, and CSMA/CD (Carrier-Sense Multiple Access/Collision Detection). The token passing ring technique passes a token (bit pattern) around a circle of nodes. When a node needs to transmit, it must wait for a free token to arrive. When one arrives, the node has a limited amount of access time. If the token is busy, it must wait until the token makes its way around the ring again. It is easy to see that in a busy network, the user may perceive a longer wait time. In a token passing bus, the token is passed along the bus in a sequential fashion rather than around a circle.

In the CSMA/CD technique, the control of the transmission is based on each node sensing whether the medium is being used. If it does not sense use, it then begins to transmit. Because it can only sense a limited distance, it may sometimes send a transmission at the same time a remote node also sends a

transmission. This leads to potential collisions. The CSMA/CD handles the collisions through retransmission direction.

All of these technical factors are determinants in the LAN selection process. It is easy to see that LAN choice can become a very complex problem. The simulation software that is being used, only addresses a small subset of these determinants. It may well be that some other factor that is not addressed by the software may be the overriding factor.

THE SIMULATION SOFTWARE

Of the three options offered by the simulation package, only two are germane to this selection process. They are maximal flow algorithm and minimal spanning tree. The shortest route algorithm is inappropriate since in most LANs the routing is fixed rather than variable.

Maximal Flow Algorithm is used to demonstrate the possible system performance degradation when additional nodes are added to a network. NET allows up to 600 branches and 300 nodes.

The NET software assumes that nodes are numbered sequentially beginning with 1. Input data can be entered and modified as needed. The data include branch number, an optional branch name, start node, end node, flow capacity from start node, and flow capacity from end node. The solution displays corresponding branches and net flows and the maximal total flow.

The minimal spanning tree helps determine the cable length requirements when all the nodes and distances between nodes are known. The input data include Branch number, an optional branch name, start node, end node, and distance between nodes (see figure 5). The output from the algorithm includes a step by step distance determination from one node to the next and also the total cable length or distance through the network (see figure 6).

Branch Number	Branch Name	Start Node	End Node	Distance
1	< >	<1 >	<2 >	<2 >
2	< >	<1 >	<3 >	<9 >
3	< >	<1 >	<4 >	<6 >
4	< >	<2 >	<5 >	<7 >
5	< >	<2 >	<6 >	<10 >
6	< >	<2 >	<7 >	<15 >
7	< >	<3 >	<5 >	<10 >
8	< >	<3 >	<6 >	<13 >
9	< >	<3 >	<7 >	<16 >
10	< >	<4 >	<5 >	<20 >
11	< >	<4 >	<6 >	<7 >
12	< >	<4 >	<7 >	<9 >
13	< >	<5 >	<8 >	<15 >
14	< >	<5 >	<9 >	<11 >
15	< >	<6 >	<8 >	<14 >
16	< >	<6 >	<9 >	<20 >
17	< >	<7 >	<8 >	<8 >
18	< >	<7 >	<9 >	<18 >
19	< >	<8 >	<10 >	<15 >
20	< >	<9 >	<10 >	<9 >

The Final Minimal Spanning Tree for MSTREE   Page: 1

Branch on the Tree	Distance
1 - 2 (B1)	2
1 - 3 (B2)	9
1 - 4 (B3)	6
2 - 5 (B4)	7
4 - 6 (B11)	7
4 - 7 (B12)	9
5 - 9 (B14)	11
7 - 8 (B17)	8
9 - 10 (B20)	9

Total distance = 68

61

A simulation is set up to determine flow capacity and cable requirements for the proposed departmental LAN. The first simulation will use the token passing ring configuration. The second simulation will use the CSMA/CD bus configuration. A comparison between the two will then be made. An assumption is made that the medium in both situations will be 10baseT wire with a data rate of 1 megabit per kilometer.

THE SIMULATION

The following section shows the output from the minimal spanning tree and maximal flow algorithms for both the ring and star topology. The results are discussed later.

<u>Token Passing Ring - Minimal Spanning Tree</u>

Minimal Spanning Tree = 930 feet

<u>Token passing Ring - Maximal Flow</u>

Maximal Flow = 93 data rate * .000304 (to convert to kilobits)

<u>CSMA/CD Bus - Minimal Spanning Tree</u>

Minimal Spanning Tree = 1458 feet

<u>CSMA/CD - Maximal Flow</u>

Maximal Flow = 139 data rate * .000304

SUMMARY AND CONCLUSIONS

From running the algorithms, it appears that the ring topology has shorter total cable length than does the star. However, the maximal flow capacity is greater in the star. Tradeoffs often occur. From these algorithms, it was difficult to make a decision.

The final decision was not based on cable length or maximal capacity. It was based on several of the other criteria, in particular; adherence to OSI standards, interoperability, and future expandability.

The proposed LAN will be a DECnet (see figure 11) with a David System Concentrator. It is based on ethernet with 10baseT wiring.

REFERENCES

Chang, Y.L., & Sullivan, R.S. (1986). <u>Quantitative Systems for Business.</u> Englewood Cliffs, NJ: Prentice-Hall.

Dordick, H.S., & Williams, F. (1986). <u>Innovative Management Using Telecommunications.</u> New York: John Wiley.

Gasman, L. (1988). <u>Manager's Guide to the New Telecommunications Network.</u> Norwood, MA: Artech House.

Grover, K.C. (1986). <u>Foundations of Business Telecommunications.</u> New York: Plenum Press.

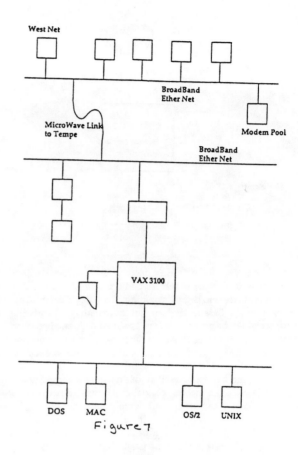

Figure 7

Mizra, J., & Belitsos, B. (1987). <u>Business Telecommunications.</u> Homewood, IL: Irwin.

Solomon, A.H. (1990). Telecommunications in the 1990s - managing networks to serve user needs. <u>Telecommunications,</u> 24(2):23-29.

Vignault, W.L. (1987). <u>Worldwide Telecommunications Guide for the Business Manager.</u> New York. John Wiley.

Weixel, S. (1990). The flesh and blood of network planning. <u>Computerworld,</u> 24(22): 77-79.

DEVELOPING A WINDOWS-BASED MANAGEMENT SUPPORT SYSTEM FOR THE FINANCIAL MANAGER

James A. Sena
School of Business
California Polytechnic State University
San Luis Obispo, California 93407

L. Murphy Smith
School of Business
Texas A&M University
College Station, Texas

ABSTRACT

This paper addresses the creation of a *windows*-based software development targeted for computerized managerial support of financial managers. Building on our previous research in financial statement analysis we utilized a database of oil and gas companies' financial information as a base for experimentation and analysis.

The focus of this paper is not on the managerial support aspects but on the philosophy, available software tools, and the ways in which a contemporary graphics user interface can be utilized to present information to the financial manager. Our objective was to present the graphics user interface, the *Window* software system and it's associated application support software, together with the financial database to indicate how these facilities could support and enhance the access of financial information.

INTRODUCTION

Business applications have played a major part in the growth and development of the computer industry. These applications have not kept pace with the deployment of new technologies such as object-oriented, icon-driven, hypercard, hypermedia, multi-screen facilities available for microcomputer software development.

The hardware environment for our approach to an object-oriented presentation advocates a PC/DOS 286 or 386 microcomputer system. The specific software framework providing the object-oriented facilities consists of several Microsoft products -- the *Windows* Operating Environment, the *Windows Software Development Kit*, and a variety of *windows*-based software packages. These systems are layered and meshed together to form a hierarchy of *windows* for the access and presentation of financial information.

OBJECT-ORIENTED PROGRAMMING

Object-oriented programming creates code that makes sense because it shifts the burden of work from the user to the processor. Early databases had a hierarchical structure in which data and structure were merged. Relational databases separated the content of the database from the structure. Object-oriented databases have, in a sense, reunited the content and the structure-- the object contains both the data and the procedures that act upon it.

From a user vantage, such a structure is desirable because it facilitates manipulation with less user effort. From a programming viewpoint, coding is modular -- providing reusable portions of code. Dealing in objects means the programmer can concentrate on what changes among objects or classes (groups of similar objects), rather than reprogramming the entire operation. Understanding the concepts of object, the methods within them that perform operations, and the messages that trigger these methods, as well as classes of objects and inheritance, is necessary in order to program object-oriented systems.

The Operating Environment

To construct an object-oriented environment suitable for a financial manager we felt that certain hardware and software products were necessary. Hardware requirements included a 286 or 386 microcomputer with a mouse pointing device, enhanced graphical display, and a communication connection to a network or mainframe computer system. Software requirements included the following products:

> o Microsoft *Windows*;
> o Microsoft Windows Development Kit;
> o Microsoft Word for Windows;
> o *Superbase*4;
> o *Excel*for Windows; and
> o *Crosstalk*for Windows.

GRAPHICS USER INTERFACE

Background

The Graphics User Interface [GUI], according to Microsoft Corporation, is a user interface that runs in a computer graphics mode. Such an interface would need to meet the following requirements:

o takes advantage of bitmapped displays, offering WYSIWYG (What You See Is What You Get) screen representations;

o s a graphically-oriented interface making extensive use of icons;

o has good screen aesthetics;

o allows direct manipulation of onscreen elements, allowing word processor users (e.g. to grab and drag left and right document margins rather than having to calculate and type in specific measurements);

o embraces the object-oriented paradigm, the user chooses an object first, then selects the action, freeing the user from an action sequence that must be completed before moving onto the next task;

o offers standard 'expected' elements -- such as menus, standard window elements, dialog control -- to provide consistency across applications;

o application support: a strong set of user-interface controls and tools to build applications;

o consistency across platforms as well as across applications;

o ease of use and visual appeal, ease of installation and configuration;

o flexibility -- support for keyboard and mouse as well as for a range of devices and peripherals; and

o user customization and personalization.

Graphical user interfaces save time, make programs easier to use, reduce learning time and make programs more powerful. GUI's offer standardized commands from one program to the next. This allows the user to master, for example, the printing of a text document in one application while that same application is being used to print a spreadsheet in another application.

THE FINANCIAL DATABASE

A database of financial information for the sixteen top oil companies for the years 1980 through 1990 have been compiled. The source of this data is the Dow Jones Retrieval Service. Data was collected on the following topics:

```
1 CURRENT QUOTES
2 LATEST NEWS ON AHC
3 FINANCIAL AND MARKET OVERVIEW
4 EARNINGS ESTIMATES
5 COMPANY VS INDUSTRY PERFORMANCE
6 INCOME STATEMENTS, BAL SHEETS
7 COMPANY PROFILE
8 INSIDER TRADING SUMMARY
9 INVESTMENT RESEARCH REPORTS
```

In previous research (Sena and Smith, 1988 and 1987) we have developed decision support and expert systems using this data in order to analyze the performance of the oil and gas industry By building on the database and those techniques we have constructed an object-oriented interface

that provides graphs, tables, charts, and other object-like presentations.

WINDOWS SYSTEMS

Microsoft Windows

Microsoft WINDOWS is one of the most popular graphical user interfaces for DOS. Windows has several versions that span the facilities and capabilities of the personal computer from 8086 to 386 architectures. In May, 1990 Microsoft released Windows 3.0 (Morse 1990). This product is the focal point from which all applications are constructed and launched as described in this paper.

Windows allows the user to work with a number of applications simultaneously. Overlapping Windows give control of any window on the screen. The user, at the touch of a button, can give control to any window on the screen and bring the active window to the front of the screen.

The main purpose of Windows is to run programs especially written for the graphical user interface, such as Microsoft *Excel* Windows runs these programs while overlapping Windows displayed on the screen, allowing the user to switch among them using the mouse or the keyboard.

Windows has a variety of user interface components consisting of menus, scroll bars, dialog boxes, and buttons. Menus consist of a list of options, where the user selects one by the push of a single key or the use of the mouse. Scroll bars allow the user to quickly scan the selected material. Dialog boxes are fill-in forms that display information and let the user supply the information necessary to carry out menu choices.

Windows has a "device independent" graphics interface to display graphics and text on the screen and on hard copy devices such as printers and plotters. Windows is equipped with device drivers that support many popular video display boards and printers. This shifts the burden of supporting various graphic output devices from the application to the operating system. Most Windows programs are written to treat the screen and printers in a device-dependent manner. Programs written for Windows can share and exchange data through the Windows clipboard (Miller, 1990).

Perhaps the most sophisticated aspect of Windows is memory management. Windows can move code and data segments in memory, discard code segments from memory and reload them from executable files (.EXE), and allows programs to share code and data located in dynamic link libraries. (The code that handles the menu logic in Windows is located in a dynamic-link library.) Only one copy of this code need be present in memory for all Windows applications (Morse, 1989). This sharing of code helps decrease the memory requirements of individual Windows applications.

Windows, when operating on a 386 computer, uses the "virtual 8086" mode to window and multitask virtually all DOS programs. Each DOS program application runs its own 640K "8086" environment and can run in the background regardless of what else is executing. This means that a user can download a file using their communication package, while working on a word processor and a spreadsheet. These various applications can be run in their own window area or they can use the full screen. Basically, a user can run in any of three modes: exclusive, foreground, or background.

In the exclusive mode the program runs just as if it were started from the standard DOS prompt and takes over the entire5re screen. The user can still copy and paste information, move from the program to Windows and toggle to the other modes.

In the foreground mode the program becomes the active window in the Windows environment, which means that it is the program actively being used. If there are other Windows on the screen, the active program is always brought to the front. When the program is in background mode, it continues to process even though another program is in the foreground. A windowed program in background mode will be overlapped by the active window and possibly by other background mode programs as well.

Besides the clipboard there are several desktop applications that are included with Windows. The Calculator enables the user to perform common arithmetic operations. The Calendar application sets appointments with alarm reminders and contains daily and monthly views. The cardfile is a filing programs containing cards as records of text or graphics. The clock is an analog which can be displayed anywhere on the screen. Paint is a full-featured drawing program and Write is a graphics based word processor. Notepad is a text scratch-pad/editor which has a date-time stamp option.

The Software Development Kit

The Microsoft Software Development Kit provides an extensive development environment with a full set of tools that assist the user in developing graphics-based applications. The kit provides a complete Windows development environment that interfaces with programming languages such as C, Pascal, and Assembler. Windows provides over 300 functions that handle menus, dialog boxes, graphics, data exchange, and memory management.

Microsoft Windows is a graphical-based environment that integrates applications, allows for easy exchange of text and graphics. Combined with the Windows features of drop-down menus, dialog boxes, icons, and overlapping Windows the development kit provides a total environment for users. Windows lets the user spend time developing their programs rather than the user interface by providing over three hundred functions that handle menus, dialog boxes, graphics, data exchange, and memory management.

The Application Program Interface (API) contains the functions, messages, data structures, data types, and files that a user employs to create programs that run under Windows. Some features provided by API include:

o Shared display, memory, keyboard, mouse, and system timer;
o Data interchange with other applications;
o Device-independent graphics through the Windows Graphics Device Interface;
o Multitasking; and
o Dynamic Linking.

Windows lets applications running simultaneously on a system share hardware resources. This eliminates the need to write specific code for each job. There are three development libraries that simplify a users development effort: the Windows Manager Interface, the Graphics Device Interface, and the Systems Service Interface.

The Windows Manager Interface function includes creating, moving, and altering Windows, menus, and system output. The Graphics Device Interface performs device-independent graphics operations within a Windows application. These functions create a wide variety of line, text, and bitmap output on output devices. The Systems Services Interface has functions that access code and data in modules, allocate and manage memory, manage tasks, load program resources, translate strings from one character set to another, alter the Windows initialization file, assist in system debugging, and create and open files.

The Windows Manager Interface has tools that allow a user to create easy to use menus in their applications. The user can also use the interface to create dialog boxes. These are fill-in forms that display information and let the user supply the information necessary to carry out menu choices. The Dialog Editor, included in the development kit, lets the user design dialog boxes on the screen and save their definitions in a resource file. The user can use the development kit to create their own fonts. When the application needs a font, the graphics device interface selects an appropriate font.

WINDOWS APPLICATIONS

One of the major selling points of graphical user interfaces is the applications platforms. Windows is a powerful foundation for productivity, but the environment can be made even more useful by launching application software programs directly within Windows.

Windows uses program information files, or PIF files, to determine how to run a standard applications that is not Windows-based. Many of the standard applications have PIF files or are provided with the Windows software installation package. Application software is the key to bringing the system together. These include for most users, and especially

the financial manager, such products as spreadsheets, databases, word processors, expert systems, desktop publishing, and communications. We will be discussing a set of packages that are being used to construct a computing environment for the financial manager. These packages are those that run under Windows such that they provide a homogeneous method of access and use and include: Microsoft *Excel Superbase* 4, *Knowledge Pro,* Microsoft *Word, Crosstalk,* and *Springboard Publisher.* Because all of these
products run under Windows a user can transfer data package to another using the Clipboard facility and can run a number of these programs simultaneously -- switching back and forth between the various programs.

Spreadsheets

Spreadsheets are both useful and necessary in the computer age. A spreadsheet can be used for bookkeeping, accounting, statistics, graphics, and even word processing. There are more than 45 different spreadsheets available for microcomputers today. Rather than discuss the various packages we will focus on *Excel* for Windows. *Excel* is both a spreadsheet and a graphics software package. Besides these two features *Excel* includes a powerful and easy to use macro capability.

Word Processors

For many users of microcomputers, their primary use is probably word processing. A word processor is the medium for the creation of everything from a memo to a novel. Similar to spreadsheets there are large number of word processing packages on the market. Microsoft provides a family of packages that work either with Windows or under Windows.

Microsoft WORD is the generic name for this family of word processors. This package approaches the capabilities of a desk top publisher. Word provides such capabilities as table formatting, customizable menus, optional automatic repagination, absolute positioning of graphics or text. There are four editing views to choose from: Outline, Gallery, Print and Page. Table handling makes side-by-side paragraphs, lists, and forms easy to construct.

Communications

Communication packages permit the user to access other computer systems through either a communication line or by the use of a modem. There are a number of packages that run under Windows. Crosstalk is one of the most popular communication packages that runs under Windows. Crosstalk's phone directory is set up using Window's dialog boxes. The script language, which is similar to programming or macros, provides user with the ability to perform a variety of communication tasks.

Imbedded in the package are several scripts which assist the user in preparing their own scripts. The pull-down menus

and dialog boxes in Crosstalk are virtually the same as in Windows. There is a dialing directory which holds all of the information Crosstalk needs to communicate with other systems. Crosstalk lists the phone entries and the user can select the one desired. Screens can be captured to a file by clicking the capture button on the screen.

Desktop Publishers

Desktop Publishing brings high-quality fonts and high-resolution to documents. Basically, desktop packages include support for laser and high quality fonts, What You See Is What You Get (WYSIWYG) editing, mouse support, and the ability to import texts and graphics files. There are number of desktop packages that work under the Windows platform. One of these desktop packages is Springboard Publisher.

Springboard Publisher works well under Windows. The program imports *Windows Paint* and *Windows Write* files. It provides a flexible layout technique that features independent frames for graphics and text.

Expert Systems

An expert system is a computer system that applies reasoning to give advice or recommendations. It is called an "expert" system because it is similar to a human expert on a particular subject. Typically, the system is a decision-making and a problem-solving package. The performance of the expert can be comparable to that of a human expert. As such Expert Systems are a branch of artificial intelligence. Expert systems can cover areas such as managing assets and liabilities, corporate planning, tax advice and bid preparation.

An expert system applies rules or conditional statements stored in its knowledge base to answer questions posed by a user. The usefulness of the program's response depends on how well the developer structures the knowledge base. KnowledgePro, a Windows-based system development tool is a powerful application-development system that uses expert system rules and hypertext but doesn't require the user to be an expert to use it.

In a sense, KnowledgePro is a knowledge processor. It uses hypertext to provide information to the user dynamically. It lets the user build a system that determines the content of the information it provides based on the user's selections. The menu system, again, is very similar to the pull-down, dialog box features of Windows.

Databases

A database is a collection of interrelated data organized in a way that provides information for specific needs. It is the organizing of files into related units that are viewed as a single storage concept. The database is available to a wide range of users. Databases can include text, number, date, time and external fields. Text and numeric fields can be formatted. Date fields can handle several different styles of expressions. Calculated fields hold arithmetic formulas, variables, or values from other fields.

Superbase 4 is a Windows-based database system. Using Superbase the user can select, build and manipulate data using a similar set of Windows menus and dialog boxes. There is a control panel on the screen that resembles a VCR. The icon choices include fast forward, forward, pause, reverse, and stop. Other buttons will take the user to the previous, first, and last records in the database. Data can be imported or exported to either the Windows based packages (e.g. *WORD* or *EXCEL*) or together popular spreadsheets and databases (e.g. Lotus and DBase III+ or IV).

Superbase has a forms editor which makes it easy to build custom data entry forms. The forms can have colored boxes, lines, text, graphics, and text form external files. The user can display data in table view, form view, or record view. *Superbase* approaches the database definition and manipulation in a manner similar to mainframe and minicomputer database management systems -- providing mechanisms for sophisticated, yet user friendly, data definition and validation, and data manipulation and access.The also provide a familiar application development language based on BASIC.

CREATING THE MANAGERIAL SUPPORT SYSTEM

In our initial system implementation we used the information extracted from the Dow Jones Services and our historical data base from earlier research to construct a series of files. Our objective was to demonstrate and experiment with the multi-application aspects of Windows. Using the files from the Dow Jones we constructed the following data sets:

---

o 5 Year Summary
o Balance Sheets for 1980 - 1990
  -- Quarterly for 1989 - 1990
  -- Annual for 1980 - 1988
o Income Statements for 1980 - 1990
  -- Quarterly for 1989 - 1990
  -- Annual for 1980 - 1988
o Disclosures
o Investment Text
o Media
o News
o Stock Market Quotations for 1989 - 1990
o Ratios for 1980 - 1989
o Standard and Poors Information

These data sets were entered into the various Windows-based software packages in the manner described in the section below.Using Communication Software

The access to the Dow Jones Service was performed by using the *CrossTalk* for Windows package. We operated

through a modem to access an IBM 3090 mainframe. On this system we extracted the data using the Dow Jones Service. The data was pulled down into a series of ASCII files on a microcomputer.

This service could have been done on a variety of non-Windows based communication packages. However, it was our intention to initially restrict our construction effort to the packages described earlier.

Text Editing Facilities

To separate and edit the extracted data we made use of Microsoft's *Word* for Windows. Under this package the data was brought into the wordprocessor as ASCII files. Depending on whether the information was to be targeted for spreadsheet analysis, text retrieval, or database manipulation the files were re-arranged and appropriately segmented.

The following sets of files were created:

Excel Spreadsheet
  Balance Sheets
  Income Statements
  Ratios

Superbase 4 Databases
  Quotations
  Disclosures
  Five Year Summaries
  Investment
  Media
  News
  Standard and Poors Information

After these data files were placed into the proper form they were saved as ASCII files on disk. At that point *Superbase* 4 and Excel software facilities were used to construct the spreadsheets and databases.

Spreadsheet Entry and Analysis

Using Excel the various ASCII files were imported and arranged in columnar fashion. A separate spreadsheet was established for each Company and Year for the Balance Sheets, Income Statements, and Ratios. Linkages were then established to provide a three dimensional effect for each Company such that the user could progress from year to year or concurrently view multiple year values on split Windows. Alternative linkages were also established to compare Companies on a yearly basis. Finally, where appropriate, (specifically the Ratios) Industry summaries were developed on a yearly basis and an overall set for all years.

Using the dialog and database features of Excel the system was customized to permit direct access and comparison of specific cell ranges from Company to Company. Finally an overall composite was constructed such that the user could inquire about a specific company and retrieve and display all of the information contained in the Excel spreadsheets for that Company for a given year.

Database Entry and Analysis

For all but the stockmarket quotations our use of *Superbase* 4 was limited to storage of records as documents or text based inquiry sources. Most of the information was stored in free text form and retrieved using the pull-down styled menus of *Superbase*.

The quotations were organized such that the user could call up a specific quote on a particular date or view changing conditions from one time period to the next. Our goal is to develop a series of graphical presentations to present the quotations in both list and graphical form simultaneously on the screen.

Combining the Products

Our last step in the initial effort was to present our work in some homogeneous fashion. From a user perspective Windows provided a made-to-order presentation to the extent that our selected products could be placed onto a single group. Using this group the appropriate software could be called and the files accessed. Such a situation, although acceptable is not optimal. It our intention to develop a series of front-end menus that would make the presentation appear as a single system as opposed to a series of software packages. At first we intended to use the Windows Development package but upon review we have noted that there are a number of menu presentation and access systems ranging from the very simple to the elaborate. At the low end is hDC's Windows Express and at the high end is Bridge by Softbridge Microsystems.

We did some experimentation with Window's Express and came to the conclusion that it was not suitable for Managerial Presentation use. At this point we are investigating the potential use of Bridge. Using Bridge a developer can construct a personalized workstation -- creating a menu system to access both Window and non-Window applications. Custom dialog boxes can also be created to prompt for input, halt or process an application, and communicate with the workstation user.

Conclusions

The potential for Windows-based systems is currently just beginning to be realized in the MS/DOS arena. The approaches and applications that we have discussed and used in this paper are to be the foundations for not only this work but for the majority of future Windows-based software developments.

BIBLIOGRAPHY

Miller, M. [1988] "Two New Windows Prove More Useful", Infoworld. January 18, 1988, pp. 50-51.

Morse, M. [1990] "Enjoying the Full Potential of Windows", PC Week. June 5, 1990, pp. 1-93.

Scannel, E. [1990] "True Believers", Infoworld. January 29, 1990, pp. 51-53.

Schindler, P. [1989] " *Superbase* 4 Fully Taps Windows", PC Week. November 6, 1989, pp. 91-97.

Sena, James A. and L. Murphy Smith, [1990] "Financial Planning Workstation", Journal of Accounting and EDP. Micros in Accounting Section, Winter

Sena, James A. and L. Murphy Smith, [1989] "The Development Process for the Creation of an Expert System for Financial Statement Analysis", Human Factors in Management Information Systems, 2nd Edition, Chapter in Readings Text, Editor: Carey, J., Ablex Publishing Company, Summer

Sena, James A. and L. Murphy Smith, [1989] "How to Design User Friendly Data Base Applications", Journal of Accounting and EDP. Micros in Accounting Section. Vol. 5, No. 2, Summer 1989

Sena, James A, and L. Murphy Smith, [1897] "The Development of a Computer Data Base of Financial Ratios to Evaluate Oil and Gas Companies", Oil and Gas Tax Quarterly, Summer, 1987.

Shaw, R. [1989] "Knowledge Pro", PC Magazine. June 27, 1989, p. 36.

Simon, B. [1989] " *Crosstalk* for Windows", PC Magazine, October 17, 1989, p. 33.

PRODUCTS

BRIDGE 286, Softbridge Microsystems, 125 Cambridge Park, MA 02140

Crosstalk for Windows, DCA/Crosstalk Communications, 1000 Halcomb Woods Parkway, Roswell, GA 30076

KnowledgePro, Knowledge Gardens Inc. 472A Malden Bridge, Nassau, NY 12123

Microsoft *Excel, Word, Windows* and *Windows Development Kit*, Microsoft Corporation, One Microsoft Way, Redmond, WA 98052

Springboard Publisher, Springboard Software, Inc. 7808 Creekridge Circle, Minneapolis, MN 55435

Superbase 4, Precision Software, Irving, TX 75063

Windows Express. , hDC Computer Corporation,, 6742 185th
Avenue, Redmond, WA 98052 |

SOCIOTECHNICAL SYSTEMS DESIGN: AN EXPERT SYSTEM PERSPECTIVE

A. B. (Rami) Shani and James A. Sena
School of Business
California Polytechnic State University
San Luis Obispo, California 93407

ABSTRACT

Over the last three decades the sociotechnical system (STS) approach has become an increasingly popular organization design tool for examining and changing the workplace environment. sociotechnical system redesign efforts indicate that STS changes have successfully increased the utilization of human and manufacturing technologies, increased productivity and quality of working life compared with traditional work designs.

Using the sociotechnical framework we formulated and developed a prototype expert system. A software development firm undergoing the transition from stand-alone to network computing is used to simulate our sociotechnical system based analysis and serves as our subject for demonstrating the use of our expert/consultative system. It is our intention that this instrument would guide the thinking of the decision maker as they construct the appropriate organizational work environment for an organization.

INTRODUCTION

This paper proposes the use of a sociotechnical system-based framework, specifically the business review and design framework, combined with an expert system shell to assist decision makers in analyzing their organization. A case study is presented which applies the expert system developed in order to examine the impact of a local area network on the organization. Following the presentation of the sociotechnical system-based framework we review the steps for the construction of an expert system using the business review and design framework. Next we examine a sample firm as the workplace is changed by the introduction of a local area network.

SOCIOTECHNICAL SYSTEMS

At the most basic level the sociotechnical systems perspective considers every organization to be made up of a social subsystem (the people) using tools, techniques and knowledge (the technical subsystem) to produce a product or a service valued by the environmental subsystem. The degree to which the technical subsystem and the social subsystems are designed with respect to each other and the environment determines how successful and competitive the organization will be.

The Business Review and Design framework, as we present it here constitutes a modified version of collaborative earlier work that has been published elsewhere by Hanna (1988) and Shani & Elliott (1988, 1989). The framework identifies seven key factors that have an impact on organizational performance. The framework is especially useful when one is attempting to understand why organization's results are what they are and to plan changes that will lead to improved results. The seven factors are:

Business Strategy
Business Design
Business Strategy
Culture
Change Strategy
Management of Change
Business Results

The first factor - *business situation* - is made up of elements and forces in the market place in which the organization competes. The factor of *business strategy* refers to the elements that spell out how the organization plans to compete in its industry. The *business design* elements are concerned with the firm's tools and organization to achieve its strategy such as technological subsystem, tasks, structure, reward systems, control systems, information systems, decision making processes, the management of human resources and, the social subsystem, The *culture* refers to elements such as as the work habits and practices, assumptions, values, rites and rituals and, emergent role systems. The *change strategy* and the *management of change* factors are concerned with how the firm plans to modify and improve its business, the specific actions taken and the specific structures and mechanisms that the firm puts in place in order to facilitate change and continuous improvements over time. Finally, the *business results* refers to the multiple methods and criteria used by the firm to measure its success.

A fundamental axiom of Sociotechnical system thinking is that whatever decisions are made about or within any one of the organizational subsystems they should meet the demands of the remaining others. Any decision about work design should meet the demands of the technical, social and environmental subsystems. A strategic decision to increase the market share of a specific product requires not only understanding of the industry, competition, customers demand and marketing know-how but the technological ability to increase production, the trained people to do the work and the organization design to support it.

In order to move towards a local area network environment as a means of conducting business requires a careful assessment and a matching process of the overall business strategy, business situation, business results together with the social subsystem. Cultural and quality issues may impact the selection and use of the most appropriate network system software. The redesign of a company's organizational structure and processes is usually warranted in order to achieve full utilization of the new systems' potential.

STRUCTURED SITUATION ANALYSIS

Knowledge Acquisition

Knowledge-based systems are designed to replicate the functions performed by a human expert (Mockler, 1989). A number of expert systems exist in various companies to give expert advice in such areas as auditing, sales management, computer configuration, and many areas of planning and decision making.

Knowledge-based systems enable a user with a problem to consult a computer system as they would an expert advisor to diagnose what might be causing a problem or to figure out how to solve a problem or make a decision. The computer system can extract information from a user by asking questions related to the problem during consultation. It can also answer questions asked by a user about why certain information is needed. Such a system can make recommendations regarding the problem decision at the end of the consultation, and when asked by the user it can explain the reasoning steps gone through to reach its conclusions.

Knowledge based systems are developed by:

Analyzing, or decomposing the decision situation;
Reformulating or reconceptualizing the decision situation; and
Putting the system onto the computer.

Decision Situation Analysis

The objectives in examining a situation are to identify the required knowledge, the reasoning process for arriving at a decision based on the knowledge, and the range of decisions outcomes that can result from the decision making process. These objectives are achieved through studying the human expert process whereby a decision is made and developing a scenario to imitate the process. This is often referred to as the decomposition or analysis phase.

The analytical process of structuring the decision situation is a continual, evolving one, involving reviewing decisions made in each area (the decomposition sub-phase) and drawing diagrams of the decision (the reformulation sub-phase). Decomposition starts out with an understanding of concepts, relationships, and definitions that appear to be relevant to the problem. Together these factors serve to explain and justify the experts' reasoning pattern. This classification and the description of how situation components are organized and structured constitutes the structure of the knowledge segments in the situation.

The next step in the analytical process is the establishment of basic reasoning strategies that are used in the search for a solution. What facts are established and in what order? What kinds of questions are asked and in what order? The reasoning strategies culminate in the specification of recommendations or actions that might be taken under the situation being studied.

Reconceptualizing the Decision Situation

As the decision situation is classified and apportioned detailed models are developed for specific areas. Each of these areas or groups of areas represent potential prototype system development candidates. The prototype systems, in turn, could culminate in stages of specific recommendations that can guide the user through the situation analysis.

Besides assisting the developer of the expert system the process of thinking about actual recommendations provides a mechanism for testing against actual examples. Thus, in each stage the thought processes regarding actual typical situations keeps the study's focus on how the situation actually works. In this way the developer can trace the expert reasoning path from the situation facts to the solution.

Structured system models developed in this way constitute the linkage between the expert situation and the computer system representing it. The models are used to conceptualize the situation in a manner that facilitates system development.

Designing the System

In the transitionfrom reconceptualization to computerization the design of the system precedes the actual computer installation. The system needs to be described, dependencies identified, decision charts developed, and the knowledge base constructed. At that point an expert system shell can be utilized to place the expert system onto the computer.

Under system description the topics of user interface, recommendations to be made by the system, and the structure of the knowledge base and reasoning processes are specified. Dependency diagrams graphically model a knowledge-based system. Knowledge segments and their relationships are shown as well as the basic reasoning processes. These diagrams are based on the structured situation models. The reasoning paths are depicted to arrive at a final decision or recommendation.

A decision chart is prepared for every rule in the dependency diagram. They serve to determine the completeness of rule sets and help to verify the accuracy and consistency between rules. Constructing the knowledge base involves selecting a representation form, recording the knowledge for the knowledge base, and preparing the data for entry into the expert system shell.

Since we are using a rule-based form of representation (as opposed to a frame-based) the selection is mandated. As the rules and other associated knowledge base entries are entered into the expert shell the system can be tested by using, as in our case, a set of sample or known actual situation elements to test the workings of the model. This provides a review and test process for generalization and refinement.

OVERVIEW OF THE SYSTEM

System Objectives

The purpose of this system is to allow managers, planners, and/or consultants to examine an organization in terms of the Business Review and Design Framework. Through an interactive dialogue the system user can respond to a series of grouped questions that could result in a set of recommendations and suggestions for organizational change.

The prototype system has several parts. Beginning with an assessment of the Business Results; proceeding to the Business Situation; examining the Business Strategy and Business Design; given these examinations the Business Culture is reviewed and recommendations for Change are generated.

The system is designed for users with knowledge of their industry. Ideally the system should be consulted by several persons familiar with the target company. The system is intended to stimulate creative interactions among the participants. This system would probably be accompanied by some form of group development and assessment of the organization.

Recommendations to be Made by the System

In the first phase of the prototype the system has the ability to determine the most obvious problem areas. Examples of possible recommendations are:

> Restructure the working relationship relationship among functional units;

> Change the pattern of decision making to greater involvement of decision implementors.

In the second and third phases the system will have the ability to provide more in-depth analysis and concomitant benefits from the use of the expert system through the treatment of more intricate problem areas. In the third phase weighted values will be used to make decisions with a greater potential for organizational improvement.

Nature of the User Interface and User Dialogue

The user consulting the system will be asked questions related to the various modules in the Business Analysis and Design Framework. Sample Questions will be similar to the following:

> Estimate the degree to which Customer needs are being meet by the current support system.

The first phase will ask whether the particular module parameter is favorable or unfavorable. In the second phase the user is asked to give one of five possible estimates: very little, somewhat, average, above average, or significantly. Using these inputs the various combination of AND values in the Rules will be averaged to give a scale value to the module or sub module. In the third phase weights can be assigned by either the developer or the user organization interactively to the various parameters, sub modules, and modules to guide the user to a more specific set of recommendations.

A Description of the System's Knowledge Structure and Reasoning Process

The knowledge base is structured around the five modules identified during the situation study: Business Results, Business Situation, Business Strategy, Business Design and Culture. An overall Design of the system is depicted in Figure 1.

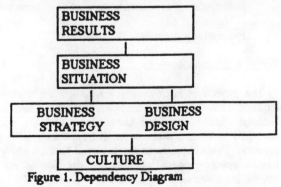

Figure 1. Dependency Diagram

For the first part of the system, factors that influence the five modules were identified. User questions were then developed for each influencing factor in each of the module areas. These questions were intended to guide users through a study of these factors. The knowledge base contains between three and seven major question groups about influencing factors related to each business module's state-of-acceptance. Figure 2 contains an outline summary of the major modules and topical areas used for questions. Figure 3 shows the Rule constructed for Business Results related to the influencing factors or variables.

```
RULE 5
  IF FINANCIAL_ASSESSMENT = OK          AND
     CUSTOMER_EXPECTATIONS = OK         AND
     COMPANY_COMPETITIVE_POSITION = OK  AND
     MANAGEMENT_EXPECTATION = OK
  THEN
     BUSINESS_RESULTS = OK
  ELSE
     BUSINESS_RESULTS = NOT_OK;

ASK FINANCIAL_ASSESSMENT: "What is your Financial
     Assessment of your Current Operation";
CHOICES FINANCIAL ASSESSMENT: OK,NOT-OK;
```

Figure 3: Sample Expert System Rule

Business Results
| Financial Assessment
| Customer Expectations
| Competitive Positioning
| Management Expectations

Business Situation
| Economic Climate
| Industry Stability
| Competition
| Customer Satisfaction
| Investor Expectation

Business Strategy
| Mission/Vision
| Operational Purpose
| Competitive Strategy

Business Design
| Technical Subsystem
| Organization Structure
| Reward System
| Human Resources
| Decision Making Process
| Information System

Culture
| Assumptions/Norms
| Attitudes & Work Habits
| Emergent Role Systems
| Socio-Task Systems

Figure 2: First Level Hierarchy of Modules
and Analysis Variables

In the second phase user will be required to give weights to each factor. Using these weights the system determines the importance of each subfactor and overall module to insure re-direction to an improved state-of-acceptance. Additional factors affecting the assessment of the degree to which the modules impact Business Results will also be identified.

Questions were then developed for each of these additional influencing force areas. They were designed to suggest areas where users (management and planners) might look for ideas, and so stimulate their thinking.

Following the second phase a third part of the system calculates cumulative values for each of the five Business module forces. They determine the potential for improving a company's performance and vitality through an assessment of the Business Analysis and Review framework.

Dependency Diagrams

Dependency diagrams constructed to document the system are shown in Figures 1 and 2. Figure 1 gives and overview of the whole system. Figure 2 shows the specific segments for the first level of the system, along with the input variables that form the questions related to these segments.

The knowledge base for this system, unlike those formed in most other knowledge systems, consists mostly of questions, supported by rules that assign quantitative values or binary choices to the input parameters and manipulate these values according to assigned weights, to arrive at recommendations. Introductory and concluding screens were developed to frame the system for the user and to give the user instruction on how to use the system. A sample section of the knowledge base showing several user questions is given.

Selecting a Computer Development Tool

The prototype of the system was to be developed using a basic expert system shell. The system needed to be able to accept word-processed material as well as entry to the system shell itself. Fore future development inputs from spreadsheets and databases were also considered desireable features. For these reasons we selected the VP Expert System.

VP Expert offers a combination of features for developing microcomputer-based expert system that meet the criteria and needs for our problem area. Special features of interest include: the ability to exchange data from dBase, Lotus, and ASCII text files; an Induction command that automatically creates a knowledge base from a table contained in a text

database or worksheet file; an inference engine that uses backward and forward chaining for problem solving; development windows that let you observe the path of the inference engine as it navigates the knowledge base to solve a problem during a consultation; and confidence factors that accommodate uncertainty factors in a knowledge base.

For our prototype system we did not create an induction table to build our initial knowledge base. Because of the diversity of our rules, a basic set of rules were constructed with the intention of modifying and expanding the rules in subsequent development phases. After the rules were entered additional embellishments such as ASK, DISPLAY and BECAUSE were added to the rules to make them more "user friendly' and informative.

The system can be deployed in one of two ways -- as a set of windows that shows the Rules, Facts or Values, and Consultation (see Figure 4); or as a single window depicting only the Consultation. The three window consultation is useful for developing a working knowledge base. However, the Rules and Values windows are not necessary in an end user consultation mode.

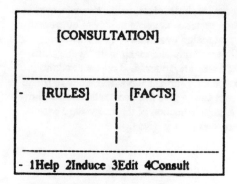

Figure 4: VP Expert Screen

TESTING THE SYSTEM WITH A CASE STUDY

Our test case is a software development firm that has recently undergone the transition from stand-alone personal computer systems to a local area network. We will examine this organization from a sociotechnical perspective in light of the changes that have taken place as a result of the introduction of the local network.

Business Situation

SDF competes in a highly volatile market, that of computer software. The success of companies prospers and wanes with each new hardware and software product introduction. The environment within the telecommunications industry is becoming increasingly competitive with IBM moving rapidly into all areas of software and service companies.

Although SDF produces a series of products that are frequently on the top ten monthly best-seller list they by no means are a dominant factor in the software industry. To a large extent they are dependent on software/hardware innovations by industry leaders (e.g. Novell's network software and hardware systems for DOS, OS/2 and other operating system platforms).

For our expert system simulation we would indicate the following to the expert system:

Economic Conditions	= Not_OK
Industry Stability	= Not_OK
Competitive	= OK
Customer Satisfaction	= OK
Investor Expectation	= OK

Business Strategy

To achieve a leadership position in its niche within the software industry SDF had to make several major decisions regarding venture capital, growth, market penetration, product concentration and diversity, and competitive positioning. The impact of these decisions needed to be examined in terms of operational efficiency, business effect and organizational innovations.

One of their major decisions was to market their products internationally. This necessitated that SDF translate their software products and documentation into multiple foreign languages. In addition, they also had to develop an international marketing and sales staff. From a network perspective these software changes, as well as all software developments, was accomplished by a shared development system. Under such a system all software versions are maintained in a single library such that all software developers and translators have access to a common, standard set of software.

The inputs to the trial run of the expert system for the Business Strategy were:

```
Mission or Vision      = OK
Operational Purpose = OK
Competitive Strategy = OK
```

Business Results

With the use of network software products SDF was able to streamline all of their operations. Electronic mail reduced the overall time lag in phone/message tag. Voice mail was introduced to accommodate external communication; facsimile transmissions via and through the network eliminated delays in the traditional mail process. Paper flow became an automated as opposed to manual process. Mailings, label generation, correspondence tracking and surveillance were accomplished at the touch of a button.

The simulation entry for Business Results was:

```
Financial Assessment     = Not_OK
Customer Expectations  = Not_OK
Competitive Positioning = OK
Management Expect'n   = Not_OK
```

These figures were based on a series of rule responses.

Business Design

The business became more effective in several ways. With the integrated accounting system inquiry, reporting and utilization of financial information is instantly available. Prior to the network implementation only one user at a time could access sales information. The orders were printed and hand-carried to Production for processing. The integrated accounting system made the entry and processing of sales orders a dynamic process. Statistics on all company information and operations were now readily available for managerial analysis. Technical Support personnel were able to handle a larger number of support calls, verify legitimate registered users, screen and classify inquiries and respond in a more timely fashion.

Software products under field testing could be monitored and tracked by marketing staff from their offices. Coordination of effort in the development of the software products was enhanced through the sharing of software modules available through the network file servers -- insuring each team member was operating with the same versions and under the same standards.

Within the support groups, the introduction of the network accounting package provided the mechanism to reduce and/or streamline the paperflow from order entry (for software products) and requisitions for materials (e.g, sales brochures, promotions, etc.) in the delivery of merchandise to the wholesalers and dealers.

With the introduction of the network inter-group and interpersonal dependencies increased. Virtually every department and each individual's work activity relied on common/shared databases. A sales order or request for material was reflected throughout the entire system -- sales results and projections were dynamically changed.

The use of a Technical Log system for Tech Support provided a barometer of support activity. This system was tied directly to the Registered Users database. As calls were made and help provided the technician could update the User database. Previous communication activity with the customer was available such that the technician could view a history of interactions. This data formed the nucleus for marketing, sales, and engineering support and enhancements. Figures on customer profiles, the nature of sales, problems and suggestions associated with products could be directed to and shared by various work groups.

Not only was there a re-design of work among the various organizational units but more specifically task designs underwent profound changes with the introduction of the network. Many of the manual or semi-automated tasks were computerized. Rather than record technical support calls on a log sheet basic information was entered into a Technical Log database. Budgets and forecasts were prepared jointly and in a common form by managers rather than each manager using their own devices and techniques.

Based on these discussions and other factors the Business Design entries for the Expert System sample were:

```
Technical SubSystem    = Not_Ok
Organizational Structure =Not_OK
Reward System          = OK
Human Resources       = OK
Decision Making Process = Not_OK
Information System     = Not_OK.
```

Conclusions

Some of the rules for the expert system are shown in the Appendix that follows this paper. We have tried to illustrate how an expert system could be used to analyze any organization especially one that is undergoing a major change (e.g. the introduction of a network system). The culture factors were not illustrated in this treatment. However, we did take them into account in the definition of our rules.l

BIBLIOGRAPHY

Hanna, D. [1988] Designing Organizations For High Performance. Reading, Mass., Addison-Wesley,

Mockler, R.J. [1990] Knowledge Based Systems for Strategic Planning. Prentice-Hall, N.J..

lShani A.B., & Elliott O [1988]., "Applying Sociotechnical System Design At The Strategic Apex: An Illustration", OrganizationDevelopment Journall Vol. 6, 2, 53-66.

Shani A. B. & Elliott O.,[1989] Sociotechnical System Design in Transition", in Sikes, Drexler & Grant (Eds.) lhe Emerging Practice of Organization Developmentl.(pp. 187-198), La Jolla; University Associates.

APPENDIX

```
ACTIONS
  FIND RECOMMENDATION;

RULE 0
  IF BUSINESS_RESULTS = OK
  THEN
    RECOMMENDATION = OK
    DISPLAY "Keep Up the Good Work";

RULE 1
  IF BUSINESS_RESULTS <> OK AND
    BUSINESS_SITUATION = OK
  THEN
    RECOMMENDATION = OK1
    DISPLAY "ReCheck Your Business Results";

RULE 2
  IF BUSINESS_SITUATION <> OK AND
    BUSINESS_DESIGN = OK   AND
    BUSINESS_STRATEGY = OK
  THEN
    RECOMMENDATION = OK2
    DISPLAY "ReExamine Your Business Situation";

RULE 3
  IF BUSINESS_SITUATION <> OK  AND
    BUSINESS_DESIGN = OK    AND
    BUSINESS_STRATEGY <> OK  AND
    CULTURE = OK
  THEN
    RECOMMENDATION = OK3
    DISPLAY "Check Business Design and Business
      Situation";

RULE 3A
  IF BUSINESS_SITUATION <> OK  AND
    BUSINESS_DESIGN = OK     AND
    BUSINESS_STRATEGY <> OK  AND
    CULTURE <> OK
  THEN
    RECOMMENDATION = OK3A
    DISPLAY "Check Business Design, Business Situation
    and  Business Culture";

RULE 4
  IF BUSINESS_SITUATION <> OK  AND
    BUSINESS_DESIGN <> OK    AND
    BUSINESS_STRATEGY = OK   AND
    CULTURE = OK
  THEN
    RECOMMENDATION = OK4
    DISPLAY "Check Business Strategy and Business
      Situation";

RULE 4A
  IF BUSINESS_SITUATION <> OK  AND
    BUSINESS_DESIGN <> OK    AND
    BUSINESS_STRATEGY = OK   AND
    CULTURE <> OK
  THEN
    RECOMMENDATION = OK4A
    DISPLAY "Check Business Strategy, Business Situation
    and  Business Culture";

RULE 5
  IF FINANCIAL_ASSESSMENT = OK        AND
    CUSTOMER_EXPECTATIONS = OK        AND
    COMPANY_COMPETITIVE_POSITION = OK  AND
    MANAGEMENT_EXPECTATIONS = OK
  THEN
    BUSINESS_RESULTS = OK
  ELSE
    BUSINESS_RESULTS = NOT_OK;

ASK FINANCIAL_ASSESSMENT: "What is your Financial
Assessment of your Current Operation";
CHOICES FINANCIAL_ASSESSMENT: OK,NOT-OK;
ASK CUSTOMER_EXPECTATIONS: "Are you meeting
Customer Expectations?";
CHOICES CUSTOMER_EXPECTATIONS: OK,NOT_OK;
ASK COMPANY_COMPETITIVE_POSITION: "Is your
Company's Competitive Position where you would like it?";
CHOICES COMPANY_COMPETITIVE_POSITION:
OK,NOT_OK;
ASK MANAGEMENT_EXPECTATIONS; "Are you meeting
Investor-Management Expectations?";
```

CHOICES MANAGEMENT_EXPECTATIONS: OK,
NOT_OK;

RULE 6
  IF ECONOMIC_CLIMATE = OK   AND
    INDUSTRY_STABILITY = OK   AND
    COMPETITIVE_POSITIONING = OK   AND
    CUSTOMER_SATISFACTION = OK   AND
    INVESTOR_EXPECTATION = OK
  THEN
    BUSINESS_SITUATION = OK
  ELSE
    BUSINESS_SITUATION = NOT_OK;

ASK ECONOMIC_CLIMATE: "Has the Current Economic
Climate Affected you?";
CHOICES ECONOMIC_CLIMATE: OK,NOT_OK;
ASK INDUSTRY_STABILITY: "What is the Stability of Your
Industry at the Current Time?";
CHOICES INDUSTRY_STABILITY: OK,NOT_OK;
ASK COMPETITIVE_POSITIONING: "Is your Company
Positioned Competitively?";
CHOICES COMPETITIVE_POSITIONING: OK,NOT_OK;
ASK CUSTOMER_SATISFACTION: "Are your Customers
Satisfied with your Product?";
CHOICES CUSTOMER_SATISFACTION: OK,NOT_OK;
ASK INVESTOR_EXPECTATION: "Are you able to attract
Investor Interest?";
CHOICES INVESTOR_EXPECTATION: OK,NOT_OK;

RULE 7
  IF TECHNICAL_SYSTEM = OK   AND
    ORGANIZATION_STRUCTURE = OK   AND
    REWARD_SYSTEM = OK   AND
    HUMAN_RESOURCES = OK   AND
    DECISION_MAKING_PROCESS = OK   AND
    INFORMATION_SYSTEMS =OK
  THEN
    BUSINESS_DESIGN = OK
  ELSE
    BUSINESS_DESIGN = NOT_OK;

RULE 7A
  IF TECHNICAL_INFORMATION = OK   AND
    TECHNICAL_ENGINEERING = OK   AND
    TECHNICAL_MANUFACTURING = OK
  THEN
    TECHNICAL_SUBSYSTEM = OK
  ELSE
    TECHNICAL_SUBSYSTEM = NOT_OK;

ASK TECHNICAL_INFORMATION: "Is your Information
Technology in your company up-to-date?";
CHOICES TECHNICAL_INFORMATION: OK, NOT_OK;
ASK TECHNICAL_MANUFACTURING: "Is the
Manufacturing Process in your company up-to-date?";
CHOICES TECHNICAL_MANUFACTURING:
OK,NOT_OK;

ASK TECHNICAL_ENGINEERING: "Is the Engineering
Technology in your company up-to-date?";
CHOICES TECHNICAL_ENGINEERING: OK, NOT_OK;

RULE 7B
  IF ORGANIZATION_FORM = OK   AND
    CUSTOMER_RESPONSE = OK   AND
    DEGREE_COORDINATION = OK   AND
    ROLE_CLARITY = OK   AND
    SKILLS_UTILIZED = OK   AND
    DEGREE_INTERDEPENDENCE = OK
  THEN
    ORGANIZATION_STRUCTURE = OK
  ELSE
    ORGANIZATION_STRUCTURE = NOT_OK;

ASK ORGANIZATION_FORM: "Is the Organization Form
(e.g. Functional, Matrix,..) commensurate with your
Organizational Goals?";
CHOICES ORGANIZATION_FORM: OK, NOT_OK;
ASK CUSTOMER_RESPONSE: "Is the Organization
Structure situated such that you can respond effectively to
Customers?";
CHOICES CUSTOMER_RESPONSE: OK, NOT_OK;
ASK DEGREE_COORDINATION: "Is there a significant
degree of Coordination among Organizational Units?";
CHOICES DEGREE_COORDINATION: OK, NOT_OK;
ASK ROLE_CLARITY: "Are Organizational Roles Clearly
Defined?";
CHOICES ROLE_CLARITY: OK, NOT_OK;
ASK SKILLS_UTILIZED: "To what extent are Skills and
Abilities Utilized?";
CHOICES SKILLS_UTILIZED: OK, NOT_OK;
ASK DEGREE_INTERDEPENDENCE: "To what extent are
Groups Interdependent?";
CHOICES DEGREE_INTERDEPENDENCE: OK,NOT_OK;

RULE 7C
  IF BEHAVIOR_REWARD = OK   AND
    PERFORMANCE_CRITERIA = OK
  THEN
    REWARD_SYSTEM = OK
  ELSE
    REWARD_SYSTEM = NOT_OK;

ASK BEHAVIOR_REWARD: "Are Appropriate Behaviors
Recognized and Rewarded?";
CHOICES BEHAVIOR_REWARD: OK,NOT_OK;
ASK PERFORMANCE_CRITERIA: "Is the criteria for
Performance Appraisal appropriate?";
CHOICES PERFORMANCE_CRITERIA: OK,NOT_OK;

SIMULATION APPLICATIONS FOR MANUFACTURING

A DEMONSTRATION OF ALTERNATIVE APPROACHES FOR AN INVENTORY SIMULATION MODEL

D. Brent Bandy and James R. Gross
Department of Information Systems and Operations Management
The University of Wisconsin Oshkosh
College of Business Administration
Oshkosh, Wisconsin 54901

ABSTRACT

A simulation model for an inventory system was formulated and solved using three basic approaches: 1) four simulation software packages (GPSS, SIMSCRIPT, SIMAN, and SLAM); 2) an electronic spreadsheet (LOTUS 1-2-3); and 3) two procedural programming languages (BASIC and FORTRAN).

The formulation and solution with each of the simulation packages was straightforward. However, the approach differed from package to package, depending on the characteristics of the packages and the features available. A comparison of the model formulations provides a basis for contrasting basic differences among these four widely-used simulation packages.

Formulating and solving the inventory simulation model using the electronic spreadsheet package was quite involved. However, an elegant formulation, which takes advantage of some of the special features of LOTUS 1-2-3, was finally developed. The fact that the inventory simulation model could be formulated and solved using LOTUS 1-2-3 is a tribute to the versatility of electronic spreadsheets in general and LOTUS 1-2-3 in particular.

Formulation and solution of the inventory simulation model with the procedural programming languages provided an interesting contrast to the other two basic approaches. On the other hand, it demonstrated the similarities of BASIC and FORTRAN, at least for certain applications.

INTRODUCTION

Various alternative approaches exist for the formulation and solution of simulation models, including simulation software packages, electronic spreadsheets, and procedural programming languages. In this study these approaches were demonstrated by formulating and solving an inventory model using four simulation software packages (GPSS, SIMSCRIPT, SIMAN, and SLAM), an electronic spreadsheet (LOTUS 1-2-3), and two procedural programming languages (BASIC and FORTRAN).

The formulation and solution of the model for all four simulation software packages was straightforward. However, there were certainly some distinct differences in the approach used by the individual packages.

The formulation and solution of the simulation model using LOTUS 1-2-3 was difficult. It required use of the random number function for sampling from the probability distributions for daily demand and lead time, a column-by-column order for the calculations, and a macro for carrying out the simulation for 1000 days. On the other hand, the versatility of LOTUS 1-2-3 is demonstrated by the fact that it could be used to formulate and solve the model.

The formulation and solution of the simulation model for both BASIC and FORTRAN was extremely straightforward. In fact, the use of procedural programming languages is the suggested approach for Monte Carlo simulation in many textbooks.

DESCRIPTION OF SIMULATION SOFTWARE PACKAGES

GPSS is a block-oriented simulation language (Shriber 1974). Among its model-building components are: transactions, blocks, facilities, logic switches, arithmetic and Boolean variables, savevalues and groups. GPSS block types include generate, mark, queue, seize, release, tabulate, terminate and others. The language provides for the orderly definition of blocks and entities, processing of entities through a system and collection and reporting of statistical measures.

SIMSCRIPT is a sophisticated programming language as well as a general purpose simulation language (Russell 1983). Organized into five "levels", the first three levels of SIMSCRIPT are quite similar to programming in BASIC, FORTRAN, or other procedural programming languages. Levels four and five provide the essential simulation-related concepts of events, entities, attributes, sets and the passage of time. In assembling a SIMSCRIPT model, various commands are used, such as create to cause an entity's arrival to the system, file to place an entity into a set, remove to remove an entity from a set and schedule to cause the occurrence of a specified event. Other SIMSCRIPT commands/statements include let, for each, loop, and destroy. Structurally, SIMSCRIPT models include such sections as a preamble, main program, event routines and other subroutines.

SLAM II (Pritsker 1986) and SIMAN (Pegden 1986) are both full featured simulation languages. Evolving from earlier languages, both SIMAN and SLAM II provide integrated frameworks for implementing models using any of three "world views": discrete event, continuous and network modeling. In SLAM II the network model component consists of nodes and branches. Branches represent activities which may include time delays. Typical SLAM II network nodes include create, queue, assign and terminate. More advanced network constructs are represented through such nodes as preempt, accumulate, batch and detect, as well as others.

Similarly, SIMAN provides for the construction of a network via blocks such as create, assign, queue, seize, preempt and group. Time delays and alternative entity routings are also represented via blocks (delay and branch). A unique feature of SIMAN is the organization of data input into two distinct "frames," the model and the experiment descriptions.

As will be observed, SIMAN and SLAM II network models seem very similar to one another, particularly for simple models such as that described herein. As is true of all four simulation software packages, more significant syntactical and practical differences are found when applied to more complex systems. Differences also exist between packages with respect to their modeling "environments", including debugging, data preparation and data post-processing features.

DESCRIPTION OF ELECTRONIC SPREADSHEET

LOTUS 1-2-3 is an integrated software package developed by LOTUS Development Corporation. It is an extremely versatile spreadsheet package that has been augmented with graphics and limited data base and word processing capabilities (Philip 1989). It has been a top selling microcomputer software package for several years. Its uses, including simulation, have been widely discussed in the literature. LOTUS 1-2-3 by itself is more user friendly than many software packages, and it can be "programmed" to be very user friendly through the use of macros and templates. It is an extremely versatile package and has capabilities for translating data to and from dBASE III, Word Perfect, and other software packages. Many other software packages have been developed as complements to LOTUS 1-2-3 to perform various functions, including optimization and Monte Carlo simulation.

DESCRIPTION OF PROCEDURAL LANGUAGES

BASIC (Beginner's All-purpose Symbolic Instruction Code) is a third-generation, procedural programming language. It was developed in the 1960s, primarily for instructional purposes. It is available on many small business minicomputers and on almost all microcomputers. Several widely different versions exist. Ease of learning and ease of use, compared to other procedural programming languages, have been the guiding principles for BASIC.

FORTRAN (FORmula TRANslator) is also a third-generation, procedural programming language. It was developed in the 1950s, primarily for scientific, mathematical, engineering, and operations management applications. It is one of the oldest procedural programming languages, yet it is still widely used and taught in the United States. Many simulation software packages, including GPSS, SIMAN, and SLAM, are written, at least in part, in FORTRAN.

DESCRIPTION OF INVENTORY MODEL

The simulation model used in the study is a textbook model for an inventory system operated by an auto supply company (Anderson *et al.* 1988). Several other simulation models from various textbooks were also considered for the study. The final selection of the model was based on the following criteria: 1) the formulation of the model had to be given clearly in the textbook; 2) the solution of the model also had to be given; 3) the model had to be fairly large for a textbook model; and 4) the model had to be as realistic as possible.

The decision variables are the reorder point and the order quantity. The costs are order costs ($20 per order), inventory holding costs ($0.10 per unit), and shortage costs for failing to meet demand ($50 per unit). The model simulates on a daily basis the arrival of items for inventory, demand for the items, updating of the number of items in inventory, and the decision of whether or not to place an order. Probability distributions for daily demand and for the lead time for the arrival of orders are given in Table 1.

Table 1

Probability Distributions for the Simulation Model

Daily Demand	Relative Frequency	Lead Time (days)	Relative Frequency
0	0.50	1	0.20
1	0.25	2	0.10
2	0.15	3	0.40
3	0.05	4	0.20
4	0.05	5	0.10

The simulation model is run for 1000 days to generate the average daily cost for a given reorder point and order quantity. A startup period of 50 days is used to randomize the starting inventory level for the 1000-day simulation. The "optimal" values for reorder point and order quantity can be determined by making several runs of the model. All the models were formulated and solved using an order quantity of 25 and a reorder point of 6 as the base case.

GPSS FORMULATION

Formulation of the model in GPSS involved the use of halfword and fullword save values, functions, fvariables (floating point variables), and several different GPSS blocks, including simulate, generate, assign, test_g, test_le, test_e, transfer, split, priority, advance, and terminate. Figure 1 shows the GPSS formulation, including the setup for running three cases using initial, start, clear, and reset commands. The three cases are for order quantities of 5, 10, and 25, respectively, with reorder points of 1, 1, and 6. The last case is the base case.

```
1         FUNCTION     RN$2,D5
          .5,0/.75,1/.9,2/.95,3/1,4
2         FUNCTION     RN$2,D5
          .2,1/.3,2/.7,3/.9,4/1,5
1         FVARIABLE    XH$4*50*(P$1-XF$2)
2         FVARIABLE    XH$4*0.1*XF$2
3         FVARIABLE    XH$4*20
          SIMULATE
          GENERATE     1,,1,1050
          ASSIGN       1,FN$1              ;Daily demand
          TEST_G       P$1,XF$2,NSHRT
          SAVEVALUE    1+,V$1,F            ;Add shortage cost
          SAVEVALUE    2,0,F               ;Set inventory = 0
          TRANSFER     ,REORD
NSHRT     SAVEVALUE    2-,P$1,F            ;Remove demand
REORD     TEST_LE      XF$2,XH$2,NOREQ
          TEST_E       XH$3,0,NOREQ
          SAVEVALUE    3,1,H               ;Make an order
          SAVEVALUE    1+,V$3,F            ;Add order cost
          SPLIT        1,NOREQ
          PRIORITY     20,BUFFER
          ADVANCE      FN$2                ;Wait for lead time
          SAVEVALUE    2+,XH$1,F           ;Add order quantity
          SAVEVALUE    3,0,H               ;The order arrived
          TERMINATE
NOREQ     SAVEVALUE    1+,V$2,F            ;Add holding cost
          TERMINATE    1
          GENERATE     ,,50.5,1            ;Simulate 50 days
          SAVEVALUE    1,0,F               ;Then reinitialize
          TERMINATE
          GENERATE     ,,0.5,1
          SAVEVALUE    1,0,F               ;Initialize total cost
          SAVEVALUE    3,0,H               ;Outstanding orders
          SAVEVALUE    4,10,H              ;Cost multiplier
          SAVEVALUE    2,XH$1,F            ;Initialize inventory
          TERMINATE
          INITIAL      XH$1,5,XH$2,1
          START        1050
          CLEAR
          RESET
          INITIAL      XH$1,10,XH$2,1
          START        1050
          CLEAR
          RESET
          INITIAL      XH$1,25,XH$2,6
          START        1050
          END
```

Figure 1. GPSS Formulation

The GPSS formulation starts with the definition of the functions for the probability distributions for daily demand and lead time, respectively. Three floating point variables are then defined for calculating shortage, holding, and order costs, respectively.

The simulate block indicates the start of the model section. One transaction is used for each of the 1050 days simulated, with daily demand stored in parameter 1. Fullword save values are used for current inventory and total costs. Halfword save values are used for

82

reorder point, order quantity, the cost multiplier, and an order-outstanding indicator. A split block is used to place an order by cloning the daily transaction. The priority block ensures that orders arrive at the beginning of the day. A transaction is generated at 0.5 days to initialize total cost, the halfword save value for outstanding orders, the cost multiplier, and the current inventory. Another transaction is generated after 50 days to reinitialize total cost to 0.

SIMSCRIPT FORMULATION

Formulation of the model in SIMSCRIPT involved the use of processes, events, random step variables, integer variables, and real variables. Figure 2 shows the SIMSCRIPT formulation, which is made up of four sections, preamble, main, the section for defining processes and events, and data, which contains the values for the probability distributions for daily demand and lead time.

```
PREAMBLE
  PROCESSES INCLUDE GENERATOR AND DAY
  EVENT NOTICES INCLUDE ORDER AND REINIT
  EVERY DAY HAS A DEMAND RANDOM STEP 2 VARIABLE
  DEFINE DEMAND AS AN INTEGER VARIABLE
  EVERY ORDER HAS A TIME.ORD RANDOM STEP 3
VARIABLE
  DEFINE TIME.ORD AS AN INTEGER VARIABLE
  DEFINE INVENTORY AS AN INTEGER VARIABLE
  DEFINE REORDER.POINT AS AN INTEGER VARIABLE
  DEFINE ORDER.QUANTITY AS AN INTEGER VARIABLE
  DEFINE OUTSTAND.ORDER AS AN INTEGER VARIABLE
  DEFINE SHORTAGE.COST AS A REAL VARIABLE
  DEFINE HOLDING.COST AS A REAL VARIABLE
  DEFINE ORDER.COST AS A REAL VARIABLE
  DEFINE AVE.COST AS A REAL VARIABLE
  DEFINE TOTAL.COST AS A REAL VARIABLE
  DEFINE TDAY.DEMAND AS AN INTEGER VARIABLE
  DEFINE T.ORD AS AN INTEGER VARIABLE
END
MAIN
  SCHEDULE REINIT IN 50 DAYS
  LET TOTAL.COST = 0.0
  LET SHORTAGE.COST = 50.0
  LET HOLDING.COST = 0.10
  LET ORDER.COST = 20.0
  LET AVE.COST = 0.0
  LET REORDER.POINT = 6
  LET ORDER.QUANTITY = 25
  LET INVENTORY = ORDER.QUANTITY
  LET OUTSTAND.ORDER = 0
  READ DEMAND
  READ TIME.ORD
  ACTIVATE A GENERATOR NOW
  START SIMULATION
  LET AVE.COST = TOTAL.COST/1000.0
  BEGIN REPORT
    PRINT 2 LINES THUS
      SIMSCRIPT MODEL
      AN INVENTORY SIMULATION
    SKIP 1 LINE
    BEGIN HEADING
      PRINT 1 LINE WITH PAGE.V THUS
        VARIABLE      VALUE
      SKIP 1 LINE
    END
    PRINT 1 LINE WITH REORDER.POINT THUS
      REORDER POINT IS ***
    PRINT 1 LINE WITH ORDER.QUANTITY THUS
      ORDER QUANTITY IS ***
    PRINT 1 LINE WITH AVE.COST THUS
      AVERAGE COST PER DAY IS ***.**
  END
END
PROCESS GENERATOR
```

```
FOR I = 1 TO 1050
DO
  ACTIVATE A DAY NOW
  WAIT 1 DAY
LOOP
END
PROCESS DAY
  LET TDAY.DEMAND = DEMAND
  IF TDAY.DEMAND > INVENTORY
    ADD SHORT.COST*(TDAY.DEMAND-INVENTORY)
              TO TOTAL.COST
    LET INVENTORY = 0
  ELSE
    SUBTRACT TDAY.DEMAND FROM INVENTORY
    ADD HOLD.COST*INVENTORY TO TOTAL.COST
  ALWAYS
  IF OUTSTAND.ORDER = 0 AND INVENTORY < =
              REORDER.POINT
    ADD ORDER.COST TO TOTAL.COST
    LET OUTSTAND.ORDER = 1
    LET T.ORD = TIME.ORD
    SCHEDULE AN ORDER IN T.ORD DAYS
END
EVENT ORDER
  ADD ORDER.QUANTITY TO INVENTORY
  LET OUTSTAND.ORD = 0
END
EVENT REINIT
  LET TOTAL.COST = 0
END
DATA
0.50 0 0.25 1 0.15 2 0.05 3 0.05 4 *
0.20 1 0.10 2 0.40 3 0.20 4 0.10 5 *
END
```

Figure 2. Simscript Formulation

The preamble section identifies the processes and events and defines the variables used in the model. The processes include generator, for the 1050 days of the simulation, and day, for simulating each day. Event notices include order, for receiving orders into inventory, and reinit, for reinitializing total costs after 50 days. Variables can be global variables or variables assigned to specific processes. For the process variables, every day has a random step integer variable named demand and every order has a random step integer variable named time.ord. The other variables are global variables and are defined as either integer variables or real variables.

The main section starts by scheduling the reinitialization event in 50 days. The global variables are then initialized and the values for the probability distributions for the random variables are read in from the data section. The generator process is activated and the simulation is carried out. Finally the average cost per day is calculated and the report for the results from the simulation run is generated.

The next section is for the processes and the events. The process named generator consists of a loop that activates the process named day for each of the days from 1 to 1050. The process named day carries out the simulation for each day. It samples from the probability distribution for daily demand and simulates appropriate actions depending on whether or not the demand is greater than the current inventory. In either case, a test is made to determine if an order should be placed. Events are for reinitializing total costs to 0 after 50 days and for the arrival of orders.

SIMAN FORMULATION

Formulation of the model in SIMAN makes extensive use of branching and variable assignments. Figure 3 shows the model description and Figure 4 shows the experiment description.

```
BEGIN;
;              *** INVENTORY MODEL IN SIMAN
;              *** FILENAME:  CABINET.MOD
;
              CREATE;                        ! Create entity
NEWDAY   ASSIGN: A(1)=DP(1,1);          ! Demand amount
              BRANCH,1:IF,TNOW.GE.X(9),ENDRUN:
                   IF,A(1).EQ.0,ENDDAY:
                   IF,A(1).LE.X(3),NORMAL:
                   ELSE,SHORTFL;
;
NORMAL   ASSIGN: X(3)=X(3)-A(1);        ! Decrease inventory
              ASSIGN: X(4)=X(4)-A(1):NEXT(DECIDE);
;
SHORTFL  ASSIGN: X(5)=X(5)+(A(1)-X(3))*50;
              ASSIGN: X(4)=X(4)-X(3);        ! Decrease position
              ASSIGN: X(3)=0;                ! Decrease inventory
;
DECIDE   BRANCH,2:
              IF,X(4).LE.X(1),ORDER:        ! Order required?
              ALWAYS,ENDDAY;
;
ORDER    ASSIGN: A(1)=X(2);                ! Set order amount
              ASSIGN: A(2)=DP(2,2);          ! Set lead time
              ASSIGN: X(4)=X(4)+A(1);        ! Increase position
              ASSIGN: X(6)=X(6)+20;          ! Add order cost
              TALLY:4,A(2);                  ! Tally lead time
              DELAY:A(2);                    ! Lead time delay
              ASSIGN: X(3)=X(3)+A(1):
;
ENDDAY   TALLY: 3,A(1);                      ! Tally demand
              ASSIGN: X(7)=X(7)+.1*X(3);     ! Add carrying cost
              DELAY: 1: NEXT(NEWDAY);        ! Repeat next day...
;
ENDRUN   ASSIGN: X(8)=X(7)+X(6)+X(5);        ! Total cost
              TALLY: 1,X(1);                 ! Reorder point
              TALLY: 2,X(2);                 ! Order quantity
              TALLY: 5,X(5);                 ! Shortage cost
              TALLY: 6,X(6);                 ! Order cost
              TALLY: 7,X(7);                 ! Holding cost
              TALLY: 8,X(8): DISPOSE;        ! Total cost
;
;
END;
```

Figure 3. SIMAN Model Formulation

```
BEGIN;
;              ***  INVENTORY MODEL IN SIMAN
;              ***  FILENAME: CABINET.EXP
;
PROJECT,INVENTORY MODEL,J. GROSS, 5/1/89;
DISCRETE,10,2,0,0;
TALLIES: 1, REORDER POINT:  2, ORDER QUANTITY:
              3, DAILY DEMAND:  4, LEAD TIME:
              5, SHORTAGE COST: 6, ORDER COST:
              7, HOLDING COST:  8, TOTAL COST;
PARAMETERS: 1, .5,0,.75,1,.9,2,.95,3,1.00,4: ! Demand distribution
              2, .2,1,.3,2,.7,3,.9,4,1.00,5; ! Lead time distribution
SEEDS: 1,21333: 2,12773;                   ! Random seeds
INITIALIZE, X(1)=6,                        ! Reorder point
              X(2)=25,                     ! Order quantity
              X(3)=25,                     ! Start. inventory
              X(4)=25,                     ! Start. position
              X(9)=1050;                   ! Run length
;
REPLICATE, 1, 0, 1050, , , 50;             ! Startup Period
;
END;
```

Figure 4. SIMAN Experiment Formulation

The model description starts by creating an entity that is used for simulating for 1050 days. Sampling is done from the probability distribution for daily demand. The branch statement sends the entity to one of four possible statements, depending on whether: 1) the simulation run is over (endrun); 2) there is no demand for that day (endday); 3) the demand is less than or equal to the current inventory (normal); or 4) there is a shortage (shortfl).

If there is a demand and sufficient inventory to satisfy it (normal), the demand is subtracted from the current inventory and from the inventory position (sum of the current inventory and any outstanding orders). If the demand exceeds the current inventory (shortfl), the shortage cost is calculated, the inventory position is decreased, and the current inventory is set to 0.

Every day there is a demand, a decision is made (decide) whether or not an order should be placed, depending on the inventory position and the reorder level. A branch statement allows for placing of an order using a cloned entity. When the order arrives, it is added to the current inventory and the cloned entity is destroyed.

Endday begins the final part of the model for each day. The inventory carrying cost is incremented based on the current inventory and the entity is delayed one day and sent to newday for the next day's operation.

Endrun begins the termination part of the model. The total cost is calculated as the sum of the inventory holding cost, the order cost, and the shortage cost. The reorder point, order quantity, shortage cost, order cost, holding cost, and total cost are then tallied and the model run is ended.

The experiment description in Figure 4 begins with control statements for identifying the model, the discrete probability distributions for daily demand and lead time, and the tallies that occur in the model description. The parameters for the probability distributions and seeds for the two random number streams are then defined. The initialize statement defines the starting values for reorder point, order quantity, inventory, inventory position, and run length in days. The replicate statement defines the 1050 day simulation run, with costs being reinitialized to 0 after the 50 day startup period.

SLAM FORMULATION

The formulation of the model in SLAM was purposely made as similar as possible to the formulation in SIMAN. Figure 5 shows the SLAM model formulation.

The formulation starts with a gen statement for identifying the model, followed by a limits statement for defining upper values for the number of files, attributes per entity, and concurrent entities, respectively. The intlc statement then defines the starting values for reorder point, order quantity, inventory, inventory position, and run length in days. The array statement defines the values for the discrete probability distributions for daily demand and lead time.

The network part of the model starts by creating an entity that is used for simulating for 1050 days. At the start of each new day sampling is done from the probability distribution for daily demand. Four act statements then send the entity to one of four possible statements, depending on whether: 1) the simulation run is over (endrn); 2) there is no demand for that day (endda); 3) the demand is less than or equal to the current inventory (norml); or 4) there is a shortage (short).

If there is a demand and sufficient inventory to satisfy it (norml), the demand is subtracted from the current inventory and from the inventory position (sum of the current inventory and any outstanding orders). If the demand exceeds the current inventory (shortfl), the shortage cost is calculated, the inventory position is decreased, and the current inventory is set to 0.

```
GEN, J. GROSS, INVENTORY MODEL, 1/1/90, 1;
;
;       *** INVENTORY MODEL IN SLAM II
;       *** FILENAME: CABNET.DAT
;
LIMITS, 1, 2, 10;
;
;  Set initial values:
INTLC, XX(1)=6, XX(2)=25, XX(3)=25, XX(4)=25, XX(9)=1050;
;
;  Set up cumulative probability distributions:
ARRAY(1,5)/ .5, .75, .9, .95, 1.0 /
      (2,5)/  0,  1,   2,   3,   4 /
      (3,5)/ .2, .3, .7, .90, 1.0 /
      (4,5)/  1,  2,  3,    4,   5  ;
;
NETWORK;
        CREATE;                         Create entity
;
NEWDA   ASSIGN, ATRIB(1)=DPROBN(1,2,1),1; Demand
        ACT,,TNOW .GE. XX(9), ENDRN;     Is run over?
        ACT,,ATRIB(1) .EQ. 0, ENDDA;     Any demand?
        ACT,,ATRIB(1) .LE. XX(3), NORML; Enough inventory?
        ACT,,, SHORT;
;
NORML   ASSIGN, XX(3)=XX(3)-ATRIB(1);
        ASSIGN, XX(4)=XX(4)-ATRIB(1);
        .ACT,,,DECID;
;
SHORT   ASSIGN,XX(5)=XX(5)+50*ATRIB(1)-50*XX(3);
        ASSIGN,XX(4)=XX(4)-XX(3), XX(3) = 0.;
;
DECID   GOON,2;
        ACT,,XX(4) .LE. XX(1), ORDER;    Order required?
        ACT,,, ENDDA;
;
ORDER   ASSIGN, ATRIB(1)=XX(2), ATRIB(2)=DPROBN(3,4,2);
        ASSIGN, XX(4)=XX(4)+ATRIB(1), XX(6)=XX(6)+20;
        COLCT(4), ATRIB(2), LEAD TIME;   Lead time
        ACT,ATRIB(2);         Time delay
        ASSIGN, XX(3)=XX(3)+ATRIB(1);    Add to inventory
        TERMINATE;
;
ENDDA   COLCT(3),ATRIB(1), DAILY DEMAND;Demand statistic
        ASSIGN, XX(7)=XX(7)+.1*XX(3);    Add carrying costs
        ACT, 1,,NEWDA;                   Repeat next day
;
ENDRN   ASSIGN, XX(8)=XX(7)+XX(6)+XX(5);Total cost
        COLCT(1),XX(1), REORDER POINT;
        COLCT(2),XX(2), ORDER QUANTITY;
        COLCT(5),XX(5), SHORTAGE COST;
        COLCT(6),XX(6), ORDER COSTS;
        COLCT(7),XX(7), HOLDING COSTS;
        COLCT(8),XX(8), TOTAL COST;
        TERMINATE;
;
        ENDNETWORK;
;
INIT, 0, 1050;                          Run length
MONTR, CLEAR, 50;                       Clear statistics
FIN;
```

Figure 5. SLAM II Formulation

Every day there is a demand, a decision is made (decid) whether or not an order should be placed, depending on the inventory position and the reorder level. The goon statements allow for placing of an order using a cloned entity. When the order arrives, it is added to the current inventory and the cloned entity is terminated.

Endda begins the final part of the model for each day. The inventory carrying cost is incremented based on the current inventory and the entity is delayed one day and sent to newday for the next day's operation. Endrn begins the termination part of the model. The total cost is calculated as the sum of the inventory holding cost, the order cost, and the shortage cost. The reorder point, order quantity, shortage cost, order cost, holding cost, and total cost are then collected, and the entity is terminated. The endnetwork statement defines the end of the network. Finally the init statement specifies the run length of 1050 days, and the montr statement specifies that statistics are to be cleared after 50 days.

LOTUS 1-2-3 FORMULATION

Formulation of the model in LOTUS 1-2-3 was difficult and time consuming, but interesting. It was based on using: 1) the random number function of LOTUS 1-2-3 (@RAND) to sample from probability distributions for daily demand and lead time; 2) a column-by-column order for the calculations; and 3) a macro to initialize the model, simulate for 50 days, reinitialize costs, and simulate for 1000 days. Figure 6 shows the LOTUS 1-2-3 formulation, in terms of the formulas in each cell, in row order. The base case values are in cell A4 for the order quantity of 25 and cell A6 for the reorder point of 6.

The macro for the model is named \C (cells A8, A9 and A10) and is contained in cells A13 through A32. The macro starts by going to cell A11, which contains the cost multiplier, and entering 0. Prior to executing the macro, the Worksheet-Global-Recalculation-Columnwise command option was chosen and the Worksheet-Global-Recalculation-Iteration command option was set to 50; thus {calc} results in 50 iterations through the model in column-by-column order, representing 50 days of simulation. At the end of 50 iterations, total cost in cell F9 is 0 because the contents of cell A11 is 0. Thus the macro next enters a 1 into cell A11, so that cell F9 will start accumulating costs. Then it goes to cell Z99 (an arbitrary location that is not in the Home Window) and then to cell D1 to position the window so that the results of the simulation can be seen. Cell A13 ends with {calc} and cells A14 through A32 all contain {calc}, which results in 1000 more iterations through the model, simulating 1000 days.

The other cells in the worksheet are set up to simulate a single day of the inventory model. Cells A1 and A2 each contain @RAND to generate random numbers each day for the daily demand and lead time, respectively. Cells B1 through B5 sample from the probability distribution for daily demand and cells B6 through B10 sample from the probability distribution for lead time.

Cells C1 through C10 use the @IF function to collect the statistics for the sampling from the probability distributions for daily demand and lead time for the 1000 days. Cell A11 is used in the formulas contained within the functions to avoid the first 50 days. Cells D5 and D10 use the @SUM function to sum the values in cells C1 through C5 and cells C6 through C10. Thus cells D5 and D10 both contain the total number of days simulated with total costs being accumulated.

Cell D1 uses the @MAX function to select the largest value in cells J1 through K5. If there is no order outstanding, cell D1 will contain 0; otherwise, it will contain the order quantity. Cell E1 is the opening inventory each day. For the first day of the simulation, it is set equal to the order quantity in cell A4. After the first day, it is set equal to the closing inventory for the previous day in cell E3. Cell E2 adds arriving orders from cell K1 to the opening inventory in cell E1. Cell E3 is the closing inventory for the day, either the inventory in cell E2 minus the daily demand in cell B5 or 0, depending on whether or not the daily demand exceeds the available inventory. Cell E4 calculates the shortage cost for the day, if there is any.

Cell E5 compares the closing inventory in cell E3 with the reorder point in cell A6, and takes on a value of 1 if an order is needed and 0 otherwise. Cell E6 checks cell D1 to see if there is an order outstanding. If so, cell E6 takes on a value of 0; otherwise, it is set equal to cell E5. If cell E6 is equal to 1, an order is to be made. Cell E7 is the order cost for the day and cell E8 is the inventory cost for the day. Cell F8 adds up the three costs for the day in cells E4, E7, and E8. Cell F9 accumulates total costs once cell A11 has been changed to 1 (after 50 days of the simulation). Cell F10 calculates the average daily costs for the model once total costs have started being accumulated.

```
A1:  [W14] @RAND
A2:  [W14] @RAND
A3:  [W14] 'Order Quantity
A4:  [W14] 25
A5:  [W14] 'Reorder point
A6:  [W14] 6
A8:  [W14] 'Alt-c
A9:  [W14] 'For simulation
A10: [W14] 'Calculation
A11: [W14] 1
A13: [W14] '{goto}a11~0~{calc}1~{goto}z99~{goto}d1~{calc}
A14: [W14] '{calc}
A15: [W14] '{calc}
  .
  .
  .
A31: [W14] '{calc}
A32: [W14] '{calc}
B1:  @IF(+A$1>0.5,1,0)
B2:  @IF(+A$1>0.75,2,0)
B3:  @IF(+A$1>0.9,3,0)
B4:  @IF(+A$1>0.95,4,0)
B5:  @MAX(B1..B4)
B6:  @IF(+A$2>0.2,2,1)
B7:  @IF(+A$2>0.3,3,1)
B8:  @IF(+A$2>0.7,4,1)
B9:  @IF(+A$2>0.9,5,1)
B10: @MAX(B6..B9)
C1:  @IF(+B$5=0,+A$11*(C1+1),+A$11*C1)
C2:  @IF(+B$5=1,+A$11*(C2+1),+A$11*C2)
C3:  @IF(+B$5=2,+A$11*(C3+1),+A$11*C3)
C4:  @IF(+B$5=3,+A$11*(C4+1),+A$11*C4)
C5:  @IF(+B$5=4,+A$11*(C5+1),+A$11*C5)
C6:  @IF(+B$10=1,+A$11*(C6+1),+A$11*C6)
C7:  @IF(+B$10=2,+A$11*(C7+1),+A$11*C7)
C8:  @IF(+B$10=3,+A$11*(C8+1),+A$11*C8)
C9:  @IF(+B$10=4,+A$11*(C9+1),+A$11*C9)
C10: @IF(+B$10=5,+A$11*(C10+1),+A$11*C10)
D1:  @MAX(J1..K5)
D5:  @SUM(C1..C5)
D10: @SUM(C6..C10)
E1:  @IF(+D5+F1>0,+E3,+A4)
E2:  +E1+K1
E3:  @IF(+E2>+B5,E2-B5,0)
E4:  @IF(+E2<+B5,50*(B5-E2),0)
E5:  @IF(+E3>+A6,0,1)
E6:  @IF(+D1=0,E5,0)
E7:  +E6*20
E8:  +E3*0.1
F1:  1-A11
F8:  +E4+E7+E8
F9:  +A11*(+F8+F9)
F10: @IF(+D5>0,+F9/D5,0)
J1:  @IF(+B$10=1,A$4*E$6,0)
J2:  @IF(+B$10=2,A$4*E$6,0)
J3:  @IF(+B$10=3,A$4*E$6,0)
J4:  @IF(+B$10=4,A$4*E$6,0)
J5:  @IF(+B$10=5,A$4*E$6,0)
K1:  +J1+K2
K2:  +J2+K3
K3:  +J3+K4
K4:  +J4+K5
K5:  +J5
```

Figure 6. LOTUS 1-2-3 Formulation

Cell F1 is set equal to 1 minus the value of cell A11 and is used strictly to initialize the opening inventory in cell E1 to the order quantity for the first day of the simulation. The logic is based on cell A11 having a value of 1 and cell F1 a value of 0 when the previous simulation ends. For the next run of the simulation, prior to the first day, the value of cell A11 is set equal to 0 by the macro. Thus during the first iteration through the worksheet (first day of the simulation), cells C1 through C10, D5, and D10 are all set equal to 0, and the opening inventory in cell E1 is then set equal to the order quantity in cell A4. Then cell F1 is set equal to 1, since cell A11 has a value of 0. For iterations 2 through 50, the opening inventory in cell E1 is set equal to the closing inventory from the previous day in cell E3. Prior to iteration 51, the macro changes the value in cell A11 to 1, to start the accumulation of total costs. Then during iteration 51 cell D5 takes on a value of 1, cell E1 is still set equal to the closing inventory for the previous day, and cell F1 is set equal to 0. Subsequently cell D5 has a value that keeps increasing, so the opening inventory in cell E1 continues to be set equal to the previous day's closing inventory.

Cells J1 through J5 and K1 through K5 handle the placing of the orders. On the iteration (day) when an order is placed, the order quantity in cell A4 is placed into cell J1 if the lead time in cell B10 is 1, into cell J2 if the lead time in cell B10 is 2, etc. If no order is to be placed that day, cells J1 through J5 all take on a value of 0. Cells K1 through K5 then handle the picking up of the orders from cells J1 through J5 and moving them forward day-by-day. When the order reaches cell K1, it is added the next day in cell E2 to the opening inventory in cell E1.

BASIC FORMULATION

Formulation of the model in BASIC was straightforward. Figure 7 shows the BASIC model.

```
100  DIM DISTDAYD(5), DISTLDTM(5), ARRIVE(5)
200  REM distdayd is probability distribution for daily demand
300  REM distldtm is the probability distribution for lead time
400  REM arrive is array for orders that have been placed
500  FOR I = 1 TO 5
600  ARRIVE(I) = 0
700  NEXT I
800  DISTDAYD(1) = .5
900  DISTDAYD(2) = .75
1000 DISTDAYD(3) = .9
1100 DISTDAYD(4) = .95
1200 DISTDAYD(5) = 1
1300 DISTLDTM(1) = .2
1400 DISTLDTM(2) = .3
1500 DISTLDTM(3) = .7
1600 DISTLDTM(4) = .9
1700 DISTLDTM(5) = 1
1800 ORDQUANT = 25
1900 REORDERP = 6
2000 REM ordquant and reorderp are decision variables
2100 REM ordquant is the order quantity
2200 REM reorderp is the reorder point
2300 INVENTRY = ORDQUANT
2400 REM initialize the inventory on hand to ordquant
2500 TOTCOST = 0
2600 REM totcost is the total cost
2700 REM run for 1050 days, reinitializing cost after 50 days
2800 FOR DAY = 1 TO 1050
2900 IF DAY = 51 THEN TOTCOST = 0
3000 REM add any arriving orders to the inventory
3100 INVENTRY = INVENTRY + ARRIVE(1)
3200 REM move any outstanding orders forward one day
3300 REM if orders outstanding, outstand is greater than 0
3400 OUTSTAND = 0
3500 FOR I = 1 TO 4
3600 ARRIVE(I) = ARRIVE(I+1)
3700 OUTSTAND = OUTSTAND + ARRIVE(I)
3800 NEXT I
```

86

```
3900 ARRIVE(5) = 0
4000 REM x is random variable for determining daily demand
4100 X = RND
4200 REM demand is the daily demand
4300 DEMAND = 0
4400 FOR I = 1 TO 4
4500 IF X > DISTDAYD(I) THEN DEMAND = I
4600 NEXT I
4700 REM subtract daily demand from inventory
4800 INVENTRY = INVENTRY - DEMAND
4900 REM if inventry is negative, total demand not met
5000 REM shortage cost is added to total cost
5100 REM and inventry is set to 0
5200 IF INVENTRY < 0 THEN                                    &
                    TOTCOST = TOTCOST-50*INVENTRY
5300 IF INVENTRY < 0 THEN INVENTRY = 0
5400 REM check to see if an order is to be placed
5500 REM if so, subroutine 8000 places the order
5600 IF INVENTRY < = REORDERP THEN                           &
                    IF OUTSTAND = 0 THEN GOSUB 8000
5700 REM add the inventory holding cost to the total cost
5800 TOTCOST = TOTCOST + .1 * INVENTRY
5900 NEXT DAY
6000 REM calculate the average total cost per day
6100 REM print order quantity, reorder point, and average cost
6200 TOTCOST = TOTCOST / 1000
6300 PRINT ORDQUANT, REORDERP, TOTCOST
6400 END
8000 REM subroutine for placing an order
8100 REM add the order cost to total cost
8200 TOTCOST = TOTCOST + 20
8300 REM x is random variable for determining lead time
8400 X = RND
8500 REM time is the lead time
8600 TIME = 1
8700 FOR I = 1 TO 4
8800 IF X > DISTLDTM(I) THEN TIME = I + 1
8900 NEXT I
9000 REM the order will arrive in time days
9100 ARRIVE(TIME) = ORDQUANT
9200 RETURN
```

Figure 7. BASIC Formulation

Arrays are used for the probability distributions for daily demand and lead time and for the arrival of the orders. At the beginning of the program these arrays and other variables are initialized. The for-next loop for the 1050 days of the simulation run follows, including reinitializing total cost to 0 after 50 days. Following the for-next loop the average total cost per day is calculated, and the values for order quantity, reorder point, and average total cost per day are printed to the screen.

FORTRAN FORMULATION

The formulation of the model in FORTRAN was essentially identical to the BASIC formulation, except for differences in syntax. Figure 8 shows the FORTRAN model.

COMPARISON OF APPROACHES

There were significant differences in the three basic approaches used to formulate the inventory model and also significant differences within the first basic approach, the simulation software packages.

With respect to the three basic approaches, the most significant differences were for using the spreadsheet package, LOTUS 1-2-3. This approach had essentially nothing that resembled the other approaches, with the possible exception of moving the orders forward day-by-day. The approach in LOTUS 1-2-3 in cells K1 through K5 does have some resemblance to the method used in the arrays in BASIC and FORTRAN for moving the orders forward.

```
      DIMENSION DISTDAYD(5), DISTLDTM(5), IARRIVE(5)
C distdayd is probability distribution for daily demand
C distldtm is probability distribution for lead time
C iarrive is array for orders that have been placed
      DO 10 I = 1, 5
      IARRIVE(I) = 0
10 CONTINUE
      DISTDAYD(1) = .5
      DISTDAYD(2) = .75
      DISTDAYD(3) = .9
      DISTDAYD(4) = .95
      DISTDAYD(5) = 1.0
      DISTLDTM(1) = .2
      DISTLDTM(2) = .3
      DISTLDTM(3) = .7
      DISTLDTM(4) = .9
      DISTLDTM(5) = 1.0
      IORDQANT = 25
      IREORDRP = 6
C iordqant and ireordrp are decision variables
C iordqant is the order quantity
C ireordrp is the reorder point
      INVENTRY = IORDQANT
C initialize the inventory on hand to iordqant
      TOTCOST = 0.0
C totcost is the total cost
C run for 1050 days, reinitializing totcost after 50 days
      DO 20 JDAY = 1, 1050
      IF (JDAY .EQ. 51) TOTCOST = 0.0
C add any arriving orders to inventory
      INVENTRY = INVENTRY + IARRIVE(1)
C move any outstanding orders forward one day
C if orders outstanding, outstand is greater than 0
      IOUTSTND = 0
      DO 30 I = 1, 4
      IARRIVE(I) = IARRIVE(I+1)
      IOUTSTND = IOUTSTND + IARRIVE(I)
30 CONTINUE
      IARRIVE(5) = 0
C x is random variable for determining daily demand
      ISTRM = -1
      X = RAND(ISTRM)
C idemand is daily demand
      IDEMAND = 0
      DO 40 I = 1, 4
      IF (X .GT. DISTDAYD(I)) IDEMAND = I
40 CONTINUE
C subtract daily demand from inventory
      INVENTRY = INVENTRY - IDEMAND
C if inventry is negative, total demand not met and
C a shortage cost is added to total cost for each unit
C and inventry is set to 0
      TEMP = 50 * INVENTRY
      IF (INVENTRY .LT. 0) TOTCOST = TOTCOST - TEMP
      IF (INVENTRY .LT. 0) INVENTRY = 0
C check to see if an order is to be placed
C if so, subroutine ORDER places the order
      IF ((INVENTRY.LE.IREORDRP).AND.(IOUTSTND.EQ.0))
     1 CALL ORDER(IORDQANT,TOTCOST,DISTLDTM,
     2 IARRIVE)
C add the inventory holding cost to the total cost
      TEMP = INVENTRY
      TOTCOST = TOTCOST + .1 * TEMP
20 CONTINUE
C calculate the average total cost per day and print
C order quantity, reorder point, and average cost per day
      TOTCOST = TOTCOST / 1000.0
      WRITE (0,60) IORDQANT, IREORDRP, TOTCOST
60 FORMAT (2I5, F15.5)
      STOP
      END
      SUBROUTINE ORDER(IORDQ,TCOST,DLDTM,IARRIVE)
C subroutine for placing an order
```

```
        DIMENSION DLDTM(5), IARRIVE(5)
C add the order cost to total cost
        TCOST = TCOST + 20.0
C x is the random variable for determining the lead time
        ISTRM = -1
        X = RAND(ISTRM)
C itime is the lead time
        ITIME = 1
        DO 50 I = 1, 4
        IF (X .GT. DLDTM(I)) ITIME = I + 1
    50 CONTINUE
C the order will arrive in itime days
        IARRIVE(ITIME) = IORDQ
        RETURN
        END
```

Figure 8. FORTRAN Formulation

There were several similarities in the BASIC/FORTRAN approach and that of some of the simulation software packages, such as the use of loops and IF statements in SIMSCRIPT, and IF statements in SIMAN. The two areas where the simulation software packages had a definite advantage over the BASIC/FORTRAN approach were the handling of sampling from the probability distributions and the handling of delaying the arrival of the orders by the lead time.

Within the basic approaches there were most significant differences among the four simulation software packages, while BASIC and FORTRAN were essentially identical, except for syntax differences, as pointed out previously. The syntax differences included DO-CONTINUE loops, Comment, WRITE and FORMAT statements in FORTRAN, while BASIC uses FOR-NEXT loops, REMark and PRINT statements. In addition all BASIC statements are numbered, while just necessary statements are numbered in FORTRAN. There are also differences in the syntax of IF statements and in handling of subroutines and variables, with FORTRAN distinguishing between real and integer variables.

For the four simulation software packages, the approach for GPSS was very much different from the approach for the other three packages. The approach using SIMSCRIPT was also quite different in many aspects. However, the approaches using SIMAN and SLAM were almost identical for this particular model.

In both the SIMAN and SLAM II formulations, considerable use of branching and variable assignments were employed to implement the model. The intent was to represent the flow chart as directly as possible, without attempting to achieve an "elegant" solution.

As stated above, the SIMAN inputs are divided into those concerning the model itself and those which provide parameters needed for the experiment. In SLAM II, all inputs reside in a single file with the network portion of the file distinguished from the remaining inputs through the NETWORK and ENDNETWORK statements. (See Figures 3, 4 and 5.)

Both models involve a CREATE element which provides a single entity to the system. In each model, this entity has a single attribute, the amount of a specific day's demand.

Each model also features another entity type representing an order for additional inventory. Attributes for these entities include: 1) the amount of the order and 2) the lead time associated with that order. This entity is "created" in the sections identified as "DECIDE" and "DECID" in the two models and is processed in the sections labeled "ORDER". Entities representing orders are removed from the systems either through the DISPOSE block modifier in SIMAN or the SLAM II TERMINATE node.

In each case, ASSIGN elements are employed to manipulate system-descriptive variables. The variables involved are:

Description	SIMAN	SLAM II
Reorder Point	X(1)	XX(1)
Order Quantity	X(2)	XX(2)
Inventory Level	X(3)	XX(3)
Inventory + Orders	X(4)	XX(4)
Accumulated Shortage Costs	X(5)	XX(5)
Accumulated Order Costs	X(6)	XX(6)
Accumulated Holding Costs	X(7)	XX(7)
Total Costs	X(8)	XX(8)
Run End Time	X(9)	XX(9)

The SIMAN model incorporates the probability distribution function via the PARAMETERS element and the DP random variable. In SLAM II, the same discrete probability information resides in the ARRAY statement and the DPROBN function expressions. Provision for a 50 day startup period has been made in each model as well. In SIMAN, this is accomplished via the REPLICATE element and in SLAM II, the MONTR statement is employed.

With the obvious exception of minor syntactical details, the SIMAN and SLAM II model formulations are essentially the same in structure and in "modeling difficulty".

REFERENCES

Anderson, D.R.; D.J. Sweeney; and T.A. Williams. 1988. *An Introduction to Management Science - Quantitative Approaches to Decision Making*, fifth edition. West Publishing Company, St. Paul, MN.

Pegden, C.D. 1986. *Introduction to SIMAN*. Systems Modeling, Sewickley, PA.

Philip, G.C. 1989. *Student's Manual for LOTUS 1-2-3*, second edition. Kendall/Hunt, Dubuque, IA.

Pritsker, A.A.B. 1986. *Introduction to Simulation and SLAM II*, third edition. Wiley and Sons, New York, NY.

Russell, E. 1983. *Building Simulation Models with SIMSCRIPT*. C.A.C.I., Los Angeles, CA.

Shriber, T.J. 1974. *Simulation Using GPSS*. Wiley and Sons, New York, NY.

BIOGRAPHIES

D. Brent Bandy is Assistant Professor of MIS at the University of Wisconsin Oshkosh. Prior to coming to UW Oshkosh in 1984, he worked for sixteen years for Amoco as a systems analyst and operations research consultant. He has extensive experience in the application of computer simulation and optimization. He received his B.S. in Chemical Engineering from the University of Illinois, and his M.S. and Ph.D. in Chemical Engineering from Northwestern University. He also has an M.B.A. from the University of Chicago.

James R. Gross is Assistant Professor of Operations Management at the University of Wisconsin Oshkosh. Prior to coming to UW Oshkosh in 1987, he worked for three years with Pritsker and Associates and seven years at Millikin University in Decatur, Illinois. He has extensive experience in the application of computer simulation and in the development of simulation software. He received B.S. and M.S. degrees in Industrial Engineering from Purdue University and his Ph.D. in Operations Management from the University of Illinois in 1987.

Using Simulation Models to Support Strategic Decision Making in the Field of Logistics

Henk A. Akkermans

Eindhoven Technical University
Faculty of Industrial Engineering and
Management Science
P.O. Box 513,
5600 MB Eindhoven, The Netherlands.

J. Wil M. Bertrand

Eindhoven Technical University
Faculty of Industrial Engineering and
Management Science
P.O. Box 513,
5600 MB Eindhoven, The Netherlands

Jac A.M. Vennix

Utrecht University
Faculty of Social Sciences
Department of Gamma-Informatics
P.O. Box 80140
3508 TC Utrecht, The Netherlands

ABSTRACT

This paper discusses the use of simulation models to support strategic decision making in the field of logistics. The growing importance of an effective logistic strategy for organizations has induced a need for tools that can support the logistic strategy process. Simulation models are very well suited for this purpose because logistic processes are relatively easy to model. In logistics simulation a lot of experience has been accumulated in the modeling of the operational and tactical levels of the organization. However, since strategic decisions are of a less structured nature, the conventional approach towards decision making that is normally taken in logistics simulation, i.e. an orientation towards simulation for analysis, is not appropriate. In this paper it is proposed that logistic models are instead developed according to the participatory user oriented methods that have emerged in the general strategic modeling area. To explain the differences and complementarities of both logistic simulation and strategic simulation, and the way in which they can support logistic strategy, a framework is presented. Here the concept of a Strategic Logistic Simulation Model (SLSM) is introduced, which is seen as a combination of simulation, logistics and strategy, or, more appropriately, as a combination of logistic simulation, strategic simulation and logistic strategy. Finally it is shown that the scepticism that is often encountered in the field of logistic simulation, whether simulation models can be of use to support decisions of a strategic nature, is not correct, since models of the higher organizational levels are relatively easy to construct because of the aggregate nature of variables at this level. Also the thought that at the strategic level too many intangible factors exist is shown to be invalid, because also at the operational levels many relevant variables are found that are very hard to incorporate in formal models.

INTRODUCTION

Because of the growing strategic importance of logistics, the development of an effective logistic strategy has become a critical success factor for many organizations (Sharman 1984, Shapiro 1984, Ernst & Whinney 1987). Not surprisingly, the use of simulation models to support strategic logistic decision making has received a lot of attention in literature on logistic simulation (Pape 1989, Renner 1989, Smook 1989, Southall et al. 1989, Akkermans and Vennix 1990, Bowersox and Closs 1990, Dangelmaier and Vollmer 1990). These models are normally aggregated versions of logistic simulation models of the operational and tactical organizational levels, of which an impressive amount of modeling experience has been accumulated. However, it is clear that although there are many similarities in the types of models involved, there are also many differences in the ways simulation models can be used effectively to support strategic decision making as opposed to operational decision making.

In this paper it is suggested that techniques that are developed for general strategy formulation, in particular participative model building (Hall 1983, Lane 1989, Richmond 1987, Morecroft 1988, Senge 1989, Vennix 1990) are employed to support the strategy process for logistic issues. For this purpose we introduce a conceptual framework for so-called Strategic Logistic Simulation Models (SLSMs), in which these are seen as a potentially synergetic combination of the fields of logistic simulation, strategic modeling, and logistic strategy (Figure 1).

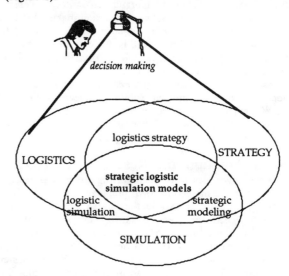

Figure 1: *The constituent fields of Strategic Logistic Simulation Models.*

In this framework we will try to provide an overview of the state of the art on these issues. The fields mentioned are themselves combinations of logistics, simulation and strategic planning. The emphasis in all this is on decision making, and on the views these different disciplines turn out to have on the nature of decision making.

It will be argued that SLSMs should be developed from a design-oriented approach, which we will describe as a systems approach in which the emphasis is both on analysis and on the cognitive and organizational limitations to organizational decision making in practice. In the field of logistic simulation scepticism whether simulation models *can* be of use to support decisions of a strategic nature is often encountered.n this paper it will be shown that the arguments presented in this case are not valid, and that indeed the use of simulation models to support strategic decision making in the field of logistics is a most promising area of research.

The structure of this paper is illustrated in the Venn-diagram of Figure 1. Strategic Logistic Simulation Models (SLSMs) are meant to support *decision making*. This basic human activity is the "search light" or "point of view" in this paper. Therefore the first section will open with some general comments on the nature of decision making. SLSMs are a combination of logistic simulation and strategic modeling, for the support of strategic logistic decisions. These three fields are combinations of logistics, simulation and strategic planning, respectively. A short description of each field will be given, as well as its prevalent view(s) on decision making. After that we will look at the intersections of these three fields, i.e. logistics & simulation, simulation & strategic planning, and strategic planning & logistics. In the final section we will return to our original theme, limitations and possibilities of strategic logistic simulation models. We will look at SLSMs from the three combinations just mentioned, i.e. logistic simulation, strategic modeling and logistics strategy.

DECISION MAKING

Decision making, or problem solving, is a basic human activity. It appears that in the literature on *strategic* decision making *behavioural science* views on decision making have had considerable impact, whereas in *logistic* decision making the approach to problem solving that is typical for Operational Research / Management Science (OR/MS) has been dominant. Russel L. Ackoff has classified these two approaches to problems as the *clinical* and the *research* approach, or as problem *resolving* and problem *solving*, respectively. (Ackoff 1981). Without wanting to present an overview of all the work performed in this area, we will discuss some concepts from the various fields that are relevant for this paper.

Problem Solving: the Research Approach

The *research approach* to problem solving emphasizes research and analysis as the method to solve problems. In this approach, "to solve a problem is to select a course of action that is believed to yield the *best possible* outcome, one that *optimizes*." (Ackoff 1981 p.354). Its practitioners abide by the Operations Research / Management Science (OR/MS) paradigm of problem solving, as formulated by Ackoff and Sasieni (1969): OR/MS problems are solved by constructing a model of the system under study which has the following underlying structure:

$$U = f(X_i, Y_i)$$

where

U is the utility or value of the system's performance
X_i are the variables that can be controlled.
Y_i are variables (and constants) that are not controlled but do affect U.
f is the relationship between U and X_i, Y_i. (Ackoff and Sasieni 1968, p. 9)

The problem solving objective is the optimization of U for given Y_i by influencing X_i.

Problem Resolving: the Clinical Approach

The so-called clinical approach on decision making is typified by Ackoff as *problem resolving*. "To resolve a problem is to select a course of action that yields an outcome that is good enough, one that satisfices." (Ackoff 1981, p.354). This approach is strongly influenced by behavioural science insights. Morecroft (1988) uses the term "behavioural decision theory" for this approach. Much of the pioneering research into human decision making has been performed by H.A. Simon, who has introduced the concepts of:

bounded rationality
The principle of *bounded rationality* is formulated by Simon as the basis for understanding human behaviour in complex systems. The principle recognizes that there are severe limitations to the thinking and reasoning power of the human mind. People do not try to find optimum solutions when they solve problems: optimality normally exceeds our cognitive capacity. Rather they look for a solution that is 'good enough', for a *satisficing* solution (Simon 1957).

intelligence-design-choice
Simon has also introduced the distinction between three different phases in the decision making process: "Decision making comprises three principal phases: finding occasions for making a decision; finding possible courses of action; and choosing among courses of action" (Simon 1960, p.1.) Simon has labelled these three phases *intelligence, design* and *choice* and as such they have become basic concepts in the literature on problem solving.

programmable and nonprogrammable decisions
Just as fundamental is Simon's distinction of "two polar types of decisions", *programmed* and *unprogrammed* decisions, respectively (Simon 1960, p.5). The idea that decisions can be seen as being more of a structured, repetitive nature or as more closely resembling "one-shot, ill structured novel, policy decisions" (Simon 1960, p. 8) has later on been elaborated by several authors.

Problem Dissolving: the Design Approach

Ackoff's own proposed approach toward problem solving he calls the *design approach*. Basically this is a synthesis of the clinical and research approaches. Analysis and formal methods are used, but in close participation with the decision makers, and while recognizing their cognitive and organizational limitations. Two other important characteristics of this type of approach are that a solution for the problem is obtained in an iterative process of designing a solution and testing if it meets the objectives, and its strong focus on systems thinking. The general ideas behind this design approach have gained much popularity in applied research in the 1980s (e.g. Bertrand and Wortmann 1981, Takkenberg 1983, Vennix 1990).

LOGISTICS

The Strategic Importance of Logistics

'Logistics' is used in this paper in a wider sense than is normally found in the American literature. In the European literature logistics is seen as an integrated systems view of all the primary processes of the organization and the control systems for these processes. The concept of *logistical management* as presented by Bowersox is more or less identical to the European conception: " (..) the managerial responsibility to design and administer a system to control the flow and strategic storage of material, parts and finished inventory to the maximum benefit of the enterprise. " (Bowersox et al. 1986, p. 4) Several other schools use different terms to denote (parts of) this broad concept of logistics, such as "production and inventory management", "materials management", "operations management" and "supply chain management". Whatever the descriptions used, it has by now become generally acknowledged that effective structuring and control of the primary processes of industrial organizations (i.e. logistics) is one of the main critical success factors for organizations in today's turbulent market environments. Effective logistic performance has become an issue of *strategic* importance.

Logistic Decision Making

Logistic theory has been strongly influenced by three other, related, fields: Operations Research / Management Science, Systems Theory and Control Theory. All these three fields have their own view on decision making.

OR/MS in logistic theory

Originally the OR view on problem solving prevailed in logistic theory. Among the earliest applications of analytical methods were the formulae developed for Economic Order Quantities and Statistical Inventory Control, but since then OR/MS has provided logistics theory with e.g. cost analysis, linear programming, waiting line models, simulation models, statistical analysis and network planning models. As has been stated by several authors, notably Ackoff (1979), the impact of these models has unfortunately not been very great in practice.

Control Theory in logistic theory

The second major influence in logistic theory in recent years has been Control Theory, or cybernetics, which may be either seen as a subset or related field of Systems Theory. The basis for Control Theory is the feedback loop, the concept of which has been developed in the technical sciences as a very effective means to control the effects of disturbances of 'technical' systems (van Aken 1978, p. 11). Perhaps the first application of Control Theory in logistics issues is described in Simon (1952). Much pioneering work in this area has also been done by J.W. Forrester, and has become known as industrial dynamics or *system dynamics* (Forrester 1961). The view of decision making in Control Theory is that of the *information-feedback mechanism*: "An information-feedback system exists whenever the environment leads to a decision that results in action which affects the environment and thereby influences future decisions (Forrester 1961, p. 14).

Systems Theory in logistic theory

In the past two decades logistic theory has also become strongly influenced by *Systems Theory*. This general use is not surprising, because logistic activities are dispersed throughout the organization and appear as "relatively low-profile, unglamourous activities" without a systems orientation towards organizing logistics. One great benefit of Systems Theory is that its application has promoted an *integral* perspective, what Williamson et al. (1990) describe as " the total cost concept, the idea of minimizing the sum of the costs of performing all activities" (Williamson et. al. 1990, p. 65). It is then not surprising that "logistics", "logistic management" and "integral logistics" are often used as synonyms in the literature.

SIMULATION

Simulation for Analysis

The field of simulation owes much to three related fields of science: to Operations Research/Management Science, to Systems Theory and to the field of Computer Science/Information Systems. The problem solving view of OR/MS, i.e. the orientation on (simulation) modeling of a problem situation for *analysis*, has been dominant in simulation.

Simulation for Understanding

However, we have seen a growing recognition of the value of simulation for understanding and explaining system behaviour. This is already apparent in Shannon's definition of simulation: "the process of designing a model of a real system and conducting experiments with this model for the purpose either of understanding the behaviour of the system or of evaluating various strategies (..) for the operation of the system" (Shannon 1975, p. 2). When simulation is meant for system understanding, models are not meant for quantitative predictions of specific events at particular future times. The idea is rather that "By constructing the model and watching the interplay of the factors within it, we shall come to a better understanding of the system with which we are dealing" (Forrester 1961, p. 56). The use of simulation models for system understanding has since 1961 developed in at least four directions:

graphical presentations

The advent of simulation environments that provide graphical representations of both the static structure and the dynamic behaviour of the simulation model have made it possible for model builders to present the model of the system under study much better than was possible before. Many simulation consultants will share the experience that an effective interactive presentation of a simulation model helps a great deal in creating greater understanding, commitment and enthusiasm within the client organization.

simulation for education and training

Just as well known will be the use of simulation models for education and training. Being a standard session topic for most simulation conferences, this use of simulation models in various areas requires no further explanation.

simulation-games

A third frequently encountered way to use simulation models for system understanding is simulation-gaming. A simulation-game is a combination of an interactive simulation model and a game scenario, which defines the actors that can take part in the game, their roles, the information they get to see from the model, the variables that they can influence in the simulation model, and a course of events that takes place in time. (Greenblatt and Duke 1981). A gaming approach can be employed to communicate insights from complex simulation models to decision makers (Vennix and Geurts 1987).

participative model building

Perhaps the most far-reaching form of using simulation for creating system understanding is the technique of participative model building. In many simulation studies it is the people that build the model, rather than the decision makers who's problem environment is being modeled, that gain most of the insights in the system under study. In the past decade several techniques have been developed to let decision makers participate in a group model-building process of the relevant aspects of the organization. This procedure is called participative or interactive modeling. In participative model building a group of managers builds a model of the organizational problem environment, guided by one or more experienced modelers, in a series of sessions. (cf. Hall 1983, Lane 1989, Richmond 1987, Morecroft 1988, Senge 1989, Vennix 1990).

STRATEGIC PLANNING

Strategic problems tend to be strongly interconnected. This means that a strategic decision should be made taking other strategic issues into considerations. This leads to the conception of a particular strategic decision as a part of a set of internally consistent strategic decisions, i.e. a strategy / strategic plan.

Although some researchers have suggested that strategic planning processes are, or should be, sequentially rational, analytical processes, most of the descriptive literature on strategic decision making confirms the views of behavioural decision theory as initially developed by Simon:

bounded rationality
Ever since its introduction, many authors have confirmed the aptness of Simon's concept of bounded rationality for strategic decision making in organizations (Saberwal and Grover 1989). Decision making in real business firms tends to be much simpler than one would anticipate based on classical models that assume objective rational behaviour (Cyert and March 1963).

decision types
Also Simon's notion of a typology of decisions has been confirmed in the strategic planning context. Simon (1960) himself has stated that decisions at the higher organizational (i.e. strategic) level tend to be of a less structured, nonprogrammable nature. Later authors have emphasized the interconnectedness of strategic problems as an additional characteristic. Ackoff speaks of *problem messes*, or systems of problems at the strategic planning level of organizations (Ackoff 1981). Mason and Mitroff (1981) use the term *wicked problems* to describe policy planning and strategy problems, which exhibit the characteristics of interconnectedness, complicatedness, uncertainty, ambiguity, conflict, and societal constraints (Mason and Mitroff 1981, pp. 10-11).

phases in strategic decision making
The *intelligence-design-choice* concept has also been applied to the strategic decision making process. E.g. Saberwal and Grover (1989) have studied the type of computer-based support for strategic decision making, and have a.o. come up with the following transitions in the strategic decision making process, going from 'intelligence' through 'design' to 'choice':
- scope / aggregation: from broad to narrow, with specific information about alternatives;
- form: from qualitative, soft, to quantitative
- level of support: from decision structuring to model-based decision making
- data/model emphasis: from data retrieval and analysis to model-based, simulation

LOGISTICS AND SIMULATION

Simulation of the Operational Level
In the field of manufacturing and logistics an impressive number of simulation studies has been performed. However, these simulation modeling studies have mostly been aimed at the modeling of the more operational levels of the organization. E.g. hardly an Flexible Manufacturing System (FMS) has been installed in recent years without a simulation study being performed to assess how the system will operate. In general, the OR/MS view on decision making is employed in these studies: every relevant variable is assumed to be known and quantifiable, and detailed analyses are be performed.

Simulation of the Strategic Level
In contrast to the large amount of attention given to these lower organizational levels, modeling studies of logistic systems at the higher organizational levels, and certainly at the enterprise level, have been relatively rare. In the late fifties Forrester's (1961) has studied goods flows and information flows in a logistic chain of organizations from an integral perspective, but after the nineteen sixties the strategic or enterprise level seems to have been abandoned almost completely by practitioners of logistics simulation. It is not until recently that logistic simulation studies of the strategic organizational level reappear in the literature in greater numbers. (Akkermans and Vennix 1989, Pape 1989, Renner 1989, Smook 1989, Southall et al. 1989 and Dangelmaier and Vollmer 1990). This rather sudden increase in activity may be due to
- the increased *experience* with logistic simulation
- the considerable progress that has been made in simulation *languages*
- the growing strategic *importance* of logistics.
- higher *awareness* of this strategic importance among top management.
- progress in the *theory* of the strategic *design* and control of logistics systems.

SIMULATION AND STRATEGY

The usage of simulation models to support the strategic planning process is not new. Forrester (1961) and Bonini (1963) are among the earliest examples. However, the way in which strategic simulation models, which are also known as corporate models or enterprise models, are employed in the strategy process, has changed considerably in the past decade. Although most corporate models are focussed on the financial / accounting aspect system of the organization, we believe that this changed attitude towards the role of models is also very relevant for the field of strategic logistic decision making.

Corporate Models
The first generation of "corporate models", as they are commonly called, appeared according to Naylor (1982) between 1965 and 1973. These models were without exception financial planning models capable of generating proforma financial statements. Most of these models were written in FORTRAN and took several man years to develop. Important advancements in computer technology in the early 1970s, such as interactive computing facilities and timesharing computing, provided the means for greater diversity and affordability in corporate

modeling. Also the emergence of simulation languages specifically tailored for corporate simulation helped to increase the number of companies that used corporate simulation to rise.

Criticism towards Corporate Models

Despite the successes in the nineteen sixties and early seventies, the popularity of strategic simulation models strongly declined in the subsequent period. Several explanations for this decline can be found in the literature.

- Shim and McGlade (1984) blame the *macro-environment* for this: as the economy entered a recession and became more unstable (less predictable) the weaknesses in the rationale underlying many corporate models were revealed" (Shim and McGlade 1984, p. 886).

Hayes and Nolan (1974) observed already in 1974 some major flaws in the *models themselves* and the way they were *developed*:

- The attempt was to create large, all-inclusive models.
- This resulted in inflexible models, which required incredible amounts of *data*, the useful life of which was often less than the collection period required.
- Moreover, they were almost impossible to understand, except for the people who created them.
- Not surprising then, that the results of the simulation runs were "piles of output that nobody bothered to look at" (Hayes and Nolan 1974, p.160).

Schrieber (1982) mentions several reasons for top management lack of confidence in using the simulation results of these corporate models:

- The model never seems to be quite done, or quite right, but the promise is made that it will soon be completed and correct.
- There is doubt whether the internal algorithms of the model really represent the original problem situation that was in the executive's mind.
- The computer model is difficult to explain in terms understandable to the executive.
- The real world and the problems to be simulated change faster than the model can be adapted.
- It is extremely difficult to define the probable range of errors in the output. (Schrieber 1982, pp. 140-141).

Strategy Support Models

All this criticism has lead to a respectable amount of "soul searching" in the model building community. The resulting new recommendations for strategic model building may be summarized as augmenting the strongly OR/MS oriented view on decision making that prevailed until recently with insights of behavioural decision theory (Morecroft 1988). Morecroft (1984) has named this new type of models *strategy support models*. The characteristics of this new type of models are direct consequences of these behavioural decision theory insights.

bounded rationality

If we for instance realize that managerial decision making has its cognitive limitations, the emphasis should be clearly on:

- simple models, that management can understand
- participation of management in the development of the model;
- treating the development and use of models as a process, not as the creation of a product.

phases in decision making

As has been shown by Sabherwal and Grover (1989), management needs different types of model-based support in its problem solving process of *intelligence-design-choice*. In the old situation management got a detailed model, which might have been useful in the analysis phase, when it was just entering the intelligence phase. In the development of strategy support models management participation starts at the beginning, and models develop gradually from very general, "Big Picture" models to more detailed models in which different policy alternatives can be explored (Richmond 1987, Senge 1989, Vennix 1990).

decision types

If problems are unstructured, or even 'wicked' (Mason and Mitroff 1981), the objective of a simulation model cannot be analysis. Instead simulation modeling and experimentation will have to focus on creating deeper understanding of the system being modeled. This goes in particular for the interactions between structure and dynamic behaviour, between model-inherent developments and policy interventions. Not the specific value of some variable at a certain point in time is important, but the general behaviour of the system (Forrester 1961). The notion that problems at the strategic level are all interconnected and that therefore a holistic approach is required (Ackoff 1979, 1981), leads to the insight that a major barrier to effective strategic planning is the functionally oriented structure of most enterprises. This is a barrier in two respects at least:

- the interplay between different functional areas is complex and dynamic. For example, changes in production operations affect inventories, which lead to reverberations in cash balance and marketing operations.
- Functional managers do not speak the same language. The day-to-day operating realities of sales, manufacturing, finance, marketing, R&D and logistics are very different. As a consequence, each operating arena has evolved his own "dialect" and way of looking at the world. (Richmond 1987).

These notions lead to the conclusions that:

- strategic decision making has to take place in a management team, comprising of the different functional managers.
- the strategic simulation model has to model all the relevant aspects of the organization, not just those aspects that can easily be identified in the "default language" of finance and accounting.

participatory simulation approaches

The participatory simulation approaches that results from these new insights, such as participative modeling and simulation-gaming, have been introduced in the previous section. We also should point out the important role that *system dynamics* (SD) is playing in the work currently being reported in participatory simulation approaches. The advantages of System Dynamics for these new approaches are obvious:

- SD is a modeling technique that is relatively easy to master to a beginner's level, because of the very limited number of simulation "building blocks" and because of its 'continuous flow' orientation, which can to a large extent be visualized by describing it in terms of e.g. water flows and levels.
- The general information-feedback control nature of SD makes it relatively easy to combine data of different functional areas, e.g. financial and physical data. This makes it possible to have a holistic modeling approach.
- SD's emphasis on the importance of the general behaviour of the model and on the importance of system understanding rather than analysis, corresponds with behavioural decision theory insights.
- One of SD's drawbacks, its inability to deal in an elegant fashion with probability, is not important if the emphasis is

on making simple, deterministic models that are easily understood.

- System dynamics models also describe organizational decision making processes, in which bounded rationality can be observed (Morecroft 1988, p.308).

LOGISTICS AND STRATEGY

Although the need to incorporate the control of the primary processes of the organization into the corporate strategy has been recognized for quite some time (Skinner 1969), elaborated notions about what the components of a logistic strategy are, and how they should be developed, are fairly new.

Logistics Strategy Process

The normative theories of the logistic strategy process still basically follow the blueprint provided by W. Skinner (1969): The general company strategy, which is determined by an analysis of external and internal strengths and weaknesses / threats and opportunities and the organizational goals, defines the task of the company logistic function, which defines, once again influenced by internal and external analysis, the company's logistic policies. The results of these policies are evaluated and appropriate action is taken. In this view logistic strategy is a functional strategy, that is derived from the corporate or business strategy. This is still the basic procedure for strategic logistic planning.

On the descriptive side only some first exploratory studies have been performed (Anderson et al. 1990). These findings indicate that in practice:

- logistics management is hardly involved in strategic planning
- *only* logistics management is involved in the translation of strategic plans into logistic plans (Anderson et al. 1990)

Logistics Strategy Content

The literature on logistic strategy content is, not surprisingly, strongly based upon concepts form Control Theory and Systems Theory. In The Netherlands much pioneering work has been done in large companies such as Philips Electronics (van Aken 1978, Hoekstra and Romme 1985). According to Van Ballegooie and De Jong (1990), who rely heavily on Hoekstra and Romme (1985), a logistic strategy should comprise of statements concerning the logistic base structure and the logistic control structure. The strategic planning and design of these structures is based upon an analysis of the desired logistic performance of product/market combinations and logistic characteristics of products and transformation processes for these product/market combinations.

PERSPECTIVES ON STRATEGIC LOGISTIC SIMULATION MODELS

Strategic Logistic Simulation Models

We see a Strategic Logistic Simulation Model (SLSM) as *a model of the strategic decision level of a logistic aspect system of an organization or a network of organizations, which is developed and/or used to support the process of strategic planning of the static and dynamic structure and control of the goods flow.* Several examples of SLSMs are mentioned in recent publications. Pape (1989), Renner (1989) and Dangelmaier and Vollmer (1990) describe attempts to model at the *enterprise* level by combining detailed models of operational subsystems. At the supply chain level modeling studies of a more aggregated nature are reported in Smook (1989) and Southall et al. (1989). Nathan (1990) describes a focused simulation approach to justify manufacturing modernization strategic plans, and Akkermans and Vennix (1990) present a participative modeling approach for SLSMs.

Depending from which related discipline one looks, different perspectives on the limitations and possibilities of SLSMs emerge. We will discuss the perspectives from the three intersections of simulation, logistics and strategic planning that have been introduced in the preceding sections.

Logistics & Simulation

In the field of simulation in logistics and manufacturing the most sceptical attitude towards SLSMs can be found. Here one sometimes hears or reads the suggestion that the development of mathematical models to support logistic decision making at the strategic level of organizations is very difficult, if not impossible, because at the *strategic* level

- it is hard to identify what is *relevant* information for strategic decision making .
- much *external* information is required which is difficult to model
- strategic *problem formulations* are normally unstructured
- information required for decision making is often of a *qualitative* nature or even *intangible*, and can therefore not be included in the models.

At the *operational* level, the argument continues,

- the modeling effort is aimed at *physical* systems,
- in which the *relevant* information is easily identifiable,
- most information is of an *internal* nature,
- and data refer to physical properties, which makes them *quantifiable*.

Although we do agree with some of the arguments made here, we certainly do not wish to draw the conclusion that all this makes modeling at the strategic level futile. We will first present some counter arguments and then illustrate what the main benefits of 'conventional' logistics simulation to SLSMs can be.

at every level are factors that are hard to model

In our view also at the lowest levels, e.g. on the factory floor, many unknown, unmeasurable or intangible factors exist that are relevant for the operation of the system under study. The major cause for this existence is the human factor. Apart from some extreme exceptions people always form part of production systems. And, happily enough, people do not behave like machines. Mental attributes such as the amount of problem solving creativity an operator has, or his work enthusiasm, his quality consciousness etc., are of paramount importance for the successful operation of any production system (Bertrand en Wortmann 1981, pp. 27-28). Such attributes can just as easily be called 'intangible'. Actually, at any organizational level factors that are undeniably relevant but relatively hard to incorporate into the model can be identified, and in our view this number does not necessarily increase for higher levels of abstraction. So either all simulation modeling of logistic systems seems futile in a sense, or we face similar kinds of problems at every level.

higher abstraction makes modeling easier

Even stronger put, we believe that, when one investigates organizational systems on an increasingly higher level of abstraction, the system under study tends to become more easy to model, because of the aggregate nature of variables at this level. Aggregation can have two important advantages:

- the underlying general behaviour of the system becomes more apparent because lots of low-level disturbances disappear out of sight. Probability, which is often difficult to determine and model, is often less important for the long term behaviour of a system (Forrester 1961).
- according to the theory of *nearly decomposable systems* (Simon and Ando 1961), no attention needs to be given to the internal workings of subsystems, but only to the interactions between the subsystems, because the long run (h.l. strategic) behaviour of the system is determined by these interactions between the subsystems, and not by the behaviour inside the subsystems.

Both considerations lead to the same conclusions: aggregation makes models simpler, and makes it easier to understand the long term behaviour of the logistic aspect system being modeled.

real intangibles do not exist

Thirdly, as early as in 1961 warnings can be heard against wanting every constant and functional relationship either to be known with high accuracy, or else to be excluded from the model. "This often leads to the omission of admittedly highly significant factors (most of the "intangible" influences on decisions) because they are unmeasured or unmeasurable. To omit such variables is equivalent to saying they have zero effect - probably the only value that is known to be wrong!" (Forrester 1961, p. 57).

combining views on decision making

The underlying rationale for this criticism may be that simulationists who adhere to the OR/MS view of decision making, which is still the dominant one in logistic simulation, are ill at ease at the strategic level, where behavioural decision theory is prevalent. Instead of saying that in the OR/MS paradigm, simulation cannot be applied to strategic logistic issues, one should say that the OR/MS paradigm should not be employed in the development of SLSMs!

similarities at different hierarchical levels

We shouldn't underestimate the potential synergy from the perspective of logistic simulation. A striking phenomenon in the field of logistics is that the ways in which the structure, dynamics and control of goods flows are modeled, is very similar on different hierarchical levels. For instance at every hierarchical level of a logistic aspect system, from shop floor to interorganizational network, models can be constructed using the building blocks of production, transport and stock, and their combinations into higher complexity, as shown in the previous section. An impressive body of knowledge has been accumulated concerning the modeling of logistics systems at the operational level, and it is safe to presume that a considerable amount of this knowledge can be applied to modeling at the strategic level.

simulation is an accepted technology for logistics issues

Another advantage is that simulation is an accepted, if not proven, technology for logistic issues. This is not the case in may other sectors, such as e.g. health care or social security (Vennix and Geurts 1987, Vennix 1990). This removes a large deal of the burden of proof for the technical, i.e. logistics, validity of the approach from the shoulders of the model builders.

Strategy & Simulation

A decade ago a sceptical attitude could also have been expected from the strategy fields. At that stage many a strategic consultant might have responded to SLSMs with remarks such as that corporate models are of little use in strategic planning because they are too inflexible, managers do not understand them, do not trust them, and as a consequence do not use them. However, as the section on strategy and simulation has shown, some very exciting developments in this area in the past few years have thoroughly changed this perspective. Participatory approaches have brought formal models right back into focus with strategic consultants.

Logistics & Strategy

The area from which the most promising sounds towards SLSMs can be heard is that of logistics strategy. Logistics has become an issue of strategic importance, and theories of content and process of logistics strategies are beginning to emerge. The use of simulation models in the logistic strategy process is promising indeed because:

- The core of logistics strategy concerns *physical chains* of products undergoing operations. These are relatively easy to model.
- In logistics, we are particularly interested in the *dynamic behaviour* of the logistic system. Strategic logistic objectives are such *process* indicators as delivery times, delivery reliability etc. . This emphasis on the behaviour of the system in time, contrasts with e.g. financial planning, where the emphasis is more on ratios over a certain period. It is very difficult to assess accurately the dynamic behaviour of a social system from its structure, since these systems tend to behave *counter-intuitive* (Forrester 1961). Simulation is a tool excellently fitted for this purpose.
- Current ideas of logistics strategy content suggest a strong emphasis on Systems Theory and Information Feedback Control Theory. For such approaches a wealth of simulation *models* is readily *available*.
-     For the strategy *process* in particular, we note that the logistics strategy is normally not integrated in business strategy, that logistics management is not involved in the business strategy process, and that other functional mangers are not involved in the logistics strategy process. Simulation models can provide the *common language* that is needed to help managers from different functional to communicate effectively from an integral, not a functional, perspective.

SUMMARY

In this paper a conceptual framework for Strategic Logistic Simulation Models (SLSMs) is presented. Logistics, and consequently logistic strategy, has become an issue of major importance for many organizations. The process of logistic strategy formulation and implementation can be supported by simulation models. Such models, called SLSMs, have roots in two applications of simulation modeling, i.e. logistic simulation and strategic modeling. Their third constituent field is strategic logistic decision making. It is shown that all these three application areas contain elements that make the use of simulation models to support strategic logistic decision making a valid and promising exercise.

Logistic simulation has established firmly that logistic structures and processes can be modeled very well, and at different levels of abstraction. Current developments in logistic strategy content indicate that a very important aspect of logistic strategy is the design of logistic structures and control systems in such a manner that the logistic processes perform confirming to certain performance indicators. Simulation is a tool eminently suited for such a design process.

A logistic strategy ought to be developed by the whole management team and in close connection with the general business strategy. Descriptive research shows that in practice this is not at all the case. Awareness and knowledge of logistics is normally fairly low in general management, and different functional perspectives within the management team inhibit the integral perspective that is fundamental to logistic design. Strategic modeling, and in particular participative modeling, can be of great help here, because it improves communication and consensus between managers of different functional areas, it deepens understanding of the logistic system, and it improves commitment to the policy recommendations that result from the simulation experiments.

ACKNOWLEDGEMENTS

We would like to thank Prof. Van Aken, Prof. Huckin, Joop Halman and Arie Nagel, who commented on earlier versions of this paper. We have benefited greatly from their remarks.

REFERENCES

ACKOFF, R.L, SASIENI, M.W. (1969) : *Fundamentals of Operations Research*, Wiley, New York.

ACKOFF, R.L. (1979) : "The Future of Operational Research is Past", *Journal of the Operational Research Society 30*, nr. 2, pp. 93-104.

ACKOFF, R.L. (1981) : "On the use of models in corporate planning". *Strategic Management Journal* 2, pp. 353-359.

AKKERMANS, H.A., VENNIX, J.A.M. (1990): "A Computer-Based Learning Environment for Logistic Management". in: S. Belardo, J. Weinroth (eds.): *Simulation in Business and Management*, SCS, San Diego, pp. 128-133.

ANDERSON, J.C., SCHROEDER, R.G., CLEVELAND, G. (1990) : "The Process of Manufacturing Strategy: Some Empirical Observations and Conclusions", in: C.Voss (ed.): *Manufacturing Strategy - Theory and Practice*. Proceedings of the 5th international conference of the Operations Management Association, pp. 1-23.

BERTRAND, J.W.M., WORTMANN, J.C. (1981) : *Production control and information systems for component-manufacturing shops*. Studies in Production and Engineering Economics 1, Elsevier, Amsterdam.

BONINI, CH.P. (1963) : *Simulation of information and decision systems in the firm*. Prentice Hall,Englewood Cliffs, NJ.

BOWERSOX, D.J. , CLOSS, D.J., HELFERICH, O.K. (1986) : *Logistical Management* MacMillan, New York, 3rd edition.

BOWERSOX, D.J., CLOSS, D.J. (1989) : "Simulation in Logistics: A review of present practice and a look to the future", *Journal of Business Logistics* 10, no 1, pp. 133-147.

CYERT,R.M., MARCH, J.G. (1963) : *A behavioural theory of the firm*, Prentice Hall, Engelwood Cliffs, NJ.

DANGELMAIER, W., VOLLMER, E. (1990) : "Integration of planning and simulation in strategic enterprise planning", in: Schmidt, B. (ed.) : *Modeling & Simulation. Proceedings of the European Simulation Multiconference*, pp. 395-407.

ERNST & WHINNEY (1987) : *Corporate Profitability & Logistics*, Council of Logistics Management, Oak Brook, IL.

FORRESTER, J.W. (1961) : *Industrial Dynamics*. The M.I.T. Press, Cambridge.

GREENBLATT, C.S., DUKE, R.D. (1991) : *Principles and Practices of Gaming-Simulation*. Sage, Beverly Hills.

HALL, R.I., MENZIES, W.B. (1983) : "A corporate system model of a sports club: using simulation as an aid to policy making in a crisis", *Management Science* 29, no.1., pp.

HAYES, R.H., NOLAN, R.L. (1974) : "What kind of corporate modeling functions best?", *Harvard Business Review* May-June 1974.

HOEKSTRA, SJ, ROMME, J.H.J.M. (1985) : *Op weg naar integrale logistieke structuren* (Towards integral logistic structures), Kluwer, Deventer (in Dutch).

LANE, D. C. (1989) : "Modeling as learning: Creating models to enhance learning amongst management decision makers", in: Murray-Smith, D., Stephenson, J., Zobel, R.N. (eds.) : *Proceedings 3rd European Simulation Congress*, Edinburgh, September 1989, pp. 321-239.

MONHEMIUS, W. (ed.) : *Logistiek Mangement* (Logistics Management), Kluwer, Deventer, Holland. (in Dutch)

MORECROFT, J.D.W. (1984) : "Strategy Support Models", *Strategic Management Journal* 5/3, pp. 215-229.

MORECROFT, J.D.W. (1988) "System Dynamics and microworlds for policy makers", *European Journal of Operational Research*, vol. 35.

NATHAN, D.L. (1990) : "A focused simulation approach to justify manufacturing modemization strategic plans", "A Computer-Based Learning Environment for Logistic Management". in: S. Belardo, J. Weinroth (eds.): *Simulation in Business and Management*, SCS, San Diego, pp. 134-139.

NAYLOR, TH. H. (1982) : "The Role of Econometric Models in Strategic Planning: The Results of a Survey of Users", in: Naylor, Th.H. (ed.) : *Corporate Strategy. the integration of Corporate Planning Models and Economics*, North-Holland, Amsterdam.

PAPE, D.F. (1989) : "Strategic Planning of Logistics Systems with Simulation", *Proceedings European Simulation Multiconference 1989*, Rome, pp. 107-112.

RENNER, R.A. (1989) : "Simulating an entire factory", in: D. Murray-Smith, J. Stephenson, R.N. Zobel (eds.) : *Proceedings of the 3rd European Simulation Congress, Edinburgh, September 1989*, pp. 562-566.

RICHMOND, B.T. (1987) : *The Strategic Forum: from vision to strategy to operating policies and back again*, High Performance Systems, Inc., Lime NH.

SABHERWAL, R., GROVER, V. (1989) : "Computer Support for Strategic Decision-Making Processes: Review and Analysis", *Decision Sciences 20* pp. 54-76.

SCHRIEBER, A.N.(1982) : "Some ways to bridge management's confidence gap in corporate planning models", in: Naylor, Th.H. (ed.) : *Corporate Strategy. the integration of Corporate Planning Models and Economics*, North-Holland, Amsterdam.

SENGE, P.M. (1988) : "Catalyzing systems thinking within organizations". MIT System Dynamics Group Working Paper, D-3877-9.

SHANNON, R.E. (1975) : *Systems simulation: the art and science*, Prentice-Hall, Englewood Cliffs NJ.

SHAPIRO, R.D. (1984) : "Get leverage from logistics", *Harvard Business Review* May-June 1984, pp. 119-126.

SHARMAN, G.(1984) : "The rediscovery of logistics", *Harvard Business Review* Sep-Oct 1984, pp. 71-79.

SHIM, J.K., MCGLADE, R. (1984) : "The Use of Corporate Planning Models: Past, Present and Future, *Journal of the Operational Research Society 35* no. 10, pp. 885-893.

SIMON, H.A. (1952) : "On the Application of servo-mechanism theory in the study of production control", *Econometrica 20*, pp. 247-268.

SIMON, H.A. (1957) : "Rationality and decision making", in *Models of Man*, John Wiley, New York.

SIMON, H.A. (1960) : *The new science of management decision*, Harper & Row, New York 1960.

SIMON, H.A. ANDO, A.,(1961) : "Aggregation of variables in dynamic systems", *Econometrica 29* no 2, pp. 111-139.

SKINNNER, W. (1969) : "Manufacturing - missing link in corporate strategy", *Harvard Business Review* May-June 1969.

SMOOK, J. (1989) : "Flexibele modelbouw en ketenmanagement" (Flexible model building and supply chain management"), *Tijdschrift voor inkoop en logistiek 5*, 1989/9, pp. 9-13 (in Dutch)

SOUTHALL, J.T. MIRBAGHERI, S., WYATT, M. (1989) : "Simulation modelling to improve supply chain management", in: D. Murray-Smith, J. Stephenson, R.N. Zobel (eds.) : *Proceedings of the 3rd European Simulation Congress, Edinburgh, September 1989*, pp. 557-561.

TAKKENBERG, C.A. TH. (1983) : *Planning en methode van onderzoek* (Planning and Research Method), Ph.D. Thesis, Groningen University, Groningen Holland (in Dutch)

VAN AKEN, J.E. (1978) : *On the control of complex industrial organizations*, Martinus-Nijhof, Groningen.

VAN BALLEGOOIE, E.D., DE JONG, J.C.J. (1990) : *SYMLAD. Systematisch management van logistieke adviesopdrachten* ("SYMLAD - Systematic management of logistic consultancy"), Samsom, Alphen a/d Rijn. (in Dutch)

VENNIX, J.A.M. (1990) : *Mental Models and Computer Models. Design and evaluation of a computer-based learning environment for policy making*, Ph.D. Thesis, Nijmegen.

VENNIX, J.A.M., GEURTS, J.L.A. (1987) : "Communicating insights from complex simulation models. A gaming approach", *Simulation and Games 18* no. 3, pp. 321-343.

WILLIAMSON, K.C., SPITZER, D.M., BLOOMBERG, D.J. (1990) : "Modem Logistics Systems: Theory and Practice", *Journal of Business Logistics 11*, no. 2, pp. 65-86.

Simulation of Operating System Reliability

David B. Hoffman
Professor of Business Administration
School of Management
University of Alaska Fairbanks
Fairbanks, Alaska 99775-1070

ABSTRACT

This paper describes using computer simulation to evaluate systems reliability under various subsystem conditions and demonstrates the use of computer simulation for evaluating redundancy conditions. The approach offers a way to evaluate the effects of "infant mortality" common to new subsystem installations.

This paper includes four simulation models. The first demonstrates subsystem and total system reliability. The second incorporates system redundancy and the third demonstrates the use of a single backup component supporting more than one main component. The fourth model incorporates the effects of infant mortality .

SYSTEM RELIABILITY

In modern integrated manufacturing systems, component reliability is essential, since failure or out-of-tolerance conditions threaten the entire system. These issues of reliability apply when dealing with integrated machinery, computer systems and office administrative systems. Consider that the removal of instability is necessary for reducing variance in any scheduling, inventory and JIT systems.

Reliability is defined as the probability that a part, component or system will function properly for a give time. The typical approaches to improving reliability are to (a) improve individual component reliability and (b) provide redundancy.

Series System

The first model represents a system made up of two components. The reliability of the system depends on all components functioning. In all of the following models
$R(t)$ is the probability that the system will function over time $[0,t]$. The performance of each component can be denoted as a random variable, X_i that takes on the value

$x_i = 1$ if functioning and
$x_i = 0$ if the component has failed.
Therefore X_i is a binary random variable defined by

$$X_i = \begin{cases} 1, & \text{if component i works during } [0,t] \\ 0, & \text{if component i fails during } [0,t] \end{cases}$$

The performance of the system is measured by the binary random variable $f(X_1, X_2, \ldots X_n)$, where

$$\phi(X_1, X_2, \ldots, X_n) = \begin{cases} 1, & \text{if system works during } [0,t] \\ 0, & \text{if system fails during } [0,t] \end{cases}$$

97

In this first model, the system reliability depends on the reliability conditions of two components. The model is represented in Figure 1.

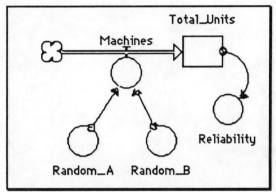

Figure 1. Series System

The two components, labelled **Random_A** and **Random_B,** have been assigned reliability of 0.9 and 0.8 respectively. Over time, the system reliability approximates the product of the component reliabilities. Therefore , system reliability; $R(t)$ = 0.72.

The formula for **Machines** is

IF (Random_A<0.9) AND
   (Random_B<0.8)
   THEN 1
   ELSE 0

Component Redundancy

In situations where component or system functioning is critical, a backup component is added to operate in the event the primary component fails. Both the primary component p_1 and the backup p_2 have reliability parameters and the combined reliability for this system is

$$R = p_1 + p_2 (1 - p_1)$$

In this example, the primary component, called **Random_A,** is p_1 = 0.9. The backup component, called **A_Backup,** is p_2 =0.8. Thus the primary component operates 90% of the time. During the 10% of the time that it is non-operational, the backup component is called upon. And 80% percent of the time, the backup

device will be able to function in the place of the primary component. The system reliability in this case is $R = 0.98$. The variation if this is monitored with Percent_Reliable in the model.

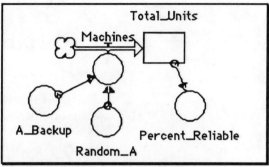

Figure 2. Component with Backup

The formula for **Machines** is

IF(Random_A<0.9)
   THEN 1
   ELSE
      IF (Random_A>.9)
     AND (A_Backup<0.8)
      THEN 1
      ELSE 0

Single Backup Redundancy

The third model combines the features of the first two. The system is operational if **Machine_A** and **Machine_B** are operational. In the event either are down a single backup (**A_B_Backup**) is available. Since each machine has its own reliability measure, system reliability is a function of having two of the three machines operational. If any two of the three are down, the system (**Line**) is not operational.

This is a common situation especially where there are limitation in resources available for providing redundancy. Where equipment is upgraded, due to space or other resource constraints, only a single backup device is left to support.

In this example **Machine_A** is given a reliability of 0.91. **Machine_B** is 0.85 reliable and **A_B_Backup** is .75 reliable. The formula for the system (**Line**) is

```
IF
    (Machine_A=1)
    AND
    (Machine_B=1)
  OR
    (Machine_A=1)
    AND
    (Machine_B=0)
    AND
    (A_B_Backup=1)
  OR
    (Machine_A=0)
    AND
    (Machine_B=1)
    AND
    (A_B_Backup=1)
THEN  1
ELSE  0
```

This model is shown in Figure 3.

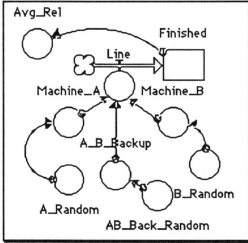

Figure 3. Single Backup Model

The system's reliability is 0.90. The effect of maintaining the backup component can be evaluated by replicating the simulation with the reliability of **A_B_Backup** set at 0.

This type of model helps to answer the question:" *When we replace old equipment, should we retain the old unit as a backup or remove it?* " In the case of computers, the plug is not pulled on the old system until the new one is fully functional because the complete loss of computer support is too expensive.

Infant Mortality

Hypothetically, component failure rates are higher in the beginning of use and higher again as the machine wears out. When new

equipment is installed, there is often a higher than desired rate of failure or "out-of-tolerance" work either because the new equipment is not setup correctly or there is a high rate of improper use(Heizer and Render, 1988).   This is represented in Figure 4.

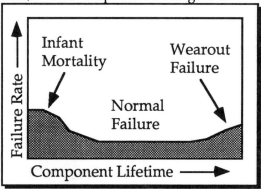

Figure 4. Lifetime Failure Rates

Adding the effect of infant mortality to a component can also be linked to the decision to "pull the plug" on the backup machine.

For this example, assume that **Machine_A** is new. As it is used, the reliability is improved. **A_B_Backup** will remain in operation until the reliability of the new machine achieves 0.90. From there, the two components are on their own. This model is represented in Figure 5.

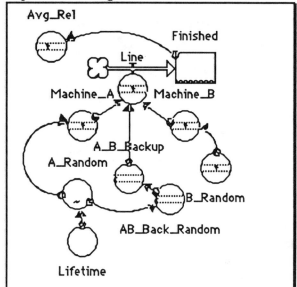

Figure 5. Infant Mortality Model

A_Random is now the lifetime reliability expected or the new machine. It is represented in the following formula and Figure 6.

A_Random = graph (Lifetime)
(0.0,0.805),(100.00,0.860),
(200.00,0.905),(300.00,0.935),
(400.00,0.945),(500.00,0.940),
(600.00,0.935),(700.00,0.930),
(800.00,0.915),(900.00,0.900),
(1000.00,0.885)

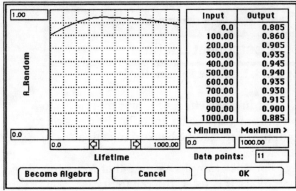

Figure 6. A_Random Reliability

The revised formula for **AB_Back_Random** is now based on both whether the new **A_Random** component is above 0.92 and the random conditions for the backup component. Thus, the backup component is taken out of service whenever the A component is above 0.92 and even when the new machine is below 0.92, there is still a 75% chance the backup machine can not support it. The formula is shown below.

AB_Back_Random =
    IF (A_Random<0.92)
           AND   (RANDOM(4)<.75)
           THEN 1
           ELSE 0

The following figure shows the average reliability of the system and the change in reliability of the new machine over time. The backup component comes out of operation around period 250. Even with the reliability of the new component improving, there is still an increased drop in the overall reliability of the system for a while.

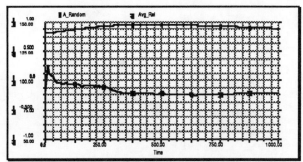

Figure 7. Lifetime System Reliability

Decisions regarding equipment replacement can be evaluated through the use of system reliability simulation. An extension of theses models could include the operational and cost tradeoffs between preventive maintenance and corrective maintenance considerations.

SUMMARY

All of these represent practical problems in industry. There is a never ending need to sustain full functioning components in any business situation and an even greater need in highly integrated systems like CIM (Computer Integrated Manufacturing). Component and manufacturing costs must be minimized and the greater the degree of subsystem integration, the greater the penalties when any one component of the process fails or comes out of tolerance. As a point, new equipment which is installed to achieve greater efficiencies is usually the main source of system unreliability. Many infant mortality failures are also not because of the equipment but the result of improper use. Increasing component and system reliability highlight the importance of understanding subsystem dependencies and proper employee training and equipment installation.

REFERENCES
Concanon, K. et.al., "Balance Maintenance Costs Against Reliability With Simulation Modeling" Insight International. Jan. 1990, pp22-26.

Heizer, J. and Render, Barry, Production & Operations Management (Allyn & Bacon, Inc.: Boston) 1988.

Hillier, F. and Lieberman, G., Introduction to Operations Research (McGraw-Hill Inc.:New York) 1990.

SIMULATION IN
BUSINESS RESEARCH

CEO: A CONFIGURABLE TOTAL ECONOMY SIMULATION

Precha Thavikulwat
Department of Management
Towson State University
Towson, Maryland 21204-7097

ABSTRACT

Total enterprise simulations are limited by dependence on a contrived market. CEO, as a total economy simulation, removes this limitation by enabling participants to be consumers as well as producers. Furthermore, CEO allows the instructor to configure the simulation to shift emphasis among three learning modes: learning through discovery, learning through perseverence, and learning through competition. The principal components of CEO are two sets of files and five computer programs. Supporting components include batch files for installation and set up, a security-enhancing program, a file-inspection program, a task-switching program, and eight Lotus 1-2-3 spreadsheets. CEO scores each participant by that participant's level of consumption, and scores each company by that company's accumulated distributions of earnings and invested capital.

INTRODUCTION

Over the past 30 years, business simulations have evolved in stages towards increasing administrative convenience, from the hand-scored stage, to the mainframe stage, and most recently, to the microcomputer stage (Wolfe & Teach, 1987). Among the many business simulations in use, total enterprise business simulations (Keys, 1987), requiring participants to decide on production, finance, and marketing, have been among the most popular. Although these simulations involve marketing decisions, such as pricing and advertising, the resulting market demand is a computed result (Decker, LaBarre, & Adler, 1987; Frazer, 1983; Gold & Pray, 1983, 1984; Golden, 1987; Goosen, 1981, 1986; Lambert & Lambert, 1988; Thavikulwat, 1989), and not a true demand dependent on human needs.

A computed demand, implying a contrived market, is a serious limitation of total enterprise business simulations, for the market plays a vital role in the success of any real business enterprise. When the market in a simulation is contrived, the simulation will tend to misdirect learning towards skills different from those required by marketing in reality. Thus, participants may learn mathematical skills instead of marketing skills.

A contrived market is unnecessary. In reality, people consume as well as produce. Business simulations can be designed to incorporate this reality. In such a simulation, the market demand will be created by the desire of participants to purchase the products their firms produced. This desire will arise from a scoring system that assigns participants scores reflecting their consumption. Thus, the participant who consumes more will score higher than the one who consumes less. By enabling participants to be both consumers and producers, the simulation completes the link between the consumption and production. Such simulations are total economy simulations.

CEO (Thavikulwat, in press) is a total economy simulation. To simplify the programming, the market of CEO allows trading in only one direction, and allows offers to go only one way. Thus, companies can sell to consumers, but consumers cannot sell to companies. Thus also, companies can state the prices they require, but consumers cannot state the prices they want. These two restrictions affect market's efficiency, but not its reality.

Besides being a total economy simulation, CEO is also a configurable simulation. A configurable simulation allows the instructor, by changing the simulation's parameters, to shift emphasis among three learning modes: learning through discovery, learning through perseverance, and learning through competition (Thavikulwat, 1988). Thus, the instructor can adapt the simulation to the student, to the setting, and to instructor's preferred method of teaching.

PRINCIPAL COMPONENTS

The principal components of CEO are two sets of data files and five computer programs. Of the files, the main data files contain data about companies; the market data

103

files contain data about products bought, sold, and offered for sale. Of the five computer programs, CEOX.EXE, REQ.EXE, and CCEO.EXE support the role of producers; BUY.EXE and CBUY.EXE support the role of consumers. A schematic diagram showing the files and programs is given in Figure 1.

Figure 1
Schematic Diagram of Principal Files and Programs

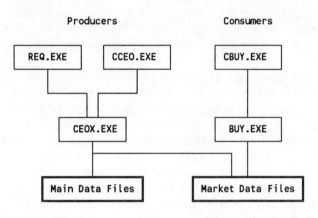

The producers are companies, generally composed of teams of participants. Each company runs CEOX.EXE to enter its decisions, execute the consequences of those decisions, save the results, see the results displayed on the screen, and obtain printouts of the results. Unlike most total enterprise simulations, CEO computes the results of decisions immediately, based on the state of the simulation at the time of execution. It does not require the instructor to collect the decisions of all companies and input them into the simulation program.

The consumers are individual participants. Each consumer runs BUY.EXE to examine the offers that producers have placed on the market. Each offer states the quantity available for sale and the selling price, and each offer is associated with an advertising expenditure that affects the random probability that the offer will appear before any one consumer. When a consumer accepts an offer, the quantity bought is transferred from the producer's account to the consumer's, and the corresponding funds are transferred from the consumer's account to the producer's.

Total enterprise simulations generally do not permit participants to change the parameters of the simulation program. CEO allows such changes, but it also allows the instructor to determine when the changes can take place and how extensive they might be. Producers enter the changes they want by running REQ.EXE. The instructor executes the changes by running the same program and entering a key password. As opposed to regular decisions, which have a tactical effect, changes in parameters have a strategic effect on the competitive position of producers.

Total enterprise simulations generally allow the instructor to change the parameters of the simulation by directly changing either a data file or the source code. These methods do not prevent the instructor from inadvertently making illogical parametric changes. In CEO, parametric changes are made indirectly through two computer programs, CCEO.EXE and CBUY.EXE. The programs guides the instructor in making changes, and prevents illogical changes.

SUPPORTING COMPONENTS

Because of differences in microcomputing hardware and operating systems, ease of use has become an important issue in simulations. CEO enhances ease of use with batch files that aid installing and setting up the simulation on networked microcomputing systems, fixed disk systems, and floppy diskette systems. A program that enhances security by hiding files (SH.COM), and a program that enables the instructor to read and edit the market files directly (INS.EXE) are also included.

With the popularity of spreadsheet programs, decision support involving such programs has become desirable. Thus, CEO includes a task-switching program (COURIER.EXE) that enables the simulation to reside in computer memory at the same time as a spreadsheet program, such as Lotus 1-2-3. Also included are eight spreadsheet templates that enable participants to solve linear programming problems (ALLOCATE.WK1) and transportation problems (SHIP.WK1); to plan material requirements (MRP.WK1); to construct pro forma financial statements (PROFORMA.WK1); and to analyze the effects of recruitment, benefits, training, and wage on the productivity and availability of labor (RECRUIT.WK1, BENEFITS.WK1, TRAIN.WK1, and WAGE.WK1).

SCORING SYSTEM

CEO's scoring system is based on the idea that the successful company enriches its shareholders, and that the successful shareholder consumes. Thus, besides a market for products, CEO has a market for shares.

Participants purchase shares in companies in the same way they purchase products. Companies can distribute their earnings back to shareholders, and can also return shareholders' invested capital.

When the simulating session has ended, each company's accumulated distribution of earnings and invested capital is its score; and each participant's accumulation of points from consumption is that participant's score. Thus, the participants' scores encompasses the companies' scores.

DISCUSSION

CEO requires that the instructor be proficient in the production, financial, and marketing aspects of business. CEO also requires that the instructor understand microcomputers enough to install and set up the simulation, to recover backed-up files as needed, and to deal with hardware problems that will arise occasionally.

CEO keeps an accumulated distribution score for each company. Because this score is comprehensive, the instructor can ask companies to make presentations and submit public reports that will have natural consequences. The companies that make the better presentations and submit the better reports will attract more investments, which, when returned to investors towards the end of the session, will raise the companies' accumulated distribution score.

CEO keeps a consumption score for each individual participant. This makes it unnecessary for instructors to rely on the contentious method of peer ratings and personal observations as a basis for individual grades.

Power and simplicity are incompatible attributes of computerized simulations. As a configurable total economy simulation, CEO is powerful. It is not simple. But it makes the computer work so that people might think.

REFERENCES

Decker, R.; J. LaBarre; and T. Adler. 1987. "The Exponential Logarithm Function as an Algorithm for Business Simulation." *Developments in Business Simulation & Experiential Exercises*, 14: 47-49.

Frazer, J. R. 1983. "A Deceptively Simple Business Strategy Game." *Developments in Business Simulation & Experiential Exercises*, 10:98-100.

Gold, S. C. and T. F. Pray. 1983. "Simulating Market and Firm Level Demand--A Robust Demand System." *Developments in Business Simulation & Experiential Exercises*, 10:101-106.

Gold, S. C. and T. F. Pray. 1984. "Modeling Non-Price Factors in the Demand Functions of Computerized Business Simulations." *Developments in Business Simulation & Experiential Exercises*, 11:240-243.

Golden, P. A. 1987. "Demand Generation in a Service Industry Simulation: An Algorithmic Paradox." *Developments in Business Simulation & Experiential Exercises*, 14:67-70.

Goosen, K. R. 1981. "A Generalized Algorithm for Designing and Developing Business Simulations." *Developments in Business Simulation & Experiential Exercises*, 8:41-47.

Goosen, K. R. 1986. "An Interpolation Approach to Developing Mathematical Functions for Business Simulations." *Developments in Business Simulation & Experiential Exercises*, 13:248-255.

Keys, B. 1976. "Total Enterprise Business Games." *Simulation & Games: An International Journal*, 18:225-241.

Lambert, N. L. and D. R. Lambert. 1988. "Advertising Response in the Gold and Pray Algorithm: A Critical Assessment." *Developments in Business Simulation & Experiential Exercises*, 15:188-191.

Thavikulwat, P. 1988. "Emphasizing Different Modes of Learning Through a Configurable Business Simulation Game." *Simulation & Games: An International Journal*, 19:408-414.

Thavikulwat, P. 1989. "Modeling Market Demand in a Demand Dependent Business Simulation." *Simulation & Games: An International Journal*, 20:439-458.

Thavikulwat, P. In press. *CEO: A Business Simulation for Policy and Strategic Management*. McGraw-Hill, N.Y.

Wolfe, J. and R. Teach. 1987. "Three Down-Loaded Mainframe Business Games: A Review." *Academy of Management Review*, 12:181-192.

BIOGRAPHY

Precha Thavikulwat (Ph.D., University of Minnesota) is Associate Professor of Management at Towson State University. He teaches production and operations management, and business strategy and policy. He is the author of *MANAGEMENT 500: A business simulation for production and operations management* (1989, New York: McGraw-Hill), and of *CEO: A business simulation for policy and strategic management* (in press, New York: McGraw-Hill).

THE HUMAN SIDE OF
COMPUTER SIMULATION

THE APPLICATION OF MODELS AND SIMULATION IN DEVELOPING QUALITY CONTROL TRAINING

George A. Johnson, Corey D. Schou, A. Davant Bullard
Idaho State University
Pocatello, Idaho

Abstract:

The demands of individual and company consumers for improved quality has required many companies to begin systems for obtaining or improving quality control. Many managers are discovering that they need training in quality control principles. We have three simulation programs with graphics and some animation that are designed to improve the effectiveness and ease of obtaining this training.

An increasing number of companies must develop an effective quality control program to meet the needs of their customers. In William Edwards Deming's celebrated fourteen points, number four states:[1] "End the practice of awarding business on the basis of price tag alone. Instead minimize total cost. Reduce the number of suppliers by eliminating those who cannot provide evidence of statistical control of processes." Many companies must to learn to deal with quality control concepts and use quality control techniques to remain competitive. Managers generally do not have to learn all the detailed mathematics, yet they must understand the basic concepts in order to implement quality control effectively. As more managers are required to understand and use quality control concepts to be effective decision makers in their organizations, it is hoped that this group of programs will make that understanding easier to obtain, clearer and more useful.

Many managers have difficulty in understanding these basic concepts. The effective use of graphical presentations with simulation of common quality control situations can significantly enhance the understanding of managers. This should be particularly true for the non-quantitative manager. This paper discusses three programs that were designed to serve this need. We have attempted to present simulations with some animation and graphs to clarify the underlying quality control concepts rather than burden the user with mathematics. We provide a relatively easy-to-follow presentation of the computations used. The unavoidable mathematics is handled by the computer, so the user can concentrate on concepts rather than having to focus first on laborious calculations or mystifying binomial or other tables.

The FUNNEL program simulates the funnel experiment as described in Gitlow, et al.[2] This experiment consists of a funnel mounted on a stand through which a ball is repeatedly dropped. The position of the funnel can be left stationary or moved after each drop. This allows the user to simulate the operation of a machine that can be adjusted in two dimensions. Five separate movement rules are included to examine the resulting patterns of machine performance. The user can actually see the points being plotted one after another on an active screen. The corresponding statility or instability is immediately apparent to the observer. The five screen patterns resulting from these rules can be saved and compared. The ability to reexamine these screens and compare them strongly emphasizes their differences and the relative effectiveness of the five rules. The first of these rules corresponds to correct operation of the machine. The other four rules correspond to incorrect rules frequently used by organizations. These four incorrect procedures arise from missunderstandings about the nature of a statistical process. These four rules "overcontrol" or improperly control the process. They usually result in lower quality and other losses to the organization. (See Appendix I for details of

1. Walton, M., *The Deming Management Method*. Mead, New York 1986, 40-51

2. Gitlow, H., et al., *Tools and Methods for the Improvement of Quality*. Homewood, IL: R. D. Irwin, 1989, 534-541.

this experiment).

Figures one and two present two sample screens of the output of this program. Figure one represents rule 1 that is the proper way to operate the machine. The spread that you see is the inherent variation in the process.

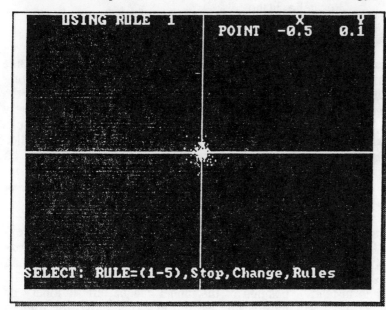

```
USING RULE 1          X      Y
                POINT -0.5   0.1




SELECT: RULE=(1-5),Stop,Change,Rules
```

Figure two represents rule 5 or a common method of control is to make the next unit like the last. A common example is the person that is cutting a series of peices of wood that are to be the same. They would cut one piece and use that piece to measure for the next piece and so on.

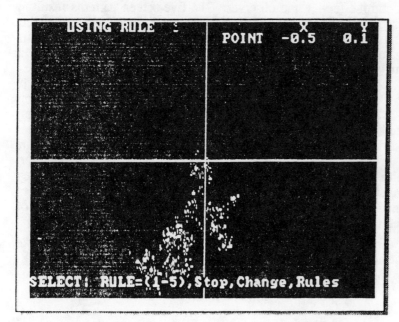

```
USING RULE 5          X      Y
                POINT -0.5   0.1




SELECT: RULE=(1-5),Stop,Change,Rules
```

The results as seen from figure two is a system dramatically out of control. Although, when viewed after the fact it seems obviously wrong, the real process often tends to hide the actual impact from the user. There are many examples of practices that in reality actually follow this strategy.

The funnel simulation allows an instructor to carry out this demonstration in the classroom without the need for physical apparatus. More importantly, attempting this experiment manually is extremely tedious and time consuming. Manually, it would take considerable time to carry out fifty trials while a sample size of 1000 can be done on the computer in a matter of a few seconds.

Program BEAD simulates the bead box experiment that is frequently used in the teaching of quality control principles. The physical bead box experiment consists of a box with a certain distribution of beads. One example may be 600 black beads, 300 red beads, and 100 white beads. A paddle having 50-bead or 100-bead depressions is dipped into the box to obtain a sample, and the sample is examined. Repeating this process allows the construction and examination of control charts, confidence intervals, sampling errors, operating characteristics, process capability, producer & consumer risks and other statistical parameters. The simulation program allows a rapid, inexpensive simulation of the bead box demonstration.

Walton[3] gives an excellent description of Dr. William Edwards Deming's use the bead box in one of his seminars. Deming recruits seminar participants for workers, inspectors, chief inspector and recorder. Deming is the production supervisor. The workers use paddles with 50 bead-sized holes to "make" white beads from a mixture of red and white beads. White beads are "made" by dipping the paddle into a mixture of 800 red and 3200 white beads. Typical fallacies and missconceptions about the nature of quality control and statistical processes are exposed by Deming as the workers one after another "make" their white beads. Obviously workers also "make" red beads (defectives), and they are praised or verbally chastized when the number of defectives seems low or excessive. The chief inspector and/or the worker may be fired for not maintaining proper quality. The point of course is that workers are often blamed and punished for problems beyond their control. Several other lessons are taught in this experiment, including the construction, interpretation and use of p-charts (control charts).

Figure three presents the view the student has when asked to make their beads. Although the student can control where the paddle is inserted, it should be obvious to the reader that this control has no effect on the underlying process. The variation that occurs is a result of the underlying process. The worker can not impact this underlying process in a statistically significant way without changing the process. This is in fact a central point of the excercise as used by Deming. To change quality one must change the process. Managerial exhortations for workers to improve

3. Walton, M., *The Deming Management Method*. Mead, New York 1986, 40-51

the quality of their output are often misguided because the worker is often unable to affect any change without a change in the underlying process. Summary data and a control chart of the results are provided as part of the end-of-simulation output. A major advantage of a computer generated exercise is of course the elimination of the need for expensive physical equipment to run the experiment. The computer exercise is also faster and includes automatic record-keeping.

Program QUINCUNX is a simulation of the quincunx training device. This is a common tool in industrial training programs in statistical quality control. The quincunx can be used to demonstrate the underlying normality of many physical situations, demonstrate process centering, demonstrate process capability studies, demonstrate that unit inspection is improper and yields poor results, and demonstrate the effectiveness of mean and range charts for control. Other important statistical quality control principles can also be demonstrated. The program QUINCUNX graphically reproduces an active animated simulation of the fall of the beads through the pin matrix to form the normal distribution.

The funnel can be moved to alter the centering of the process, and the pin block can be changed to alter the process standard deviation (change the process capability). While the physical device is an extremely effective demonstration tool, it is expensive and cumbersome to transport. Microcomputers are commonly available in many sites, so only a computer disk is needed to transport these experiments to various locales. These demonstrations can thus be performed using simulation without the difficulty and expense of transporting the physical device.

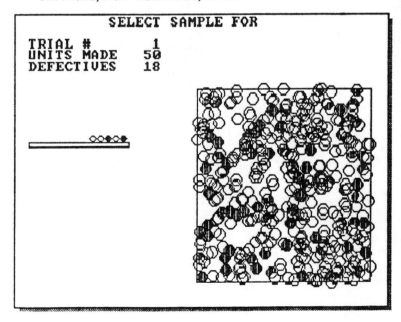

SELECT SAMPLE FOR

TRIAL # 1
UNITS MADE 50
DEFECTIVES 18

Appendix 1
The Funnel Experiment

You are in charge of a machine that operates on a certain part in two dimensions, say length and width. Your measuring device is set to read (x,y) = (0,0) with perfect part. A reading of (x,y) = (.005,-.003) means that the part is too large in the x value by .005, and the part is too small in the y value by .003.

This process can be simulated roughly by the funnel experiment. A funnel is placed on a stand, and a ball is dropped through the funnel onto a cartesian coordinate system. The position of the ball is then marked on the coordinate system. The funnel "makes" a perfect part if the ball is at (0,0).

There are several ways or rules that you might choose to adjust the machine (or the funnel) to try to produce the best output.

Rule 1: Set the machine (or the funnel) at (0,0), and make no changes as the machine makes parts (or as the ball is repeatedly dropped).

Rule 2: After each part is made (or each drop), reset the machine (move the funnel) from its current position to correct the error of the last part (drop). for example, if the machine makes a part that measures (x,y) = (.005, -.003), adjust the machine (move the funnel) from its current position in the x direction by -.005 and in the y direction by +.003. (this is to "correct" for the last "error" in the process.)

Rule 3: Adjust the machine (funnel) as in rule 2 only if there is "too much" error. That is, if the part (or ball) distance from (0,0) is greater than some fixed amount, then adjust as in rule 2. Otherwise make no change in machine (or funnel) setting.

Rule 4: This rule appears to be similar to rule 2, but it differs in that rather than adjust the machine (move the funnel) from its current position, the machine is adjusted (or the funnel is moved) from (0,0). To further contrast rule 2 and rule 4: rule 2 says adjust the machine from its current

position by the amount of the error. This "corrective" process remembers its last position. If the machine is currently set at (.002, -.004) and the part comes out as (.005,-.003), then the machine is adjusted by (-.005,.003) from its last position to (-.003,-.001).

Rule 4 says adjust the machine from (0,0) by the amount of the error. Since the adjustment is from (0,0) rather than from the last position, the machine has no memory of its last position. If the machine is currently set at (.002,-.004) and the part comes out as (.005,-.003), then the machine is adjusted with no regard for its previous position to (-.005,.003).

	Current Machine Setting	Part Measurement	New Machine Setting
Rule2	(.002,-.004)	(.005,-.003)	(-.003.-.001)
Rule 4	same	same	(-.005,.003)

Rule 5: If the part is (.005,-.003), make the next part like the last part (move the funnel to that point).

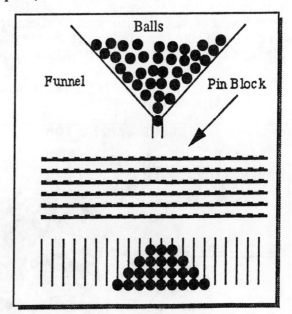

112

SIMULATION-NEURAL NET INTERFACES FOR MANAGEMENT SUPPORT: RESEARCH IN PROGRESS

Jay Weinroth
Gregory Madey
Vijay Shah
Thomas Rathbun
Scott Lloyd
Graduate School of Management
Kent State University
Kent, Ohio 44242 USA

ABSTRACT

At the Graduate School of Management at KSU, a research effort is underway to achieve a synergistic set of goals which will contribute to an effective simulation-based system for management support. This paper reports on the stages of progress of these parallel research efforts and their implication for future use in management support.

METHODOLOGICAL DEMANDS

Simulation shares with all other programming technologies the characteristic of being dependent on the construction and implementation of code applied to a specific problem domain, which obviously requires the time and skills of someone expert in that technology, i.e., a simulationist. However, after a long process of study and development, even when the simulation model is constructed and made available, there remain a number of difficulties which stand in the way of an easy access to modeling for daily decision support. These include validation, experimentation, output interpretation, public domain knowledge, and domain expertise.

The result is that the dependence of the decision maker on a professional simulationist does not end with the act of receiving the finished model. Output interpretation from model experimentation requires a special expertise, with respect both to the need for multiple runs and random number control and also the type of statistical output parameters produced by a simulation. Experimentation also requires expertise in simulation methodology in more than one way. Selecting parameters as dependent and independent, specifying simulation length, number of iterations, statistical controls, and finally, altering the model code may all be required.

It is an open issue whether validation is more important to simulation models than it is to their deterministic counterparts. In any case, in the simulation profession, an established practitioner sense of responsibility requires us to pay careful attention to statistical and face validity measures.

Concerns over domain expertise are extremely important to simulation precisely because simulation models permit such high degrees of operational, tactical and strategic realism. Strategic models are found in abundance in the realm of military modeling. With the RAMP modeling activity at Rand, highly complex and realistic models which operate on all 3 levels of management activity are given extensive meaning through the inclusion of expert systems content which puts artificial copies of expert competitor behavior in the game. Concerns over public domain knowledge are surely shared by other forms of modeling. However, the fact that simulation models tend to be much less burdened with deterministic assumptions and other theoretically imposed constraints usually leads to a much wider demand for domain knowledge in model construction and configuration.

EFFORTS AT COMPUTER SUPPORTED MODELING

Based on these and similar concerns, simulationists have been working over the past few years to link models with expert systems (ES) and other artificial intelligence (AI) software, in order to provide technological support to users of models. In its broadest scope, this effort has aimed at delineation and progress toward an automated modeling environment. Many more narrowly focused efforts have also gone forward, toward providing automated output analysis, automated advice on statistical procedures, natural language interface, and simulations embedded in object oriented code. More imposing projects have involved environments in which additional human expertise can be captured by the software complex in order to enhance the effectiveness of knowledge bases driving the simulation. In general, the concept of intelligent simulations and automated modeling environments has captured a great deal of attention.

With few exceptions, these new efforts have not focused specifically on management support. It is also true that the impressive work done in this new area linking simulation and ES/AI has tended to involve very complex programming outside of traditional simulation languages and very labor-intensive and hardware-intensive installations. Furthermore, while there is clear aspiration for a general automated modeling environment, thus far all the progress appears to have been made on very localized fronts. Finally, where progress is made in support of simulation through linkage with ES/AI technology, we go from an old difficulty to a new one, inasmuch as knowledge engineering is difficult, often limited in results, and often productive of results which do not adapt well to rapidly changing real world domains.

NEW RESEARCH STRATEGIES

All of these considerations have led several colleagues at the Graduate School of Management at Kent State University to pursue some parallel research efforts aimed at having simulation models which are accessible for automated daily decision support.

There are a few parallel research strategies here, each with its own prototype project or projects, but usually sharing programming technology.

1. Hypertext is being used as the basis for a code generator which, on one hand, enables us to retain the built-in strengths of a traditional simulation language such as GPSS/H and, on the other hand, captures a tutorial approach and context-sensitive help of hypermedia variety. Such a tool can be used by decision maker and professional simulationist alike. Without our becoming involved in object oriented coding, this approach enables us to select modules of generic code, modify these, and reuse them for model modification or construction of new models.

2. Experimentation is being done with use of neural nets for the capture of expertise, as an alternative to the difficult and time-consuming task of hand crafting knowledge bases. It turns out that simulation modeling and neural nets have several tendencies to lend each other a special sort of synergistic support. One such synergy is in the use of a simulation model to provide training sets for the neural net. Where the data and domain knowledge is already sufficiently available for construction of and experimentation with a realistic and valid model, then domain expertise can be captured by having the model provide a fairly large number of scenario results, in place of having to gather data from an equally large number of experiments with the real world system.

3. Related to strategy 2 but in a different direction, research is being conducted with embedded trained neural nets in simulation models. This is a situation where the net learns which experimentation strategies were successful under a variety of problem scenarios. The result is that the net will then select very good strategies for other scenarios which it has not seen. Since a feed-forward portion of a neural net is a set of formulas, these can be written in simulation code as well as in any other programming language. In fact, a language such as GPSS/H appears particularly well-suited for this purpose, through the modeling entities of the MATRIX and the SPLIT and ASSEMBLE blocks. The result is an automation of discovering a particular configuration for a model which will amply satisfy the decision maker's performance standards.

4. Building on the techniques of strategy 3, simulation models may also be able to incorporate a neural net training procedure, such as the feed-forward, back-propagation method. Once again, we are required to produce some appropriate code and use a modeling strategy. The value of this development is the potential achievement of a completely self-contained, self-educating model. Once data about the domain is gathered in some way, randomly generated experiments can produce a number of optimal results representing effective strategies for the real world system. An experimental result is saved only when it meets the appropriate criteria. The next phase is further randomization in order to effect the training of the embedded neural net. Again, stopping and saving criteria are based on input standards of system performance. Ultimately the model will have trained itself to produce high-performance strategies for new problem scenarios. Ironically, it will no longer be necessary to run the model itself to get a recommendation, since the embedded neural net gives the answer

in real time. However, running the model under the selected parameter settings provides the rich detail of predictions about the real world system characteristic of traditional simulation.

5. Another strategy involves replacing the simulation model with a neural net. In principle this is another task in which we want a neural net to capture underlying patterns between inputs and outputs. Given specific configuration of certain key parameters and the underlying nature of probability distributions and event interactions of the modeled system, the simulation model produces a range of output results, rather than one specific result. Teaching these related sets of inputs and outputs to a neural net should enable the researcher to replace the entire simulation model with a trained net. One result would be attainment of the elusive quality of real time performance for complex simulations, even for simulations which require very long run times.

6. As of this date, the overall list of strategies being pursued is completed with the description of one additional approach. Domain knowledge for the simulation model can be constructed through neural computation. An example is expert behavior in the domain to be simulated. Capturing complex expert behavior in rule based technology is both very difficult and usually doomed to incompleteness. However, it is plausible that submitting a set of input/output scenarios to a neural net for training will produce a set of mathematically derived relations which can be used to generate activity patterns within the simulation model. The converse of strategy 2, this approach requires accurate and ample data from the real world system. Once this data is acquired, we can proceed rapidly to imitate expert patterns of behavior for the domain to be modeled, without having to develop a complex set of rules and specify these in code. Rather, configuration of action parameters in the model will be dictated by the trained net, from configurations of scenario parameters input by the decision maker.

An ultimate objective of this research is to make available to the user an integrated, complete system of developed components. A diagram of such an integrated system is shown in figure 1.

A hypermedia product can provide an overall interface which links software and files as needed, and steps the user and the software through the exact task sequence required. The anticipated result is a self-contained system, constructed in a comparatively non-complicated sort of programming approach, which achieves the objectives widely sought in the simulation profession for a completely empowered automated modeling environment, including code generation.

REFERENCES.

1. O. Balci, "Requirements for Model Development Environments," Computers & Operations Research, 13 (1986), pp. 53-67.
2. P.K. Davis, "A New Analytic Technique for the Study of Deterrence, Escalation Control, and War Termination," Simulation, 50 (1988), pp. 195-202.
3. P.A. Luker & H.H. Adelsberger (eds.), Intelligent Simulation Environments, Society for Computer Simulation, 1986.

4. G. Madey & J. Weinroth, "Neural Networks and
General Purpose Simulation Theory," Proceedings of the
IJCNN, Jan. 1990.
5. T. Rathburn & J. Weinroth, "Desktop Simulation:
Modeling for Managers," Simulation (May 1991), in
press.
6. J. Weinroth,"Model-Based Decision Support and User
Modifiability," IEEE Transactions on Systems, Man, and
Cybernetics, 20 (1990), pp. 513-517.

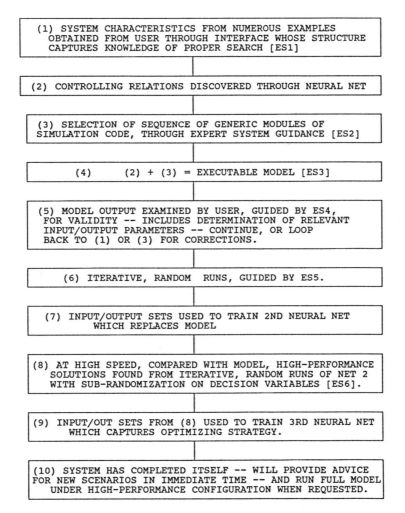

FIGURE 1. LONG RANGE DESIGN FOR AN INTEGRATED SYSTEM

SIMULATION IN
UTILITY MANAGEMENT
(AND MISCELLANEOUS)

SIMULATION OF PLANT RECORDS FOR THE DEPRECIATION OF INDUSTRIAL PROPERTY

Dr. Thomas A. Barta and Dr. Harold A. Cowles
Department of Industrial and Manufacturing Systems Engineering
Iowa State University
Ames, IA. 50011

ABSTRACT

Determination of the proper amount of depreciation expense is important to a regulated public utility because of the influence of depreciation on the level of allowed revenues and, hence, the rates for service provided. Simulation of the retirement experience to determine the proper amount of depreciation is accomplished by use of a set of generalized retirement dispersion models. The simulation model utilizes different survivor curves and determines the best curve based on a goodness of fit technique. One of these techniques compares simulated account balances with actual balances for a set of test years. The model that has the minimum sum of squared differences simulates the account activity best.

INTRODUCTION

Rates are designed to generate sufficient revenue to cover all costs of production, including annual depreciation expense, plus a return on the undepreciated investment in production facilities, a function of accumulated depreciation.

Adequate and proper depreciation for a company is related to a number of factors, but most significant are the life forecasts made for each class of property. Life forecasts are usually accomplished by evaluating and modifying as needed the results of life analysis studies made on relevant property retirement data. In many instances, these studies are similar to those conducted by life insurance actuaries in their quest for indications of human mortality trends.

Unfortunately, accounting records sometimes are not of actuarial quality and do not provide the ages of property items at retirement, a requisite of the data for an actuarial-type study. The lack of a proper age means the date of installation is not known and thus neither is the proper price to assign to the retirement. In these cases, the unknown age-related retirement data is generated by simulation and life indications are determined in the process.

SIMULATION AND LIFE ANALYSIS

The term simulation has been defined in many different ways but the following seem to be the most appropriate for the purposes of the present paper.

"Simulation is the process of designing a model of a real system and conducting experiments with this model for the purpose either of understanding the behavior of the system or of evaluating various strategies for the operation of the system." (Shannon 1975).

119

"Computer simulation is the process of designing a mathematical-logical model of a real system and experimenting with this model on a computer." (Pritsker 1986).

It is recognized that the familiar life analysis process of analyzing property retirement data and representing the resulting life indications with a survivor curve is exactly the procedure described in the above definitions. The model is the survivor curve and the system is the property record-keeping process which in turn represents the retirement activity of the property itself.

The selection of the appropriate model to represent the system is critical to obtaining satisfactory results, obviously. The selection can vary depending upon the models adopted and the type of data available. This paper concerns itself with the selection process utilized with unaged retirement data. The two approaches to be considered are both known as Simulated Plant-Record (SPR) techniques. Specifically they are the balances and the period retirements methods.

THE SYSTEM TO BE MODELED

The activity which is to be simulated is the retirement behavior of the various property categories involved in a firm's activities. Because of the complexity of these properties as well as the requirements of the uniform system of accounts, it is not possible to work with the retirement of the items of property themselves. Rather, the retirement activity reported in the property accounting systems which records the investment in these properties is analyzed to give the desired behavior indications.

This indirect approach of analysis does introduce the possibility of some misleading information arising from any modeling process no matter how successful it is. The extent of this depends upon the precision with which the accounting records reflect actual property retirement experience.

Even with perfect modeling results this data problem could possibly lead to some minimal distortion but to an extent this is countered by the fact that the principal use of the life indications is in the development of depreciation accrual rates which are applied to dollar amounts from the property accounts and not to any count of the number of items of property in service. That is, the use of the life indications is consistent with their source.

It appears that records which permit the aging of retirements, and, hence, the correct pricing of the property retirement, will produce the most dependable indications. The retirement data extracted from this type of property record is termed actuarial.

Table 1 illustrates an array of actuarial data. Note that the account additions are given year by year as are the surviving balances for each of these vintage placements from the date of installation to the study date. The sum of the respective surviving vintage balances as of a date gives the account balance at that time. Total account retirements by year are accumulated similarly.

Table 1 Example of Aged or Actuarial Retirement Data

Account E656: Special Equipment, Placements and Retirements by Calendar Years

UPPER FIGURES: Plant remaining in service at end of the indicated calendar year
LOWER FIGURES: Plant retired during indicated calendar year

Year of Placement During Year	Plant Installed During Year	1977	1978	1979	1980	1981	1982	1983	1984	1985	1986	1987
1977	378	378	378	373	370	345	299	219	144	91	44	31
		0	0	5	3	25	46	80	75	53	47	13
1978	392		390	390	390	380	350	305	213	132	94	63
			2	0	0	10	30	45	92	81	38	31
1979	670			664	664	662	646	600	505	365	230	150
				6	0	2	16	46	95	140	135	80
1980	690				690	689	680	655	627	495	341	226
					0	1	9	25	28	132	154	115
1981	340					340	340	337	329	299	237	189
						0	0	3	8	30	62	48
1982	416						412	412	411	401	349	311
							4	0	1	10	52	38
1983	365							365	364	358	343	319
								0	1	6	15	24
1984	355								349	348	347	330
									6	1	1	17
1985	605									603	602	598
										2	1	4
1986	710										710	708
											0	2
1987	890											890
												0
TOTALS: In Service End of Yr		378	768	1427	2114	2416	2727	2893	2942	3092	3297	3815
Retired During Yr		0	2	11	3	38	105	199	306	455	505	372

121

In contrast, property record systems are frequently utilized which do not permit the aging and thus the correct pricing of retirements. In these cases, much of the information available in the actuarial format is lost. Table 2 (transparency) illustrates, relatively, the missing information if the property activity summarized in Table 1 had been kept in this less precise manner.

Table 2 illustrates the property accounting system which is to be modeled by the Simulated Plant-Record life analysis techniques. Note that it consists of a chronological listing of annual gross additions, annual account balance and annual retirements.

SURVIVOR CURVES

The mathematical expression that is needed to form the basis of the simulation model is one that relates age to the portion of plant surviving. Figure 1 (transparency) shows the graphical representation of such an expression. As indicated, this plot is of a survivor curve and it shows for any age what portion of an original placement remains in service.

If discrete values from the mathematical expression or from the plot are tabulated, a life table is produced. The first two columns of Table 3 (transparency) illustrate this format. Since life table values indicate the portion remaining in service at any age, the difference between successive life table values must indicate the portion of the original placement which was retired over the age interval involved. Column 3 of Table 3 shows these retirement frequency percentages for this particular model. Since a model of this nature can predict the ages at which retirements will occur, it is frequently termed a retirement

dispersion or a retirement behavior pattern.

To illustrate the use of this model assume that additions costing in total $21,800 were installed in 1981. To find the investment remaining in service as of December 31, 1987, according to the model, the investment must first be aged. Most property accounting systems utilize the so-called half-year convention. That is, property activity, installation or retirement, is assumed to take place at mid-year.

Therefore, the $21,800 is assumed all to be installed as of July 1, 1981. The age of surviving investment as of December 31, 1981, would be one-half, one and one-half at December 31, 1982, and on December 31, 1987, it would be six and one-half years. The life table of the model indicates 76.9 percent of the original investment will be remaining in service as of age six and one-half, or in terms of dollars for the investment, ($21,800) (0.769) = $16,764. This and similarly calculated amounts are found in Column 5 of Table 3. The column amounts to a life history of the $21,800 investment as simulated by the assumed survivor curve model.

To find the number of dollars of the investment retired during the year 1986, that is the 4 1/2 - 5 1/2 age interval, $21,800 is multiplied by 6.1%, the difference between the percent surviving at age 4 1/2 and at age 5 1/2. This and other calculations of this type are illustrated in Column 6 of Table 3.

AVERAGE SERVICE LIFE

The average service life of a particular dispersion pattern is simply the weighted average of the possible lives. Since the assumption has been made that retirement activity takes place at mid-year,

122

retirement is assumed to take place at the middle of the age interval, that is at age 2 for the 1 1/2 - 2 1/2 interval, age 3 for the 2 1/2 - 3 1/2 interval, etc.

In the case of the model illustrated in Figure 1 and in Table 3, the lives range from 1/4 year to 13 years. If each life is weighted by the portion of the placement anticipated to be retired at that age, the average service life can be found by dividing the sum of the %-age products by the sum of the weights, or

Average Service Life = Sum of Col. 4/
        Sum of Col. 3
        = 800.0/100.0
        = 8.0 years

Since the entries in column 4 of Table 3 amount to areas of horizontal strips under the survivor curve of Figure 1, the summing of column 4 amounts to finding an estimate of the area under the survivor curve, or

Average Service Life = Area Under
        Survivor Curve/100%

This expression is perhaps a more familiar one for calculating an estimate of Average Service Life.

GENERALIZED SURVIVOR CURVE MODELS

By varying only the scale of the age axis, related survivor curves can be obtained. The curves are alike, relatively, in all respects except for the average service life. By doubling the age scale, for example, average service life would be doubled.

If the dispersion pattern model is plotted or tabulated for a 100 year average service life, the resulting age scale is the same as though age is expressed as a percent of average service life. This particular version of the model is known as a generalized survivor curve. It is useful because all other average service life versions can be obtained from it by simply converting the age of the desired life curve to a percent of the average service life and then interpolating for the corresponding percent surviving values from the generalized curve or life table.

IOWA TYPE SURVIVOR CURVES

The Iowa type curves are a set of generalized retirement dispersion models. These curves were developed on the basis of analyses of actual retirement experience and represent typical retirement behavior patterns likely to be encountered. When originally presented the Iowa system consisted of 18 type curves. However, research and industrial practice has increased the number to 31.

Most applications of the SPR life analysis technique incorporate the Iowa type curve system to provide a range of possible life dispersion models. The Iowa system has been adopted for the demonstration in this paper.

THE SIMULATED PLANT RECORD METHOD (SPR)

The ease with which to select an appropriate survivor curve to represent the retirement behavior of an account, as well as the confidence placed in that choice, is much greater in the case of actuarial data than with unaged retirements. (Cowles 1988).

However, as noted earlier, this paper is concerned only with the modeling of unaged data.

The analysis process utilized by the SPR methods is one which expands the data as shown in Table 2 to the extent needed so that they appear as the data in Table 1. The behavior of each vintage investment through time, of course, is unknown with the unaged data. To accomplish the expansion the basic assumption is made that all vintages behave alike with respect to the retirement dispersion pattern.

This is a fairly restrictive and somewhat unrealistic constraint to impose upon the modeling process. However, it is usually justified because of the procedural complications which would result from a less restrictive assumption. Also, since the objective is a model representative of the composite behavior of the entire account, the constant behavior assumption may not be that bad, provided it can be shown that the model does a reasonable job in duplicating actual recorded account retirement activity.

The two most common selection criteria make use of the notion of "goodness of fit" based on minimum sum of squared differences. In the balances approach the simulated account balances are compared with actual account balances for a set of test years and each year's difference is squared to remove the effect of positive or negative differences. These squared differences are summed and are tested against comparable sums generated by other models. By definition that model which has the minimum sum of squared differences simulates the account activity best.

In the second SPR approach, the period retirements method, the ranking criterion is based upon the sum of the differences between the simulated annual retirements and the corresponding actual account retirements for a period of years. Again the model which produces a minimum sum of squared differences is by definition the most representative.

It is important to note here that these two criteria are based on different measures yet both are used to select an appropriate model to represent the retirement activity in the account category. It is not unexpected then that inconsistent indications are frequently encountered in using the two SPR methods on the same account's retirement data and that considerable judgement needs to be exercised in attempting to evaluate them.

THE SIMULATION PROCEDURE

The SPR balances method attempts to duplicate the annual balances of a plant account by distributing the actual annual gross additions over time according to an assumed mortality distribution. To be specific, the units (or dollars) remaining in service at any date are estimated by multiplying each year's additions by the successive proportion surviving at each age as given by the assumed mortality distribution. For a given year, therefore, the accumulation of survivors from all vintages is an estimate of the actual plant balance for that year. This process is repeated for different mortality distributions until a pattern is found which produces a series of "simulated" balances most nearly duplicating the set of actual plant balances experienced by the account over a test period of years. Generally, this determination is based on the distribution producing the minimum sum of squared differences between the simulated balances and the actual balances. (White 1971).

In the balances approach a number of end-of-year (or beginning-of-year) dates are chosen on which the simulated balances will be checked against balances the account actually had obtained on those dates. These dates may be four or five in chronological order or they may form a sequence of every other year for, say, 10 years, or every third year, etc. The number and patterns are decisions for the analyst, chosen to develop the most realistic evidences of retirement behavior.

When the period retirements method is used a representative period of time is usually specified. Retirements are then simulated for each year in the period. A preliminary study may first be done comparing just the sum of all retirements simulated with the total actually reported over the full test period.

To illustrate the simulation process, assume SPR studies are to be made on the data in Table 2. The balances method test dates are chosen to be the end of year balances for 1985, 1986, and 1987. An R_3 Iowa type survivor curve with an 8-year average service life will be the simulation model used.

Table 4 (transparency) summarizes the necessary calculations. Columns 1 and 2 give the age in percent surviving data for an R_3-8 curve. Column 3 identifies the Table 2 vintages which will be at the age shown in Column 1 as of December 31, 1985. Column 4 gives the initial investment of the respective vintages and Column 5 is the simulated survivors as of the end of 1985, the product of Column 2 and Column 4. Columns 6, 7 and 8 accomplish the same thing for the December 31, 1986, test date and Columns 9, 10, and 11 generate December 31, 1987, simulated survivors.

Simulated values in Columns 5, 8 and 11 are comparable to the actual surviving amounts shown in the columns of Table 1 headed by 1985, 1986 and 1987. The sum of the surviving balances of Column 5 is the simulated plant account balance for December 31, 1985, using an R_3-8 curve as the model. Similarly, the sums of Column 8 and 11 give simulated balances for December 31, 1986 and December 31, 1987.

The period retirements approach can be illustrated by assuming the period over which retirements are to be compared is made up of the years 1986 and 1987. A chart similar to Table 4 could be prepared to calculate the simulated retirements. Column 2 would have to be changed to show retirement frequencies rather than percent surviving.

However, the computer is aware of the basic accounting equation:

Annual retirements = account beginning balance - account ending balance + additions.

Thus, no further simulation is needed. Simulated retirements are found as follows:

1986 Annual Retirements=3556-3919+710
$$= 347$$
1987 Annual Retirements=3919-4375+890
$$= 434$$

From Table 2 it is seen that the actual number of retirements recorded for 1986 was 505 and 372 for 1987. The sum of squared differences then is $(347-505)^2 + (434-372)^2 = 28,808$.

RANKING PROCESS

The model considers each of the possible survivor curves, e.g., all 31 of the Iowa type survivor curves, and adjusts the average service lives for each by first 10% increments and then 1% increments to find the life combination with each type curve which produces the minimum sum of squared differences. This is done in the case of either the balances or the period retirements approach.

A printout is then produced giving the rank of the 31 models (Iowa type curve and average service life), the one with the least sum of squares listed first. In some cases, when the period retirements approach is used, the sum of squares results for average service lives from 3 to 99 years for each Iowa type is reported.

INTERPRETATION OF THE RESULTS

The SPR results represent outcomes of analyses on retirement history only. They do not indicate proper life estimates for whole life or remaining life depreciation purposes. These lives must be forecast by judgement from, among other factors, the historical results and future expectation.

Each of the 31 "winners" in an SPR study represent the best service life estimate for the respective survivor curve type to match the specified balances or retirements. Thus, all are possible choices in the judgmental selection of what best represents the subject retirement experience to date. However, because of the likelihood of at least some relationship between the matching of a balance as done in an SPR analysis and the more correct but impossible to accomplish matching of the vintages making up that balance, it seems safe to say that the choice probably should come from the top half or third of the outcomes as ranked by the Index of Variation. Thus it is seen that the analyst must exercise judgment at two distinct steps in arriving at an estimate of life. She must first select which service life and curve type best represents the past retirement

experience of the account and then she must combine that with her estimate of future factors to produce her final forecast of the whole life of the account.

Tables 5 and 6 (transparencies) indicate the results obtained by submitting the data in Table 2 to the computer for analysis. Table 5 gives the results of the balances method and Table 6 the period retirements approach. The rankings and model selections noted in Table 6 were obtained by the two-step selection process.

REFERENCES

Cowles, H. A. 1988. "Computation Procedure for the Simulated Plant-Record Methods by Life Analysis." A.G.A. Depreciation Committee and E.E.I. Depreciation Accounting Committee Conference, San Diego, CA.

Pritsker, A. A. B. 1986. "Introduction to Simulation and SLAMII." John Wiley & Sons, New York, N.Y.

Shannon, Robert E. 1975. "Systems Simulation the Art and Science." Prentice-Hall, Englewood Cliffs, N.J.

White, R. E. 1971. "The Simulated Plant-Record Method of Life Analysis." Regulatory Information Systems Conference, St. Louis, MO.

Drive-up Banking:
A Simulation of Protocols and Service

Robert S. Roberts and R. Wayne Headrick
Business Computer Systems
New Mexico State University
Las Cruces, NM 88003-0001

ABSTRACT

This paper focuses on simulating the operations of a drive-up bank. As the queuing system of a drive-up banking operation has both unique constraints and uncommon flexibilities, it represents a particularly interesting system to model and study. The paper investigates several rules for selecting the next customer to be served in a multi-server, multi-queue service system, where there are two servers (tellers), but four queues and service positions (customer drive-up lines). The study's emphasis on the implications of the various customer selection rules on system efficiency and customer fairness. Although the selection rule did not significantly affect system throughput, it was shown to have an impact on the customer's time in system, as well as the level of fairness (measured by the degree to which service varied from first-come, first-served).

INTRODUCTION

The post office and the bank are classic examples of queueing systems. A few years ago, USPS post offices adopted the convention of having multiple servers work on jobs arriving through a single first-come, first-served (FCFS) queue. This queueing system is often modeled using the M/M/k model. Many banks have also adopted this queueing discipline for customers of their inside teller operations. This classic multi-server, single-queue system is efficient and popular for several reasons. It has the desirable attributes of being fair (FCFS), it utilizes each server to the maximum extent possible, it avoids having a customer getting 'stuck' behind the occasional long job, and line jumping is avoided simply because there is only one queue.

Unfortunately, physical constraints often preclude the use of the multi-server, single-queue system. For example, it is usually considered to be impractical in the grocery store checkout line situation. It is also seldom considered for use in the popular drive-up banking operation. Instead, drive-up banking customers are usually presented with a choice of waiting lines, each with its own server station. Although

this would appear to constitute a typical multi-server, multi-queue environment, the drive-up banking operation has some unique operational constraints and flexibilities that cause it to be quite different. The most important difference between it and the multi-server, multi-queue system is that it is not necessary for a single server (teller) to be assigned to each queue. Because servers are typically connected to the customer service stations via a system of microphones, speakers, and pneumatic tubes, a great variety of server-to-queue assignment rules are possible. For instance, drive-up bank facilities often allow each of the tellers to serve a customer at any of the service stations (see Figure 1). Another possible scenario is one in which each serves the customers in a particular set of queues. Of course, many other server assignment/customer selection rules are possible.

This paper presents the results of a series of simulation experiments that explore several server assignment/customer selection scenarios under a wide range of system loading conditions. The merits of the various scenarios are evaluated on the basis of both efficiency and fairness, concerns of the bank and its customers alike.

THE MODEL

As noted above, the thrust of this study is simulating the operations of a small drive-up bank to evaluate the performance of several server assignment/customer selection scenarios at different levels of system loading. Figure 1 shows a diagram of a small drive-up bank teller operations in which the entrance is located to one side, and four service stations and their queues are available to arriving customers. The drive-up bank houses two tellers who each have the capability to provide service to all four queues. If it is assumed that arriving customers are unaware of the server assignment/customer selection rule in use, it can also be assumed that they will enter the shortest available queue. If there is not a unique shortest queue, they will randomly choose one of the qualifying queues. Of course, it is assumed that a teller can

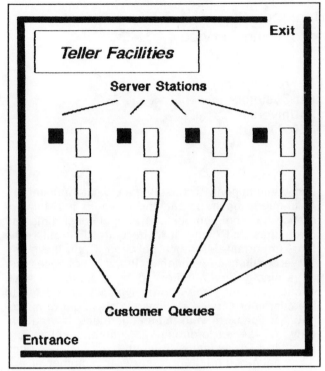

Figure 1. Drive-In Bank Schematic

provide service to only one customer at a time; and only one customer from a queue can be served at a time.

The four server assignment/customer selection scenarios included in this study are:

- CYCLE - The server assignment for this scenario is *both tellers serve all four customer queues,* and the customer selection rule is *cyclical.*

- CYCLE/2 - The server assignment rule is *one teller serves two customer queues and the other teller serves the other two queues.* The customer selection rule is *cyclical within assigned queues.*

- FCFS - The server assignment for this scenario is *both tellers serve all four customer queues,* and the customer selection rule is *first-come, first-served of the customers at the front of the queues.*

- LONGNXT - The server assignment rule is *both tellers serve all four customer queues.* The customer selection rule is *serve the customer at the front of the longest queue next, with random selection from among non-unique longest queues.*

Because customer interarrival time is one of the variables in this study, it was assumed to be exponentially distributed, with four different means ($1/\lambda$) to provide for the four levels of system loading. To inject as much reality as possible into the study, data on actual customer service times was collected at a local drive-up bank and used to develop the service time distribution subsequently incorporated into the simulation model. The resultant distribution is illustrated in Figure 2.

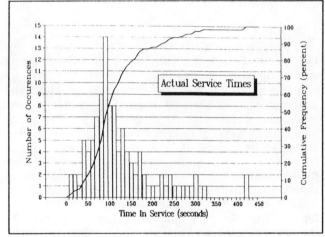

Figure 2. Actual Service Time Distribution

Although the queueing system being studied is not an M/M/k system (Taylor 1982), it can be argued that as the system's utilization ratio ($\lambda/k\mu$) increases to the point where the average number of customers in the system (L) is as least as great as the number of queues, the M/M/k steady state equations can give reasonable estimates of the relationship between L and $1/\lambda$ for the system being studied. Figure 3 depicts this relationship where the exponentially distributed service time has a mean ($1/\mu$) equal to 120.3 seconds and the number of servers (k) is equal to 2.

Using the curve provided in Figure 3, four values of $1/\lambda$ (77.05, 64.03, 62.06, 61.10) were chosen for use in the study because they are associated with L values of 4, 16, 32 and 64. The four levels of system loading represented by these values of $1/\lambda$ are subsequently referred to as light, moderate, heavy and very heavy.

THE EXPERIMENT

To compare and contrast the performance and fairness of the four different drive-up banking server assignment/customer selection scenarios detailed above, four simulation models were developed and exercised under four different levels of system loading. The measure of system performance selected for use was the average time a customer spends in the system (W). System fairness was measured by

128

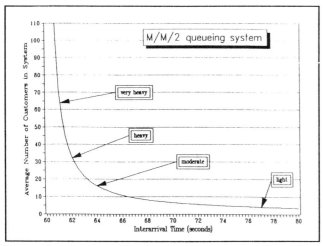

Figure 3. Average Number in System vs. Interarrival Time

the degree to which customers are served in the order of their arrival in the system (S).

The SIMAN language (Hoover and Perry 1989) was used to develop simulation models of the various system scenarios and loadings. The 16 combinations of scenarios and loadings were subsequently run through 10 simulations of 20,000 time units (seconds) each to generate the data needed to evaluate the scenarios. Because each of the 10 runs was accomplished using a different random number stream, it was possible to test the hypotheses that there are no significant differences in system performance or fairness using the paired observations t-test (Shannon 1975).

PROGRAMMING THE MODELS

At first glance, the SIMAN simulation language appears to be ideal for use in programming our simple simulation model. A close approximation of the basic model of the drive-up bank can be quickly constructed using SIMAN blocks (see Figure 4). The QPICK block and the shortest number in queue (SNQ) queue selection rule (QSR) are used to send the entering entity (customer) to the shortest of the four queues. The PICKQ block is also used to choose the next customer to be served, with built-in QSRs easily accommodating both the cyclic (CYC) and longest queue (LNQ) customer selections. Of course, as an entity is selected for service, it moves from the queue to SEIZE a server and start a DELAY which corresponds to the service time. After service is completed, the teller is released to serve another customer.

As development of the detailed model progressed, it became apparent that there were some significant problems with the basic model that could not be

easily overcome. In languages like SIMAN and SLAM, the entry of an entity into service is accomplished with a QUEUE-SEIZE mechanism (Hoover and Perry 1989, Pritsker 1986, Pegden 1987). Unfortunately, this mechanism removes the entity from the queue and passes it on to the following DELAY block to simulate the time necessary for service. In the process of removing the entity from the queue, the number of entities in the queue is decremented. In many modeling situations this would be correct, but in a drive-up banking operation, the model is not quite realistic. In a drive-up bank, the customer appears to be in the queue until service is completed and he drives away. Although this is not a major problem, it would affect the assignment of customer to queues because the model sends arriving customers to the shortest queue. As entering customers visually include all customers in the system (even those in service) in their shortest queue selection process, this pattern of customer behavior must be correctly modeled. A second, related problem is that when a customer is selected, and removed from the queue, it is possible for another server to select the next customer to be served from the same queue before the previous customer has completed service. This is, of course, not physically possible in the drive-up banking operation.

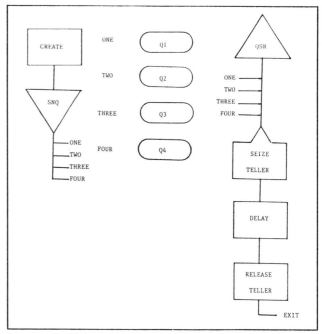

Figure 4. Basic SIMAN block model of the drive-up bank.

As there were no simple fixes that could make the original model acceptable, it had to be totally rewritten, making it significantly longer and more complex (see Figure 5). As part of the rewrite, FORTRAN subroutines to determine the next queue to serve for each of the four scenarios were incorporated into the model. This new model accurately represents the drive-up bank, with the queue length including the service position (the queue length only changes at the end of service), and no more than one customer in a queue being able to be served at the same time. The EVENT block in the revised model is a FORTRAN subroutine called whenever there is an arrival or departure. When called, it checks to see if service can be started on another customer, and determines which queue should be served next. That information is then passed back to the SIMAN program.

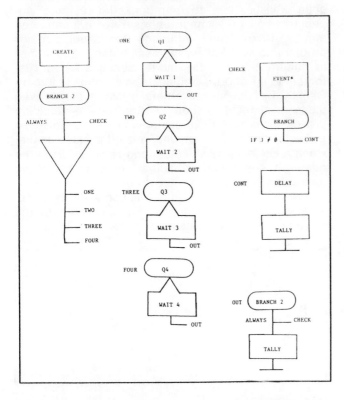

Figure 5. Representative SIMAN block model of the drive-up bank.

RESULTS

The model was set up to tabulate several performance measures, including the two measures of primary interest: average time in the system and average degree to which FCFS is achieved. The FCFS score (S), a sequence score designed to evaluate the degree to which customers were served in the order in which they arrived, is calculated as:

$$S = \frac{\sum_{i=1}^{N} |S_i - S_{i-1} - 1|}{N},$$

where S_i = system entry sequence number of the ith customer served,
$S_0 = 0$ and
N = total number of customer.

In other words, whenever a customer enters service in the correct sequence (relative to the previous customer), a zero is entered as that customer's **unfairness** score. As the service sequence of customers moves away from the correct sequence, the score will increase in increments of one.

Table I presents the results of the 10 simulation runs for each of the four server assignment/customer selection scenarios under light system loading; Table II, moderate loading; Table III, heavy loading; and Table IV, very heavy loading. W is, of course, the average time a customer is in the system, and S is the average degree to which FCFS is achieved. Table V presents the results of the tests of hypothesis that there are no significant differences in average time in the system among server assignment/customer selection scenarios for the various levels of system loading. Table VI presents the results of similar tests of hypothesis related to the degree to which the server assignment/customer selection scenarios achieve FCFS.

An analysis of the results presented in Table V indicates that the average time a customer is in the system under the server assignment/customer selection scenario known as CYCLE/2 is significantly greater than that found under the other three scenarios, regardless of which level of system loading was in use. As the CYCLE/2 scenario assigns a teller to each of the two sets of two customer queues and doesn't allow an idle teller to help the other, busy teller, this result is not entirely unexpected. Similarly, Table V indicates that, in general, there are no significant differences among the average times in the system for the CYCLE, FCFS and LONGNXT scenarios, all of which allow both tellers to serve all four customer queues. These results are illustrated in Figure 6. In addition, Figure 6 clearly illustrates a result that is intuitively obvious, that under any particular server assignment/customer selection scenario, the time a customer expects to remain in the system increases as the loading on the system increases. Even though few significant differences were found in the average time customers were in the system under the CYCLE, FCFS and LONGNXT scenarios, there were manor differences in the **fairness** of those scenarios as measured by S. In fact, there were significant differences in the average degree to which FCFS was achieved between all four server assignment/customer selection scenarios across all but one of the four levels of system loading (reference Table VI). As illustrated by Figure 7, FCFS is the fairest of the four scenarios, with LONGNXT being the least fair. It is particularly interesting to note that the fairness level of FCFS remains essentially unchanged as the system loading goes from light to very heavy. The level of fairness of the LONGNXT scenario, on the other hand, is quite adversely impacted by increased system loading.

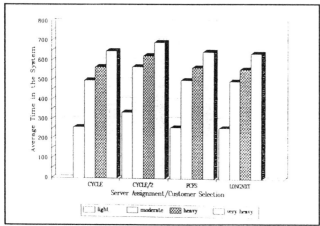

Figure 6. Average Time in System by Scenario/Loading

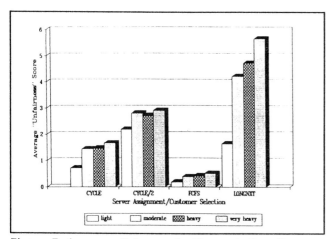

Figure 7. Average Fairness by Scenario/Loading

CONCLUSIONS

The primary purpose of this effort was to investigate the relative efficiencies and fairness levels of various drive-up banking server assignment/customer selection scenarios under a number of system loading levels. Toward that end, models of the selected scenarios were written in the SIMAN simulation language, the models were exercised, and the results were analyzed. As noted above, statistical analysis of the simulation results shows that the efficiency levels, measured in terms of average time a customer is in the system, of all three scenarios that allow all tellers to service all customer queues are essentially all equal.

Analysis of the **fairness** of the various scenarios, measured by the degree to which FCFS is achieved, revealed significant differences among all four server assignment/customer selection scenarios. The FCFS scenario was by far the fairest of all, with

a customer having a greater likelihood of being served in order under the heaviest system loading than that same customer would have with any other scenario under even light loading.

Since the FCFS scenario is significantly fairer than the others, and it is not significantly less efficient, it is obvious that it should be the server assignment/customer selection scenario of choice. There is, however, one major impediment to its implementation, it is not a trivial task to determine which of the customers at the front of the queues was the first to enter the system. Unlike customers in a walk-in environment, drive-up customers cannot easily be provided with sequential identification. Unless this limitation can be overcome, the second most fair scenario (CYCLE) must be considered as the best choice for implementation.

The second purpose of this study was to explore the ability of a readily available simulation language such as SIMAN to correctly model a system such as a drive-up bank. As noted earlier, the situation in which an entity is in service, but is also still considered to be in the queue by other entities entering the queue, is not easily modeled using the normal functionalities of SIMAN. Because the beginning of service for an entity normally causes the number of entities in the queue to be decremented, and the number of entities in the queue affects the queue selection of arriving entities, the normal functioning of SIMAN must be modified to accurately reflect the situation being modeled.

This research is presently being expanded in several directions. Other performance and fairness measures are being explored in detail. The use of animated simulation models to help better understand the dynamics of more complex server assignment/customer selection scenarios is being evaluated. Of course, other server assignment/customer selection scenarios are being developed and evaluated. Current efforts are also underway to collect additional information on the distribution of service times for several local drive-up banking situations.

REFERENCES

Hoover, S.V. and R.F. Perry. 1989. *Simulation - A Problem-Solving Approach.* Addison-Wesley Publishing Company, Reading, MA.

Pegden, C.D. 1987. *Introduction to SIMAN.* Systems Modeling Corporation, State College, PA.

Pritsker, A.A.B. 1986. *Introduction to Simulation and SLAM II.* Halsted Press, New York.

Shannon, R.E. 1975. *Systems Simulation - The Art and Science.* Prentice-Hall, Inc., Englewood Cliffs, NJ.

Taylor, B.W. 1982. *Introduction to Management Science.* Wm. C. Brown Company, Dubuque, IA.

TABLE I

Light Loading Simulation Results

Simulation Run	Server Assignment/Customer Selection Scenario							
	CYCLE		CYCLE/2		FCFS		LONGNXT	
	W	S	W	S	W	S	W	S
1	181.10	0.441	265.42	1.847	180.68	0.076	180.68	0.873
2	626.49	1.656	671.08	3.119	626.24	0.430	626.17	5.199
3	197.59	0.723	268.84	1.823	197.93	0.125	197.59	1.107
4	162.11	0.245	234.72	1.984	161.71	0.049	161.71	0.555
5	256.74	0.912	327.07	2.192	256.74	0.199	257.07	1.787
6	339.12	0.881	400.34	2.209	339.56	0.336	339.19	2.433
7	241.57	0.579	328.61	2.333	241.80	0.301	241.66	1.331
8	236.57	0.812	346.23	2.348	238.52	0.165	235.43	1.444
9	169.81	0.354	234.76	1.933	170.91	0.110	169.81	0.748
10	186.45	0.413	280.47	1.858	186.47	0.050	186.55	0.818

TABLE II

Moderate Loading Simulation Results

Simulation Run	Server Assignment/Customer Selection Scenario							
	CYCLE		CYCLE/2		FCFS		LONGNXT	
	W	S	W	S	W	S	W	S
1	330.91	1.251	420.87	2.398	331.77	0.286	326.18	2.544
2	812.10	1.687	824.80	3.102	812.10	0.458	811.16	6.898
3	266.45	1.195	344.09	2.703	263.32	0.239	263.39	2.267
4	475.94	1.312	540.75	2.840	471.10	0.457	469.50	3.880
5	541.78	1.457	595.81	2.454	541.78	0.377	537.41	4.785
6	765.27	1.698	848.63	3.472	765.87	0.464	757.43	6.218
7	393.15	1.371	489.53	2.555	400.23	0.334	394.15	3.291
8	258.62	0.983	341.44	2.603	258.62	0.245	258.43	1.929
9	337.30	1.446	422.24	2.556	379.01	0.409	377.48	2.911
10	805.38	1.926	877.58	3.267	798.69	0.588	794.89	7.256

TABLE III

Heavy Loading Simulation Results

Simulation Run	Server Assignment/Customer Selection Scenario							
	CYCLE		CYCLE/2		FCFS		LONGNXT	
	W	S	W	S	W	S	W	S
1	394.62	1.502	486.11	2.352	394.75	0.454	391.45	3.142
2	835.53	1.780	926.22	3.320	835.73	0.654	833.02	7.511
3	313.59	1.212	373.25	2.545	306.98	0.437	304.64	2.431
4	511.75	1.269	572.53	2.839	511.72	0.415	511.35	4.771
5	626.82	1.356	705.33	2.808	626.82	0.360	626.33	5.126
6	1193.38	2.039	1193.79	3.093	1192.82	0.600	1156.34	9.439
7	313.08	1.252	371.45	2.252	313.84	0.268	313.02	2.422
8	300.64	1.182	363.02	2.314	301.55	0.293	298.35	2.128
9	351.79	1.251	425.11	2.421	351.87	0.309	350.32	2.794
10	850.57	1.663	868.93	3.091	850.57	0.333	836.11	7.314

TABLE IV

Very Heavy Loading Simulation Results

Simulation Run	Server Assignment/Customer Selection Scenario							
	CYCLE		CYCLE/2		FCFS		LONGNXT	
	W	S	W	S	W	S	W	S
1	433.49	1.623	514.71	2.108	433.19	0.407	425.85	3.222
2	922.24	2.006	954.78	2.976	923.39	0.695	920.90	8.168
3	325.60	1.252	417.97	2.907	324.59	0.284	323.12	2.551
4	562.62	1.318	608.92	2.938	561.16	0.495	561.73	5.171
5	718.01	1.416	757.88	2.750	718.25	0.540	711.12	5.686
6	1416.81	2.483	1395.85	4.475	1417.26	0.749	1392.61	13.851
7	325.49	1.462	404.70	2.325	325.40	0.327	325.08	2.615
8	410.97	1.289	472.88	2.565	411.43	0.269	409.27	3.452
9	491.98	1.772	529.88	2.755	493.13	0.563	484.60	4.114
10	900.84	1.858	902.58	3.224	901.80	0.800	889.55	7.610

TABLE V

Average Time in System Comparisons

Hypothesis	Level of System Loading$_a$			
	Light	Moderate	Heavy	Very Heavy
CYCLE = CYCLE/2	reject	reject	reject	reject
CYCLE = FCFS	-	-	-	-
CYCLE = LONGNXT	-	-	-	reject
CYCLE/2 = FCFS	reject	reject	reject	reject
CYCLE/2 = LONGNXT	reject	reject	reject	reject
FCFS = LONGNXT	-	reject	-	reject

Note: a - table entries indicate whether the hypotheses were rejected at the $\alpha = 0.05$ level.

TABLE VI

Average degree to Which FCFS is Achieved Comparisons

Hypothesis	Level of System Loading$_a$			
	Light	Moderate	Heavy	Very Heavy
CYCLE = CYCLE/2	reject	reject	reject	reject
CYCLE = FCFS	reject	reject	reject	reject
CYCLE = LONGNXT	reject	reject	reject	reject
CYCLE/2 = FCFS	reject	reject	reject	reject
CYCLE/2 = LONGNXT	-	reject	reject	reject
FCFS = LONGNXT	reject	reject	reject	reject

Note: a - table entries indicate whether the hypotheses were rejected at the $\alpha = 0.05$ level.

SIMULATION IN
FINANCIAL PLANNING

WARRANTY COST ESTIMATION WITH WARRANTY EXECUTION FUNCTION: A SIMULATION APPROACH

Dr. Keith A. Klafehn and
Dr. Jayprakash G. Patankar
The Department of Management
The University of Akron
Akron, OH   44325-4801

ABSTRACT

The purpose of this paper is to incorporate a warranty execution function in a warranty cost estimation problem. A consumer may not exercise the warranty if the cost of doing so exceeds the benefit derived. Two types of warranty execution functions are considered. One is based on the cost of exercising the warranty and the other is a function of time. Two types of rebate plans: a linear pro rata and a combination of a linear pro rata and a lump sum rebate plan are compared. The effect of warranty execution on warranty costs is studied. If the management judges that the warranty execution may be less than perfect, the warranty cost incurred should be appropriately estimated using warranty execution function.

INTRODUCTION

The innovation in consumer products continues to expand each day with consumer products becoming more and more complex. Consequently, the average consumer is unable to adequately determine or judge the quality of the product he or she is buying. To alleviate this uncertainty in the minds of consumers, manufacturers are offering some kind of warranty with their products at the time of sale. The Magnuson-Moss Warranty Act of 1975 also mandates that manufacturers must offer warranty for all consumer products sold for more than fifteen dollars. The warranty statement assures consumers that the product will perform its function to their satisfaction up to a given amount of time (i.e., warranty period) from the date of purchase. Manufacturers are offering many different warranties to promote their products. Thus, warranties have become a significant promotional tool for manufacturers. Warranties also limit the manufacturer's liability in the case of product failure beyond the warranty period.

Although warranties are used by manufacturers as a competitive strategy to boost their market share, profitability, image, etc., they are by no means inexpensive. Warranties cost manufacturers a substantial amount of money. The cost of a warranty program must be estimated precisely, and its effect on a firm's profitability must be studied. Warranty programs must be revised from time to time to meet consumers' needs and the firm's profit goal and to compete with competitors' warranty programs.

Warranties also serve another very important function for the manufacturer. Warranty claims provide an important feed back on the quality of the product itself. Top management in many corporations meet routinely to assess the warranty claims. This valuable information reveals where the product is not conforming to its design and purpose. This information may be used to improve the product design, which may lead to improved product quality.

Various authors have studied the warranty cost estimation problem. (Menke, 1969) estimated warranty cost for nonrepairable products using linear prorate and lump sum rebate plans. (Amato and Anderson, 1976) extended Menke's research by incorporating present value analysis in their warranty cost estimation. (Lowerre, 1968) developed a formulation of the warranty reserve model for repairable products. His model assumed that a selected percentage of revenue is used to meet warranty claims. Expected repair cost for the consumer over the life of the product was considered by (Heschel, 1971). (Patankar and Worm, 1981) developed prediction intervals for warranty reserves and cash flows associated with selected warranty policies. (Blischke and Scheuer, 1981) applied renewal theory to estimate warranty cost for free replacement and pro rata rebate policies under selected failure distribution functions. (Mamer, 1981, 1987) estimated short run total costs and long run average costs of products under warranty. Mamer also studied pro rata and free-replacement warranty policies under different failure distributions. He showed that the expected warranty cost depends on the mean of the product lifetime distribution and its failure rate. Mamer extended his previous research with present value analysis and analyzed the tradeoff between warranty and quality control. (Balachandran et al., 1981) used a Markovian approach to estimate repair and replacement costs of a warranty program. The warranty cost attributable to a given accounting period is discussed with the model. Warranty cost problems were studied by (Mitra and Patankar, 1988) through a goal programming approach where multiple goals were considered. (Frees and Nam, 1988) found expressions for expected warranty costs under free-replacement and pro rata policies in terms of distribution functions. (Patankar and Mitra, 1989) used a goal programming model to determine the price, warranty time, and production quantity of the product in the context of satisfying multiple objectives. The goals included minimization of warranty reserve cost per unit, offering of a minimum level of warranty time based on an allowable proportion of failures within a warranty period, and achieving a minimum proportion of market share. (Patankar and Mitra, 1989) also developed a multi-objective model for warranty cost problems in a multi-product environment. Interrelationships among different products have been incorporated in this study. (Blacer and Sahin, 1986) used renewal process to estimate warranty cost under pro rata and free-replacement warranty policies. (Frees, 1988) showed that estimating warranty cost is similar to estimating renewal functions in the renewal theory. He also estimated the variability of the warranty costs using parametric and non-parametric estimators.

(Udell and Anderson, 1968) concluded that warranties serve as a promotional as well as a protectional marketing tool. (Wiener, 1985) conducted an empirical study and concluded that warranties accurately predict product quality. (Shimp and Bearden, 1982) studied the effect of warranty quality, warranty reputation, and price on the consumer's perception of financial and performance risks.

MODEL FORMULATION

The purpose of this paper is to incorporate the warranty execution function in a warranty cost estimation problem. A consumer may not elect to exercise the warranty for various reasons. If the cost of exercising a warranty exceeds the benefit derived, then there is no incentive to exercise that warranty. Sometimes consumers may decide to switch brands due to dissatisfaction with the product. Sometimes consumers may forget to exercise a warranty during the warranty period.

In this paper we have looked at two types of warranty execution functions. One is based on the cost of exercising the warranty. If the cost ($X) of exercising the warranty exceeds the benefit received ($Y), then it is assumed that the consumer will not exercise the warranty. So this function takes the form of 0-1 warranty execution function. That is,

$$g_1(t) = \begin{array}{ll} 1 & \text{if } x \geq y \\ 0 & \text{if } x < y \end{array}$$

where $g_1(t)$ is the probability of warranty execution at time of failure.

The second form of the warranty execution function is defined as follows:

$$g_2(t) = \begin{array}{ll} 1 & \text{if } t \leq w_1 \\ 1 - \dfrac{t-w_1}{w-w_1} & w_1 < t \leq w \end{array}$$

Here a consumer will exercise warranty up to time w_1. From time w_1 to warranty period w, the probability of warranty execution will be less than one and will be estimated by the function given. At time w, the probability of warranty execution is zero since no benefit will be received at time w.

Two forms of rebates are considered. One is a linear pro rata rebate plan given by

$$r_1(t) = C \left(1 - \frac{t}{w} \right) \qquad 0 \leq t \leq w$$

where C is the unit price, t is the time of failure, and w is the warranty period. The other rebate plan offers a full refund up to time w_1, and then linearly pro rata rebate from time w_1 to w and is given by

$$r_2(t) = \begin{array}{ll} C & t \leq w_1 \\ C\left[1 - \dfrac{t-w_1}{w-w_1} \right] & w_1 \leq t \leq w \end{array}$$

We will call this rebate plan the "modified rebate plan".

The parameters of the simulation model are as follows. A unit price of ten dollars and a warranty period of five years are assumed. For the rebate function $r_1(t)$, the rebate will start at $10 and decrease to zero at the end of the warranty period. For the rebate function $r_2(t)$, a full rebate of $10 will be given up to two and one half years, and then the rebate will decrease linearly from $10 to $0 during the later two and one half years. The product failure time, t, is assumed to follow an exponential probability distribution with a mean of ten years.

For simplicity, the warranty period is divided into sixty months. Five different cases of the warranty execution function $g_1(t)$ are considered, i.e., full warranty execution and if rebate exceeds either $1, $2, $3, or $4. Similarly, five different

$g_2(t)$ are considered, i.e., full warranty and warranty execution fully up to either 10 months, 20 months, 30 months, or 40 months.

The simulation model was developed using General Purpose Simulation System (GPSS) Language and utilized GPSS/PC[TM] software to run on a personal computer. The model is an extension of the work done by (Patankar and Klafehn, 1988). Each simulation run depicted an analysis of 5000 units and was replicated ten times for each of the specified parameters indicated above. The results from each series of runs were averaged to provide the information that is noted below.

RESULTS:

Table 1 shows the total warranty costs for the linear rebate plan and the modified rebate plan. If we assume that there will be full warranty execution, then a warranty cost of $10875 will be incurred under the linear rebate plan. The same cost will be $15557 under the proposed rebate plan, an increase of 43%. If we assume that the customer will exercise the warranty if the rebate exceeds $1, then the warranty costs are $10362 and $15346 under the linear rebate plan and the modified rebate plan, respectively. This translates into an increase of 48%. For cases where warranty is executed fully if the rebate exceeds $2, $3, or $4, the percentage increases are 48.6%, 56%, and 62%, respectively. This shows that if fewer people exercise warranty, then the modified rebate plan is relatively more expensive than the linear rebate plan.

We also find that for a linear pro rate rebate plan, there is a 19.4% increase in warranty cost if we assume that all customers will execute warranty versus the situation where only those will execute the warranty where the rebate exceeds $4. The increase for the modified rebate plan is only 5.2% for similar situations. This indicates the modified rebate plan is not as sensitive to the warranty execution function $g_1(t)$ considered for the above discussion.

The second form of warranty execution function $g_2(t)$ assumes that customers will execute warranty with probability of one up to time period w_1 and then this probability will decrease linearly to zero at time w, the warranty period. Table 2 shows the warranty costs for the linear prorated rebate plan and the modified rebate plan for selected values of w_1. If $w_1 = w$, then we assume full warranty execution. The costs are $10875 and $15557 under linear pro rata and the modified rebate plan, respectively, as indicated before. If we assume that there will be

a full warranty execution up to 10 months and then a linearly decreasing probability as defined by function $g_2(t)$, the warranty costs are $8280 and $11351 under the linear pro rata and the modified rebate plan, respectively. This shows that the proposed rebate plan is 37% more expensive. If we consider cases where w_1 = 20, 30, or 40 months, then Table 2 shows the modified rebate plan is 39.5%, 43.2%, and 46% more expensive than the linear pro rata rebate plan, respectively.

We find that for a linear pro rata plan, the full execution is 31% more expensive than a case where warranty execution is full for 10 months. The modified rebate plan, full warranty execution, is 37% more expensive than a case where warranty is executed with a probability of one up to 10 months. We note that the difference in the linear pro rata plan and the proposed rebate plan is not as significant for this form of warranty execution ($g_2(t)$).

CONCLUSION:

This paper has added the concept of the warranty execution aspect to the determination of warranty costs. Linear pro rata and the modified rebate plans are compared. Two types of warranty execution functions are explored. The warranty execution function defined on the basis of dollar amount, $g_1(t)$, influences warranty costs under the two rebate plans quite substantially. The warranty execution function, $g_2(t)$, based on w_1 ad w, also shows the differences in warranty costs between the two rebate plans. The percentage increase within a plan from w_1 = 10 months to full execution is about the same for both plans. If management judges that the warranty execution may be less than perfect, the warranty cost incurred should be appropriately estimated using warranty execution functions.

Table 1

Dollars	Linear Pro-Rata Rebate Plan	The Proposed Rebate Plan
X*		
0	$ 10875	$ 15557
1	$ 10362	$ 15346
2	$ 10231	$ 15204
3	$ 9720	$ 15120
4	$ 9107	$ 14785

*Warranty is not executed if the rebate is less than X dollars.

Table 2

w_1* (month)	Linear Pro-rata Rebate Plan	The Proposed Rebate Plan
10	$ 8280	$ 11351
20	$ 9088	$ 12685
30	$ 9781	$ 14006
40	$ 10104	$ 14747
60	$ 10875	$ 15557

* Warranty is executed with a probability of one to w_1 months. The probability of execution decreases linearly to zero at the end of the warranty period (w = 60 months).

REFERENCES

Amato, H. H., & Anderson, E. E. 1976. "Determination of Warranty Reserves: An Extension." *Management Science*, 22 (12), 1391-1394.

Balachandran, K. R., Maschmeyer, R. A., & Livingstone, J. O. 1981. "Product warranty period: A Markovian approach to estimation and analysis of reair and replacement costs." *The Accounting Review*, 56(1), 115-124.

Blacer, Y., & Sahin, I. 1986. "Replacement Costs Under Warranty: Cost Moments and Time Variability." *Operations Research*, 34(4), 554-559.

Blischke, W. R., & Scheuer, E. M. 1981. "Applications of Renewal Theory in Analysis of the Free-replacement Warranty." *Naval Research Logistics Quarterly*, 28,193-205.

Frees, E. W. 1988. "Estimating the cost of a warranty." *Journal of Business & Economic Statistics*, 6(1), 79-86.

Frees, E. W., & Nam, S. H. 1988. "Approximating expected warranty cost." *Management Science*, 43(12) 1441-1449.

Heschel, M. S. 1971 "How Much Is a Guarantee Worth?" *Industrial Engineering*, 3(5), 14-15.

Lowerre, J. M. 1968. "On Warranties." *Journal of Industrial Engineering*, 19(3), 359-360.

Mamer, J. W. 1982. "Cost Analysis of Pro Rata and Free-replacement Warranties. *Naval Research Logistic Quarterly*, 29(2) 345-356.

Mamer, J. W. 1987. "Discounted and Per Unit Costs of Product Warranty." *Management Science*, 33(7), 916-930.

Menke, W. W. 1969. "Determination of Warranty Reserves." *Management Science*, 15(10), 542-549.

Mitra, A., & Patankar, J. G. 1988. "Warranty cost estimation: A goal programming approach." *Decision Sciences*, 19(2), 409-423.

Patankar J.G. and K.A. Klafehn. 1988. "Warranty Cost Estimation Using Stimulation." *Proceedings , Winter Simulation Conference*, San Deigo, CA. Dec. 12-14, 857-859.

Patankar, J. G., & Mitra A. 1989. "A Multiobjective Model for Warranty Cost Estimation Using Multiple Products." *Computers and Operations Research* 16(4), 341-351.

Patankar, J. G. & Mitra, A. 1989. "A Warranty Cost Estimation and Production Problem Using Multiple Objectives." *Journal of Cost Analysis*, Vol. 8, Fall, pp. 55-70.

Patankar, J. G., & Worm, G. H. 1981. "Prediction Intervals for Warranty Reserves and Cash Flows." *Management Science*, 27(2), 237-241.

Shimp, T. A., & Bearden, W. O. 1982. "Warranty and Other Extrinsic Cue Effects on Consumers' Risk Perceptions." *Journal of Consumer Research*, 9, 38-46.

Udell, J. G., & Anderson, E. E. 1968. "The Product Warranty as an Element of Competitive Strategy." *Journal of Marketing*, 32, 1-8.

Wiener, J. L. 1985. "Are Warranties Accurate Signals of Product Liability?" *Journal of Consumer Research*, 12, 245-250.

BIOGRAPHIES

KEITH A. KLAFEHN is a Professor of Management and Health Care Systems in the College of Business Administration at The University of Akron, in Akron, Ohio. He also serves as the editor of The Akron Business and Economic Review. He received a B.S. in Industrial Distribution and an M.S. in Industrial Management from Clarkson University in 1961 and 1968 respectively, and the DBA from Kent State University in 1973. Dr. Klafehn's research interests include the building of simulation models for health care administrative purposes, for industrial product flows, for evaluating critical paths, for evaluating warranty plans, for observing systems operations, and the like. Dr. Klafehn has published in Hospital Topics, Journal of Nursing Administration, Operations Management

<u>Review</u>, and other journals. Dr. Klafehn is a member of the Decision Sciences Institute, The Institute of Management Sciences, The Academy of Management, and The Society for Computer Simulation.

JAYPRAKASH G. PATANKAR is Professor of Management at The University of Akron. He received an undergraduate degree in Textile Technology from the University of Bombay, Bombay, India. Dr. Patankar received an M.S. in Textile Science and a Ph.D. in Management Science from Clemson University, Clemson, South Carolina. He has published in <u>Management Science</u>, <u>Decision Sciences</u>, <u>European Journal of Operational Research</u>, <u>Computers and Operations Research</u>, <u>Journal of Cost Analysis</u>, <u>Socio Economic Planning Sciences</u>, <u>Tax Adviser</u>, <u>Akron Tax Journal</u>, and other journals. Dr. Patankar is a member of The Institute of Management Sciences and the Decision Sciences Institute.

SERTS OPERATING ENVIRONMENT (SOE): A CASE IN INTEGRATING PROJECT MANAGERS AND COMPLEX BUSINESS-ORIENTED SIMULATION MODELS

James W. Richardson, Peter T. Zimmel, Daniel R. Sechrist, and Clair J. Nixon
Texas Agricultural Experiment Station and Departments of Agricultural Economics, and Accounting
Texas A&M University
College Station, Texas 77843

ABSTRACT

The development of inexpensive, high speed microcomputers offers the potential for moderate size companies to take advantage of simulation models. The number of generalized, complex simulation models capable of simulating many different facets of a business has grown, however, their widespread adoption among small and moderate size companies has not kept pace. One of the reasons cited for the slow rate of adoption is the need for user-friendly data base managers. It is our hypothesis that in addition to the obvious data problem, the major reason for the slow rate of adoption is the veil of mystery created by simulation and the extensive use of input and output files. SOE (SERTS Operating Environment) was created to overcome these problems.

SOE is a user-friendly, intelligent, menu-driven operating environment that allows managers and developers to interface easily with complex Monte Carlo simulation models. SOE allows users to: input an extensive data set that is column and row specific, manage multiple data files with a limited amount of DOS expertise, examine the stochastic output in a condensed form, and accomplishes all of this in a user-friendly environment. The intricacies of SOE and SERTS are discussed in this paper.

Simulation has been used, for the past three decades, by consultants and managers to analyze the consequences of alternative decisions in both business and government. Numerous examples of simulation models developed to analyze the consequences of management decisions on the profitability of a business exist, e.g., Anderson 1974; Naylor 1971; Affleck-Graves and McDonald 1989; Baer and Ingersoll 1990; Conger 1988; Schuyler 1990; Richardson and Nixon 1986; Cochran, et al. 1990; Nixon, et al. 1990; and Bailey and Richardson 1985. In the 1960s, only a handful of companies used simulation models but, by 1970, over 100 companies had adopted simulation models as analytical tools. In 1979, the number of companies using simulation models had exceeded 2,000, and it is estimated that virtually every major company and organization currently uses simulation in one form or another (Moser 1986).

Early simulation models were developed to address a single problem (e.g., McKenny 1962) while complex models capable of simulating a wide variety of business problems were developed and used in the 1980s (e.g., Cochran, et al. 1990; Richardson and Nixon 1986; and Baer and Ingersoll 1990). Complex models which simulate many different facets of a company can be used to both train managers and to evaluate the probable consequences of management's actions. Once a model is validated to the satisfaction of management, it can be made even more useful by incorporating risk (Cochran, et al. 1990, Richardson and Nixon 1986). Incorporating production and marketing risk into a business model greatly expands the usefulness of the results but at the expense of increasing the model's data requirements, the complexity of the results, and the task of running a Monte Carlo simulation model. These problems increase exponentially the more detailed (or complex) the simulation model. The extensive demand for data and problems associated with using complex Monte Carlo simulation models threatens to move business simulation models back to the era of single purpose models that are unable to cope with complex intricacies of management problems in the 1990s.

Data base management systems have been suggested as a means of coping with the increased complexity of data required for simulation models (Richardson, et al. 1990; O'Keefe 1986; Kerckhoffs and Vansteenkiste 1986). Simple data base managers are not adequate for handling and pre-processing complex data requirements. Artificial intelligence (AI) assisted data base systems, however, can provide management a user-friendly tool to process data required for a complex simulation model, by creating an interactive environment for the user. This environment not only allows the user to create a data set, but has an added feature which allows data processing and display. However, the author's experience with two complex business simulation models, SERTS (Small Business Economic, Risk and Tax Simulator) and FLIPSIM (General Farm Level Income and Policy Simulator), has proven that an intelligent data base manager is not sufficient to gain use by business managers.

To bridge the gap between simulation model application and management, complete operating systems for the simulation model are required. An intelligent operating system for SERTS, which includes an AI augmented data base manager, report writers, and supporting computer software, has been developed to bridge the gap between the model and management. The purpose of this paper is to describe the SERTS Operating Environment (SOE) in sufficient detail so it can be used as a prototype for developing user interfaces for complex business simulation models.

The remainder of this paper is separated into three sections. The next section provides a brief description of SERTS to give the reader a flavor for the model. The subsequent section includes a detailed description of SOE. The final section provides a brief summary.

DESCRIPTION OF SERTS

The Small Business Economic Risk and Tax Simulator is a firm level, recursive, simulation model which simulates the annual production, marketing, financial, management, growth, and income tax aspects of a business over a multiple-year planning horizon (1-10 years). The model is designed to be used to quantify the effects of

alternative management strategies and economic policies on the economic viability (probabilities of survival, economic success, and increasing real net worth) of a business. The model recursively simulates a business by using the ending financial position for year 1 as the beginning financial position for the second year, and so on. Risk associated with production and marketing of the firm's output is incorporated by drawing annual prices and outputs (yields) at random from a multi-variable empirical (MVE) probability distribution for these variables.

A schematic diagram of the SERTS model is provided in Figure 1 to demonstrate its complexity. The model is sufficiently general to simulate a sole proprietor or partnership business which produces up to 10 different products or services (enterprises) that are dependent or independent of each other. At the outset of each year, SERTS determines how much of each product will be produced based on the analyst's business plan. These planned output levels are used as means to develop stochastic values for actual output; stochastic realizations of prices for products are based on the analyst's projections of their means, and the MVE probability distributions. Annual variable costs and fixed costs are calculated based on initial values and projected rates of inflation for the factors of production (fuel, labor, utilities, raw inputs, etc.). Annual debt servicing expenses are calculated for long- and intermediate-term debts assuming constant payments using the remaining balance formula. Annual interest costs for operating loans are calculated assuming simple interest mortgages.

Each depreciable asset (machinery, equipment, buildings, etc.) is depreciated separately for income tax purposes. Options are available so the analyst can evaluate alternative depreciation methods, replacement schemes, and expensing options. Replacement of depreciable assets is calculated one item at a time based on the analyst's specified economic life for the asset. Income tax and depreciation provisions in effect for 1975-1989 are incorporated in the model so the manager can analyze the effects of different tax-depreciation laws on the business.

The market value of fixed assets and equipment is updated annually based on the analyst's projected rates of inflation for these assets. The value of land can increase while the value of buildings and equipment can decline at independent rates. Property taxes are calculated using a fixed tax rate (based on market value), the lagged market value of land, and the manager's assumed inflation rate for property taxes. Receipts for the individual enterprises are calculated annually using the stochastic values for output sold (output times the fraction sold) multiplied by stochastic prices. Inventories are valued for balance sheet purposes based on stochastic prices for the current year.

Income for the business (receipts less cash expenses) is summarized prior to calculating profits (income less depreciation allowance) available to the owner/operator (or partners). Annual cash flows are calculated based on net cash income plus other income (interest, royalties, etc.) less down payments for equipment replacement, principle payments, owner (partner) withdrawals, and income/self-employment taxes. If the business experiences a cash flow deficit, the deficit is financed by obtaining a mortgage on real estate or equipment. When insufficient equity exists to cover cash flow deficits or the firm's equity to asset ratio falls below the manager's threshold level, the business is declared insolvent. If the business has a cash surplus, the analyst can elect to apply excess cash to the remaining debt or carry a cash balance forward. Accrued federal and state income tax and self-employment taxes due in the next year are calculated based on the analyst's selected income tax provisions (1986 Tax Act or others), form of business, taxable income, and number of tax exemptions. (A corporate version of SERTS is under development.)

The market value balance sheet for the business is calculated at the end of the tax year. At the end of each year, the model updates the financial situation for the subsequent year by using year ending debts and assets as beginning values for the next year. At the end of the last year in the planning horizon, SERTS summarizes the simulated values for 100 key output variables (Figure 1). The multiple-year planning horizon is repeated 100 times (iterations) to insure a sufficiently large sample size to calculate statistics for the output variables. Statistics for the probability distributions of the 100 key output variables are calculated after the last iteration. The statistics are stored to disk for later retrieval and comparison to other scenarios.

Due to the complexity of SERTS and its predecessors (FLIPSIM and FLIPSIM V), it has not been used widely by business consultants and managers. The reasons have been: data requirements, complexity of the output, and extensive use of data files. To simulate a business with SERTS requires a large complicated data base with more than 5,000 values to describe the initial business, the economic projections, and the stochastic variables affecting the business. Output for a deterministic analysis of SERTS is straightforward (Income Statement, Balance Sheet, and Cash Flow Statement); however, for a stochastic analysis, the output is complex and comparison of alternative scenarios is not straightforward. Business managers tend to be overwhelmed by a model which uses numerous files to store the different types of simulated results and input data. A user-friendly, menu-driven Operating Environment for SERTS (SOE) was developed to overcome these and other problems.

SERTS OPERATING ENVIRONMENT (SOE)

The main objective of SOE was to bring a complex simulation model to a non-technical user. Several problems emerged when trying to do this. The first was how to allow the manager to input an extensive data set that is column and row specific. The second was managing multiple data files without the manager having to do this manually using DOS commands. The third problem was presenting the stochastic output to the manager in a condensed form. The final, and possibly most critical, problem was to make the system user friendly and easily accessible to users with limited DOS skills. The solution to these problems was SOE.

The first problem was to develop a data input system so the manager could easily develop an extensive column and row specific data set in ASCII format. This was done by developing a user-friendly, menu-driven data entry system named CARMS (Computer Assisted Records Management System). (See Richardson, et al. 1990, for an extensive description of CARMS.) CARMS prompts the user for the required data and then builds the data set using the manager's current data, economic projections for the planning horizon, and historical prices and outputs for the MVE probability distribution.

The second problem, managing multiple files for the analyst, was handled by keeping track of all input and output files in a text file accessed by SERTS and SOE (see PROJECT.PRO in Figure 5). This solution to the file handling problem allows one to easily add files as the system expands for additional applications.

The third problem, presenting the output to the manager in a condensed form, was handled using a FORTRAN program named TABLE. TABLE builds a summary report of stochastic analyses. TABLE develops a summary table from data in the direct access file generated by SERTS. The final problem, making the system user friendly and easily accessible for managers with limited DOS skills, was the most challenging. A commercially available window development package was used to develop menu driven screens for SOE. Selectable menus allow the manager to proceed through the system without knowing DOS and having to develop an indepth understanding of the data structures required for SERTS.

Programming Considerations

The SOE shell was written in C and all of the screens were built using the Windows for C® and Windows for Data C® function libraries. The operating environment centers around a main hub (Figure 2) which allows the manager to move the highlighted bar to the desired option and select it by pressing <ENTER>. SOE then leads the manager to one of three sub-hubs (Figures 3 and 4). Each sub-hub is like the main hub in that it gives the manager the option of selecting which function to perform next. Each option in a sub-hub performs a particular task in SOE. These tasks include such things as accessing a menu-driven, user input system (CARMS), running the SERTS

simulation model, building a summary output table, etc.

SOE keeps track of 22 data files using the text file PROJECT.PRO in Figure 5. This file contains the names and paths of all input and output files accessed by the programs in SOE (SERTS, TABLE, and UPDATE). The current location of the PROJECT.PRO file on the hard disk is determined by reading the FLIP.PRO file at the root directory.

The FLIP.PRO file is updated each time SOE is activated by the manager. SERTS can be accessed from any directory on the hard disk because SOE updates FLIP.PRO and, during installation, the location of all executable programs in SOE is placed in the Path statement of the autoexec.bat file. The SOE system will run on a MS-DOS based 80386 micro-computer with at least 4 meg of RAM, a math co-processor (80387 or Weitek), and a hard disk.

SOE Menus

The SOE menus center around a main hub that allows the manager to do one of three things: *Business Analysis Using SERTS*, *Summarize Results*, and *Update Economic Projections* (Figure 2). This main hub is the first screen that appears when the manager enters the system. F1 help screens are available to remind the manager what each option does and the order in which an analysis should proceed. Once an option is selected, the system moves to the relevant sub-hub. Upon exiting a sub-hub, the computer returns to the main hub. The manager once again is able to make a choice from the menu or exit SOE.

The Business Analysis Sub-Hub. To complete a business analysis using SERTS, the manager must go through several steps. The first step is to develop or update the data which describes assets, liabilities, production capacity, and costs of the business to be analyzed. Second, the manager must enter projected values for average annual market prices, annual rates of inflation, and annual interest rates over the period to be analyzed. Third, the manager must assemble this information into a SERTS input file and run the model using DOS commands. Once the model is run, the manager must preview the simulation results and either print all of the 30 plus pages of output or print selected output tables. Saving the input data set to a backup file prior to doing another scenario is something managers find useful.

The Business Analysis sub-hub (Figure 3) enables the manager to perform all of the tasks necessary to simulate a business without using DOS commands to merge and move files, to execute the model, and to print the results. The first option in the sub-hub, *Review and Modify Business Data via CARMS*, allows the manager to use a menu-driven, user input system to enter new data or modify an existing data set for the business. CARMS uses the same type of main hub and sub-hub menu system as SOE (Richardson, et al. 1990). Managers can easily move around in the menus to modify the necessary variables for the desired management strategy being analyzed. As the manager exits CARMS, a data set for SERTS is developed and stored in input file FLIP.INP.

The second option, *Review and Modify Business Data Via Brief®*, allows the user to edit the SERTS input file (FLIP.INP) using the text editor Brief®. Managers who master the data base taxonomy and wish to develop data for alternative scenarios more rapidly have learned to use the programmers/users manual with the editor. This option in the sub-hub is much faster than using the CARMS data base manager if the analyst is familiar with the data requirements of SERTS and is changing only one or two variables. The option is particularly useful for the developers. Brief® is a text editor sold by Solution Systems and must be purchased and installed on the hard disk prior to using this option on the sub-hub.

The third option, *Review Simulated Output*, allows the user to preview the output of a SERTS analysis. When this option is selected, the operating system calls the SERTS output file into the Brief® editor. By using the arrow keys, the manager can preview the simulated output. Brief® commands allow the manager to mark and print selected parts of the output file from this option of the sub-hub.

The fourth option, *Print Simulated Output*, prints the output from a SERTS analysis (FLIP.OUT). A sub-menu allows the manager to configure the printer if a laser printer is being used. The sub-menu sets the margins based on the number of years simulated (indent or not indent the left margin) and changes the printer to a compressed line printer mode.

The fifth option, *Copy Input Data to Backup File*, allows the user to copy the SERTS input file (FLIP.INP) to a backup location. A sub-menu allows the manager to name the backup file and asks if the backup should be stored on a floppy disk or the hard disk. This option is particularly useful if the manager is analyzing a series of alternative management decisions and wishes to maintain backups.

The final option, *Run SERTS*, causes SERTS to simulate the manager's input data stored in FLIP.INP. The SERTS model generates several output files that are useful to the manager and accessed through SOE. The simulated results (Income Statement, Balance Sheet, and Cash Flow Statement) are stored in FLIP.OUT and accessed through the third and fourth options of the sub-hub. A statistical summary of the 100 key output variables generated by a stochastic analysis are stored in FLIP.STA. A cumulative distribution of the business's net present value is stored in FLIP.NPV after a stochastic analysis. Several debug and intermediate result files are written by SERTS and are useful for diagnostic purposes.

Summarize Results Sub-Hub. The second option in the main hub brings the manager to the second sub-hub depicted in Figure 4. The purpose of this sub-hub is to assist the manager in developing final summary tables for stochastic scenarios using a FORTRAN program named TABLE. The first option in the sub-hub, *Select Variables and Scenarios for Summary Table*, leads the manager through the critical process of specifying the output variables and the scenarios to include in each summary table. The manager selects the desired output variables for the table (the stubs) using a '+' to select a variable and a '-' to unselect. The columns of a summary output table consist of different scenarios, so the manager is asked to enter the scenario identification number for the scenarios to include in each table. Additional options allow the manager to specify which statistics (mean, standard deviation, coefficient of variation, minimum, and maximum) should be printed and whether footnotes defining the output variables in the table should be printed. The information obtained from the manager is stored in the TABLE.INP file. The more frequently used output variables in the tables are: After Tax Net Present Value, Present Value of Ending Net Worth, Long and Intermediate Term Debt to Asset Ratio, Average Annual Cash Receipts, Average Annual Cash Expenses, Average Annual Net Cash Income, Average Annual Income Taxes, Probabilities of Survival, Economic Success, and Increasing Real Net Worth. The second option, *Preview Variable and Scenario Selection via Brief*, enables the manager to view and modify the TABLE input file (TABLE.INP) inside the Brief editor. This option is available for the experienced manager who has established which variables to include in the tables and wishes to change only the scenario identification numbers.

The third option, *Review Summary Table*, enables the user to preview the results of Table (TABLE.OUT). At this point, the manager can use the Brief editor to type the appropriate table titles and column headings for each of the scenarios. The final product is then ready for inclusion in reports and viewgraphs. The fourth option, *Print Summary Table*, prints the TABLE output file (TABLE.OUT).

The final option, *Build Summary Table*, constructs the summary tables. In this option, a FORTRAN program, TABLE, is run to generate the summary tables. TABLE reads from two data files. The first file, TABLE.INP, contains the list of key output variables and scenario identification numbers to be included in the summary tables. The second file, FLIP.STA, is a direct access file created by SERTS which contains the statistics of key output variables that summarize their results for stochastic analyses. TABLE creates an output file, TABLE.OUT, which contains the completed summary tables and a diagnostic file, TABLE.OT1.

Update Economic Projections. The process of updating annual prices, interest rates, and rates of inflation has been automated for SERTS by including this option. When the manager selects this option, SOE automatically updates the business data base (FLIP.INP) using the economic projections in MASS.POL.

SUMMARY

The development of inexpensive, high speed microcomputers offers the potential for small and moderate size companies to take advantage of simulation models for management training and analysis of management decisions. The number of generalized, complex simulation models capable of simulating many different facets of a business has grown, however, their widespread adoption among small and moderate size companies has not occurred. One of the reasons cited for the slow rate of adoption is the need for user-friendly data base managers to reduce the burden of data preparation and maintenance.

It is the hypothesis of the authors that in addition to the obvious data problem, the major reason for the slow rate of adoption is the veil of mystery created by the volumes of output generated by Monte Carlo simulation and the extensive use of input and output files. In many cases, managers must be well trained statisticians to utilize the results of a stochastic analysis and an expert in DOS to find the results after the simulator has finished its task. To bridge the gap between managers and complex simulation models, user-friendly operating environments must be developed and implemented.

The purpose of this paper was to describe the SERTS Operating Environment (SOE) in sufficient detail so that it can be used as a prototype for developing user-friendly operating environments for complex simulation models. The SERTS model is described briefly to provide background as to the complexity of the model. The primary screens used by SOE to assist managers in utilizing SERTS for business analysis and report preparation are described in detail. Programming considerations in developing SOE are detailed as well.

The results of using SOE have been very positive. The development scientists have adopted SOE in place of using the more direct DOS commands due to the increased accuracy and reduced fatigue. The time required to teach a manager how to use the SERTS system has been cut from a week to a few hours. As a result, more time can be spent teaching the new user what SERTS does, and how it can be used to address particular problems. Managers gain confidence in their abilities to use SERTS without direct supervision in about one-tenth as much time.

An added benefit is that SOE has greatly reduced the need for over the telephone diagnostics and has reduced the time necessary to diagnose problems over the telephone. Because users are not dealing directly with the files created by the SERTS system, they do not get overwhelmed by the number of files. This has allowed the developers to add useful diagnostic files that can be accessed while diagnosing problems.

Although SOE is not directly portable to other complex simulation models, it can serve as a prototype for developing user-friendly operating environments for complex simulation systems.

REFERENCES

Affleck-Graves, John, and Bill McDonald, 1989. "Nonnormalities and Tests of Asset Pricing Theories", *Journal of Finance*, vol. 44 (Sept.), pp. 889-908.

Anderson, Jock R., 1974. "Simulation: Methodology and Application in Agricultural Economics", *Review of Marketing and Agricultural Economics*, vol. 42, pp. 3-55.

Baer, Harold, and Gerald T. Ingersoll, 1990. "A Strategic Planning Model can Improve Management Decision making", *Pulp and Paper*, vol. 64 (Apr.), pp. 184-187.

Bailey, D. V., James W. Richardson, 1985. "Analysis of Selected Marketing Strategies: A Whole-Farm Simulation Approach", *American Journal of Agricultural Economics*, vol. 67, pp. 813-820.

Cochran, Mark J., James W. Richardson, and Clair J. Nixon, 1990. "Economic and Financial Simulation for Small Business: A Discussion of the Small Business Economic, Risk, and Tax Simulator", *Simulation*, vol. 54, no. 4, pp. 177-188.

Conger, James L., 1988. "Using Financial Tools for Nonfinancial Simulations", *Byte*, vol. 13 (Jan.), pp. 291-292.

Kerckhoffs, E.J.H, and G. C. Vansteenkiste, 1986. "The Impact of Advanced Information Processing on Simulation - An Illustrative Review", *Simulation*, vol. 46, no. 1, pp. 17-26.

McKenny, J. L., 1962. "An Evaluation of a Business Game in an MBA Curriculum", *Journal of Business*, vol. 35, pp. 278-286.

Moser, Jorge G., 1986. "Integration of Artificial Intelligence and Simulation in a Comprehensive Decision-Support System", *Simulation*, vol.47, no. 6, pp. 223-229.

Naylor, Thomas H., 1971. *Computer Simulation Experiments with Models of Economic Systems*, John Wiley and Sons, Inc., New York.

Nixon, Clair J., James W. Richardson, and Mark J. Cochran, 1990. "The Impact of Changing Tax Laws on Different-Sized Farming Operations", *Journal of Agricultural Taxation and Law*, Fall, pp. 268-277.

O'Keefe, Robert., 1986. "Simulation and Expert Systems - A Taxonomy and Some Examples", *Simulation*, vol 46, no. 1, pp. 10-16.

Richardson, James W., and Clair J. Nixon, 1986. "Description of FLIPSIM V: A General Firm Level Policy Simulation Model", Texas Agricultural Experiment Station Bulletin B-1528, College Station, Texas, July.

Richardson, James W., Peter T. Zimmel, Delton C. Gerloff, Mark J. Cochran, and Siew C. Goh, 1990. "CARMS: Computer-Assisted Records Management System for Expert Simulation Systems", *AI Applications*, vol. 4, no. 2, pp.85-93.

Schuyler, John R., 1990. "Using a Simulation Model to Plan Property Acquisitions: Evaluation vs Bid Practices", *Oil and Gas Journal*, vol. 88 (Jan. 8), pp. 78-81.

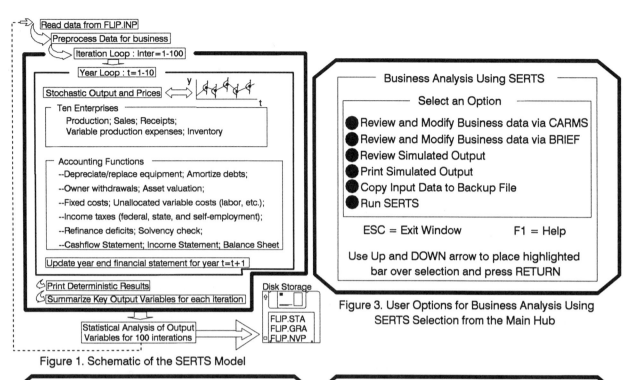

Figure 1. Schematic of the SERTS Model

Figure 3. User Options for Business Analysis Using SERTS Selection from the Main Hub

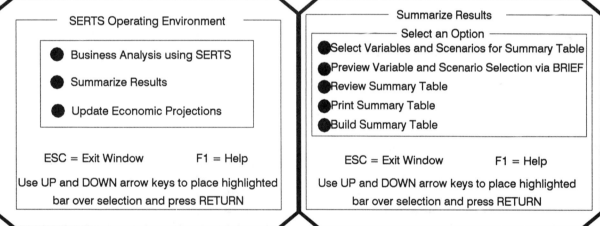

Figure 2. Main Hub of SERTS Operating System (SOE)

Figure 4. User Options for Summarize Results Selection from the Main Hub

D:\JR\FLIP.INP	D:\CS\NDATA\MASS.POL
D:\JR\FLIP.OUT	D:\CS\NDATA\MASS.ABV
D:\JR\FLIP.DBG	D:\CS\NDATA\MASS.DBG
D:\JR\FLIP.LP	D:\JR\MASS.OUT
D:\JR\FLIP.MAP	D:\CS\NDATA\MASS.DIA
D:\JR\FLIP.NPV	D:\JR\MASS.INP
D:\JR\FLIP.STA	D:\JR\FLIP.GRA
D:\CS\SUBNAM.DAT	D:\JR\GRAPH.INP
D:\JR\TABLE.INP	D:\JR\GRAPH.OUT
D:\CS\NDATA\TABLE.OT1	D:\CS\NDATA\MASTER.ABV
D:\JR\TABLE.OUT	D:\JR\UPDATE.OUT

Figure 5. List of Files Required by the SERTS Model and the SERTS Operating System

INTRODUCTION OF SIMULATION MODELING TO BANKING QUEUES IN OIL-RICH DEVELOPING COUNTRIES

Masood A. Badri
Department of Business Administration
United Arab Emirates University
P.O.Box 15990, Dubai, United Arab Emirates

ABSTRACT

A common phenomenon in Oil-Rich developing countries is the absence of waiting lines in banking services. For those banks which do appreciate the benefits of waiting lines, no models are available to study these systems. This study was motivated by bank management's concern with the need to access the current levels of customer services.

For the first time, simulation is introduced to banking services in Oil-Rich developing countries. Ninety four percent of the bank managers admitted their lack of knowledge about simulation modeling. For the managers that accepted to participate in the study, several lectures were given on simulation modeling. Moreover, the animation feature of SLAMSYSTEM removed a great deal of their fear of the unknown and enhanced their understanding of the models.

The developed models are of great benefit to bank service managers in helping to decide the required capacity of the service system. Given the forecasts of demand patterns, it is possible to evaluate various possible combinations of capacity and queue length.

The models can also help in developing decision rules for increasing and decreasing service acility capacity in the short term. In addition, it is possible to consider the alternative queue discipline policies and demand management policies that can be applied.

INTRODUCTION

Waiting lines are a common situation, and take different forms. In banking operations, managers recognize the tradeoff that must take place between the cost of providing good service and the cost of customer waiting time.

Managers want waiting lines short enough so that customers do not become unhappy and get frustrated with the banks service image - which might cause customers to terminate their dealings with these banks and go to other banks.

An understanding of the queue phenomenon is necessary before creative approaches to the management of banking service systems can be considered. An appreciation of the behavioral implications of keeping customers waiting reveals that the perception of waiting is often more important than the actual delay (Fitzsimmons and Sullivan 1982). An understanding of each feature of the system will provide and identify management options for improving consumer services.

Systems simulation helps answering "what if" type questions about existing or proposed banking systems. For example, what if another teller is added?, What if some tellers handle check cashing?. The response to these changes can be observed over an extended period by means of simulation without any changes in the real system.

SIMULATION MODELING

Many practical waiting line problems occur in service systems have characteristics that make them practical candidates for the application of queuing models. The most common case of queuing problems involves the Single-Channel, Single-Phase model. In this type of a system, it is often possible to assume that certain conditions exists.

For example, arrivals are independent of preceding arrivals, arrivals follow the Poisson probability distribution and come from an infinite source, units are served on a first come first serve basis, service rate is faster than arrival rate, service times are independent of one another, and they follow the negative exponential probability distribution.

Often, however, variations of this specific case are present. Service times for example tend to follow the normal distribution. Some services are based on other queue disciples. In other words, many real world applications are too complex to be modeled analytically. In these instances, analysts turn to computer simulation. Using simulation, many hours, days, or years of data can be developed by the computer in few seconds.

Computer simulation allows analysis of controllable factors, such as adding another service channel without actually doing so physically (Murdick et al. 1990). Moreover, several special purpose simulation languages have been developed that provide extensive modeling capabilities. Simulation models don't guarantee mathematically optimal solutions, but they can lead to more realistic, near-optimal solutions. In addition, simulation models are not limited to restrictive assumptions compared to mathematical models. Since many trials or experiments can be made with a computer, simulation can be used to expand or compress time. Finally, simulation may be less expensive and involve less risk than an actual experiment.

SIMULATION IN PRACTICE

A survey of Fortune 500 companies revealed that 176 of them used operations research techniques, and 73 respondents applied simulation in at least one area in the operations unctions (Ledbetter and Cox 1977). About 36 percent of firms used simulation in capacity scheduling. In a study which was motivated by managements concern of maintaining high levels of customer service, a waiting line model was used to examine teller staffing policies (Bennett and Melloy 1984).

PSYCHOLOGY OF WAITING IN BANKING

In waiting, one is forced to be idle to forego more productive or rewarding pastimes. Hence, even when consumers have nothing else to do, they detest delays. Many researchers have investigated waiting from the perspective of psychological punishment, ritual insult, and social interaction when waiting with others (Schwartz 1975).

Waiting is an anticipatory state. It is an activity where time appears to pass more slowly precisely because it is tentative. Banking usually is done in highly productive hours. As a result, it is a very challenging problem to use waiting time in a constructive manner. Moreover, waiting usually is performed standing up and not setting down which limits opportunities for innovative ways to eliminate boredom.

In waiting, consumer's desire

can be consummated only upon the initiative of the server. The sever, therefore, has power over the consumer, and waiting acts to reinforce the consumer's subordinate status. In banking, an apology is seldom provided by the server who keeps the customers waiting. The sensitive customer will promptly interpret this as an insult. Thus, the opportunity for banking service personnel to enlarge their egos at the expense of clients needs to be avoided.

Several approaches could be taken: training employees to be courteous and attentive, creating an organizational atmosphere that reinforces proper employee attitude, and avoiding the appearance of ignoring waiting consumers.

BANKING QUEUES AND EXPERIENCES FROM DEVELOPED COUNTRIES

Few businesses have taken more ard shots about bad management of lines than banks. In an interview with the New York Times, Mr.Mooney, senior vice president of Chemical Bank said "our research indicates that people don't like to spend time in bank branches, it is probably second in their disdain to waiting to see the dentist." To reduce lines, most banks have installed teller machines and tried to persuade employees to alter their check distribution, or to directly deposit payroll checks in the bank. The lines, however, persist. One way to take some of the sting out of waiting is to entertain customers.

Since 1959, the Manhattan Saving Bank has offered live entertainment during the frenzied noon time hours. In 13 branches, a pianist performs and one branch has an organ player. Occasionally, to make waiting lines even more wonderful, the bank has scheduled events

such as fancy-cat exhibit, a pureb-red dog show and a boat show.

BANKING QUEUES IN OIL-RICH DEVELOPING COUNTRIES

This study is performed in Dubai, a state considered by many experts to be the business center of the Middle East. Table 1 shows the numbers of local and foreign banks and their dealings with queues. About 56.7 percent of the banks don't have organized waiting lines, and only 27 percent of the local banks have some sort of queues, while about 66 percent of foreign banks do form queues.

Most of the foreign banks have centralized operations dictated to them by their headquarters in the United States or Europe. Local banks have more branches than do foreign banks. Local banks also carry the accounts of various governmental agencies which include monthly payroll. At the end of each month, these banks are seen very crowded with queues failing quickly. Most of the banks' managers, meanwhile, don't attempt to organize queues in these situations.

Banks that don't organize queues have either tried to force them once or twice or have never tried to do so. Their waiting line arrangement is shown in Figure 1. In these type of arrangements, most of the time the people in the line do respect the right of who ever they believe was present before them, but they would not mind being served first. On the other hand, sometimes human qualities such as nationality, strength, personal contacts with servers, and sex of the customer play an important role in who is served first.

For those banks that do form queues, most of the arrangements are Single Channel - Single Phase types. The sever provides all the required services but might require the help of another server for cashing purposes. Some banks utilize the arrangement of only one line forming in front of several servers that can perform all of the tasks. In addition, few banks have organized multiple-line arrangements, where the servers provide a limited set of services. These arrangements are shown in Figure 2.

THE STUDY

In spite of the importance of the study, only 8.7 percent of the banks accepted to participate. Two major national banks and three major foreign banks participated in the study. These banks had 25 branches altogether. Some of the reasons for not participating are cited here: 1) failure to accept responsibility; the top person in most banks asked one of his employees to talk to the researcher and these employees would not and could not accept responsibility, 2) lack of knowledge and understanding about simulation modeling, even though they were offered free lectures, 3) fear of the outcome; almost all bank authorities admitted that the study would reveal major shortcomings with regard to their systems. Moreover, most managers were not ready to try new alternatives even if they proved to be more efficient, 4) time and effort; few managers cited that such a study might consume lot of effort and time and their time would not allow it.

For those who accepted to participate, daily lectures on simulation modeling were given. The lectures were carried out by the researcher for one week and covered topics such as probability and statistics, simulation applications, network modeling, simulation languages, simulation support systems, random sampling from distributions, statistical aspects of simulation, and simulation animation.

THE MODELS DEVELOPED

To accommodate the various arrangements shown in Figure 2, four models were developed, tested, and implemented. The models replicated these systems in an effort to 1) evaluate various combinations of variables and policies, and 2) provide possible alternatives for future policies to the management of these banks based upon the results of the model's simulation.

SLAMSYSTEM was used to translate these models. It was chosen primarily because it is a comprehensive simulation language that offers total modeling flexibility.

DATA COLLECTION

All the banks that participated in the study cooperated to the fullest extent. Data for the various elements in the models were collected for one year. The probability distributions for the arrival and service rates were identified and tested.

VERIFICATION AND VALIDATION

The performance of the simulation models verified and validated. The verification task involved the use of the "TRACE" option provided by SLAMSYSTEM to determine that the translated models execute on the computer as the modeler intended.

The validation task consisted of determining that the simulation models were reasonable representations of the systems. The validations were performed on data inputs, model elements, subsystems, and interface points. In making these validation studies, the comparison yardsticks encompassed both past system outputs and experiential knowledge of system performance behavior.

EXPERIMENTAL CONDITIONS

For each policy, the following estimates were calculated using the models: 1) the time an entity spends in the system, 2) the number of entities that pass through the different subsystems, 3) the average utilization of the service activities, 4) the average length of each queue involved in the operations, and 5) the average waiting time in the queues.

The models considered variations in the number of channels, number of phases, queue disciplines, channel arrangements, service rates, and size of queues. Thus, the simulation models were designed to evaluate different variations in these variables only.

EXPERIMENTATION AND ANALYSIS OF RESULTS

In most of the experiments that were carried out, the files could not absorb the large number of entities (customers or jobs) that were lining up to demand service. For example, it was observed that in most cases, the service rates were too slow to catch up with the increased demand for services. In reality, most of the banks stayed open longer than the scheduled times. From a scientific point of view, some of the channel arrangements caused this kind of a break down in the systems (it was determined later that minor changes in these arrangements were only needed).

The One-Window Arrangement

In this type of an arrangement the server provided all the required services, except for check cashing which sometimes was carried out by another server. This system was applied only in the smaller branches. Because of the small business loads of these branches, the current practices were found to be adequate.

The Two-Window Arrangement

Here, when a check is cashed, the request is made through the first server, and the cash is obtained from another server (the cashier) by the customer. This type of an arrangement required the customer to wait twice, and was found to be highly inefficient. Server utilization was almost 100%, and customer waiting was about 15 minutes for the simplest service that was required.

Several scenarios were investigated. One alternative required both servers to perform all the tasks. Another alternative involved, in addition to the first one, having one line formed in front of the servers.

One-Line, Several-Servers

The analysis showed that this arrangement was the best, but required highly trained personnel. Only an American bank operated in this manner. This type of an arrangement has the advantage of maintaining the utilization of servers at a high level and giving the customer a sense of fairness (Krajewski and Ritzman 1987). The only drawback to this type was the layout of the bank that could not permit for a line longer than 15 people.

Multiple-Lines

In this arrangement some of the servers provided a limited set of services. Most local banks operated in this manner. In theory, this arrangement should be adequate and efficient provided that enough servers were available. Again server utilization was almost 100% and the queue files were full most of the time. These banks offered several services including utility bill payments and credit card services. The scenarios considered with these systems showed that more servers were needed to handle the jobs. This alternative was also examined to be cost effective in the long run.

COMMON RECOMMENDATIONS

Several recommendations were provided with respect to all the systems evaluated:

1) Increased training and a greater level of responsibility at the front line- service representatives should routinely be empowered to do what needs to be done for the customers.

2) Greater attention should be given to selecting people who are likely to perform successfully in customer service situations.

3) To enhance banks commitment to quality, excellence awards could be given to employees who provide meritorious service to their customers- where the names are displayed in the lobby of banks corporate headquarters.

4) Banks, on periodic basis, should continue to talk and listen to their customers- and for those banks that have centralized decision making processes, it makes a point of doing that at the branch level so unique situations don't become ignored and lost. Specific, measurable objectives can then be set at each level. Some targets are measured by the percentage of customers surveyed who report they are satisfied with the services that have been provided to them- the measurement is from the customer's point of view.

POLICY IMPLEMENTATION

Top management of the banks that participated in the study reviewed the various strategies suggested by the simulation models. Only two banks implemented these new suggested strategies, one national and one foreign. The national bank was recommended the implementation of the fourth arrangement type with additional servers than was available. This policy also required the changing of the bank layout to accommodate the changes.

The foreign bank was recommended to stay with the third arrangement type. The only change was to have a separate line formed for draft orders which constituted only 5% of their business. Draft orders usually demanded longer service times than other transactions.

The new changes were implemented at the branch level of the local bank. A month later those changes were implemented at their headquarter level. The foreign bank implemented the changes at all levels at the same time. In August 1990, the researcher received a call from the largest bank in Dubai, which refused to participate in the study earlier, to perform the study.

CONCLUSIONS

For the first time simulation modeling was introduced to banking queues in Oil-Rich developing countries. The developed models and the ease of scenario generation did provide bank managements the ability to evaluate many alternative policies within a relatively short time period. Simulation modeling enabled those decision makers to easily change the number of variables to be considered or the number of subsystems included. Furthermore, through the use of simulation models management was able to analyze "what if" type questions and enhance their competitive advantage.

REFERENCES

Bennett, G. and B.J. Melloy. 1984. "Applying Queuing Theory Helps Minimize Waiting Time and Costs of Available Resources." Industrial Engineering, 16, no. 7 (Jul.):86-91.

Fitzsimmons, J.A., and R.S. Sullivan. 1982. Service Operations Management. McGraw-Hill Book Company, New York, N.Y.

Foot, B.L. 1976. "Queuing Case Study of Drive-In Banking." Interfaces, 6, no. 4 (Aug.):31.

Krajewski, L.J., and L.P. Ritsman. 1987. Operations Management Strategy and Analysis. Addison-Wesley Publishing Company, Inc., Reading, Ma.

Ledbetter, W.N., and J.F. Cox. 1977. "Are OR techniques Being Used?." Industrial Engineering, (Feb.):19-21.

The New York Times, 1988. "Conquering those Killer Queues." (Sunday, Sep. 25):11.

AUTHER'S BIOGRAPHY

Dr. Masood A. Badri received his Ph.D, in Production and Operations Management from the University of Mississippi in 1989. He is currently an Assistant Professor of Management at the United Arab Emirates University. He has published and presented papers at national meetings of Decision Sciences Institute, the Institute of Management Sciences, the Operations Research Society of America, the Society for Computer Simulation, and the Production and Operations Management Society. His main areas of research are computer simulation of service or manufacturing industries, quality control studies, location analysis, and transfer of technology studies.

Table 1: Number of Local and Foreign Banks

Type	They Form a Queue	They Don't Form Queues	Total
National	45	122	167
Foreign	79	40	119
Total	124	162	286

Figure 1: Customers Arriving at Banks with no Queues

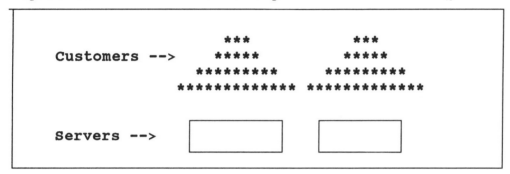

Figure 2: Arrangements of channel of queues

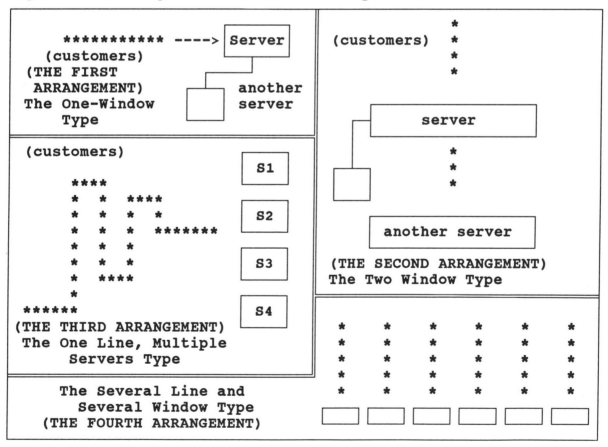

AUTHOR INDEX